Democracy on the Move?

Democracy on the Move?

Reflections on Moments, Promises and Contradictions

Edited by

Manindra Nath Thakur

Dhananjay Rai

Democracy on the Move? Reflections on Moments, Promises and Contradictions
Edited by Manindra Nath Thakur and Dhananjay Rai

First Published, 2013

ISBN 978-93-5002-218-4

Published by
AAKAR BOOKS
28 E Pocket IV, Mayur Vihar Phase I, Delhi 110 091
Phone : 011 2279 5505 Telefax : 011 2279 5641
info@aakarbooks.com; www.aakarbooks.com

Printed at
Mudrak, 30 A, Patparganj, Delhi 110 091

Contents

Acknowledgements

This book is the culmination of a collective effort. It would not have been possible sans the generous and quick support of contributors who were readily available for articles and interviews despite their busy schedule. The encouragement on the part of contributors kept us motivated to finish the book as soon as possible.

We are grateful to *Economic and Political Weekly* and *Mainstream* wherefrom four articles are included in this book. The swift consent of the respective authors for the inclusion of their articles published in these two journals has beyond doubt augmented this collective endeavour. From, *Economic and Political Weekly,* Manoranjan Mohanty's article *People's Movements and the Anna Upsurge* (17 September 2011 Vol. XLVI No. 38) and Sukumar Murlidharan's article *Media as Echo Chamber: Cluttering the Public Discourse on Corruption* (10 September 2011, Vol. XLVI No. 37) are included. Anand Teltumbde's article *The Neoliberal Revolution* (Vol. XLIX, No. 39, 17 September 2011) and Satish K. Jha's article, *Democratic Meaning of the Anna Movement: One View* (Vol. L, No. 1, 24 December 2011 (Annual 2011)) were published in *Mainstream.* We are indebted to the authors for their invaluable consent.

This book could not have been conceptualised, had it not been discussed in the milieu of Jawaharlal Nehru University, New Delhi. Directly and distantly, this book has an imprint of *JNU's* discursive and egalitarian ambience. Moreover, the conceptualisation could not have been materialised, had we not received the much needed support from vibrant and radical-argumentative researchers and scholars of

JNU. We are obliged to (alphabetically) Abhay Kumar, Manu Puthur, Manzoor Ali, Pavel Tomar, Rityusha Tiwary, Ruchi Shree and Shashank Chaturvedi for their indefatigable efforts. Sivadasan was of a great help. Finally, K.K. Saxena, publisher of Aakar, deserves much credit for bearing many missed deadlines on our part and remaining patient and hopeful towards completion of the book.

Introduction

The contemporary moment of democracy is full of contradictory trends. At a time when the collapse of the Soviet Union is being celebrated as an extraordinary triumph of liberal democracy, the world is witnessing fresh mobilisation of people against the liberal democratic system. The marriage between capitalism and liberal democracy seems to be in danger. It is a difficult moment for analysts as it is risky to jump to quick conclusions about anything. Everybody is moving around with a lot of questions in mind. They are trying to explore if mobilisations for Jan Lokpal in India, the questioning of the government's economic policies in Europe and North America and the change of regime in the Arab world are fragmented acts of venting out a longstanding dissatisfaction or indications of something new emerging. Nobody knows how such huge mobilisations are possible—whether they are the media's creation or are spontaneous; or whether they have some organisational base or are quite anarchic. We know that the indicators of the health of the economy show that the economy is not in good shape but we do not know the exact link between this and the kind of mobilisation we are seeing. It is difficult to comprehend the totality of the moment. One can only try to make sense of the things happening in their own locations and keep one's fingers crossed to see if that contributes to making sense of the total picture.

Whatever it may be, one thing is quite obvious: these mobilisations are going to have huge implications for democracy and we need to understand democracy in its wider connotations. It has many theories and innumerable practices; there are many contestations as well. One of the caveats to discern democracy is not reduction to its institutional success. The institutional success, like periodical electoral practices, is sine qua non process of democracy whereby the nature of power relations among social groups, the participation of marginal classes/ castes, the deliverance of essential goods and the glossiness of the economy can be fathomed. Nonetheless, institutional perspective can be one of the criterions of democratic functionalism but not the absolute measure. One of the lacunae in the institutional perspective is its wide ignorance or at best only partial recognition of churnings prevalent in the everyday life of any society, as everyday churning should not be treated only as a 'postscript' of institutional success. In other words, they do not need passing reference after the glorification of institutional success. The political theory of democracy cannot be confined to merely unfurling of niceties of procedural successes. It has to confront each day as well as a simplified political claim wherefrom people's struggles renew their interest by way of many means.

This book has a particular context and a special allusion. The particular context is a departure from institution-oriented political theory to that of everyday churning; and the special allusion is the anti-corruption crusade led by Anna Hazare and his team. It is not difficult to accept that there is utter theoretical confusion and practical bafflement concerning naming itself: whether it can be christened as moment, a movement, a mobilisation, an agitation or a confrontation. We know that etymologically and valuably, each stands apart when the question of strategy and larger vision comes in. This book does not solve this dilemma of naming and valuing the idea, respecting and debating these visions. Instead, it takes a theoretically neutral standpoint. A theoretically neutral standpoint does not entail that editors and respective authors do not have a point of view with respect to 'Team Anna' and the crusade led by it. It only suggests that the book, instead of taking a singularity of standpoint, would like to put an emphasis on the plurality of perspectives and standpoints. This, we think, will help the reader to draw her/his conclusion and association with the struggle against corruption. Thus, the epithet 'mobilisation' will be used as far as the introduction is concerned.

This issue needs some clarity. We know that 'movement' has non-ephemeral characteristics whereas, 'agitation' is issue-specific and ephemeral in nature and 'mobilisation' would involve the congregation of a large number of people. 'Mobilisation' is means whereas 'movement' and 'agitation' have strategy and respective visions. Mobilisation as means is present in both movement and agitation. There cannot be movement and agitation sans mobilisation. For theoretical convenience, we will use the term 'mobilisation' in the Introduction to highlight both the perspectives, inter alia, 'mobilisation' and 'agitation' schools. It will also help us in refraining from imposing a singular outline regarding the Anna Hazare-led mobilisation.

Put differently, there is emphasis on content in lieu of form and, it does not set the agenda. The unity of the book lies in the fact that all the contributors are reflecting on recent developments which took place in the form of the first hunger strike by Anna Hazare, ex-serviceman of the Indian Army and known for experiments in his village, Ralegan Siddhi, which has attracted both adulation and condemnation on 5 April 2011 for the enactment of laws popularly known as the *Jan Lokpal Bill* (People's Ombudsman Bill). The title of the book, *Democracy on the Move,* is self-explanatory wherein contributors have *reflected* on *moments* of recent churning while evaluating the *promises* and exhibiting the *contradictions.*

The nature and purpose of the book is two-pronged. Since it departs from 'institutional melody', the nature of the Jan Lokpal Bill, its ambit and lacunae will not be discussed. The core of the book is not to discuss the profundity of the bill. It does not mean it will not attract the attention of the respective authors but that they will be treated as an 'allusion'. Regarding the second purpose, it has many sub-layers. This book is a reflection on the mobilisation and on its dynamics in the context of larger implications of the democratic theory and its practice in India. These reflections encompass both entities, that is, theory to practice and practice to theory. The reflections encapsulate whether the idea of democracy (theory) is confirming the practice or whether the practice is moulding the nature of democracy. We are using the epithet 'reflection' due to the one consideration that the timeline of mobilisation is uncertain and it is encapsulation from the midst. More concerted postulations by academicians who are witnessing it closely will definitely take more time. The timing of the book also needs illustration. Even the people involved in the mobilisation have no idea of its direction. Nevertheless, the book will most likely also inform the mobilisation about how academicians view it and the possible direction it might take.

Besides, media and technological expansion have transmogrified the public sphere. Opinions are prioritised over substances of news. These days, news is becoming synonymous to views: editorials are placed before information and information is edited. Many people have noticed that the Anna-led mobilisation and its representation in the print and electronic media have significantly influenced the mobilisation and opinion about it. Yet, it is not very clear that round-the-clock coverage by the media has played a significant role in mobilisation or that they have had no option but to cover it as it was important for their own survival in the competitive atmosphere. The representation by the media has not only produced a rainbow of opinions but also an uncertainty about them. One of the corollaries of such representation by the media is that it has created a huge amount of confusion.

Since the mobilisation seems to be pregnant with new possibilities and is unfolding itself, these contributions have to be read as a process of thinking rather than a finished product. Scholars from different disciplines and 'antithetical' worldviews are included to unwind the heterogeneity of opinion. The importance of the book does not lie in the fact that it has analysed the mobilisation but in the fact that it places the mobilisation in the larger perspective of functioning of the project of democracy. One may find it useful for forming one's own opinions at a time when democracy to facing large numbers of contradictions due to emerging global dominance of capital. One may find it useful for forming one's own informed opinion.

II

As stated above, heterogeneity of opinion is the fulcrum of the book. It is not necessary that authors would resonate the opinion explained by the editors in their respective contributions. Likewise, editors may differ with some of the chapters while finding affinity with others. The entire academic-reflective endeavour is to place many views indiscriminately before the reader.

The first chapter, 'People's Movements and the Anna Upsurge', contributed by Manoranjan Mohanty, explicates the divergence between people's movements and the Anna Hazare upsurge, the possibility of convergence and what is to be done. Mohanty suggests that the Anna Hazare campaign has to reflect upon why dalit and adivasi movements have kept their distance from it. Moreover, minority groups and leaders were critical and indifferent. Forest workers' organisations and workers from organised sectors did not participate. Conversely, all of these movements do identify themselves with Irom Sharmila. It is also important to ask whether these groups were right while not recognising the democratic element in the Anna Hazare upsurge against corruption as a part of the democratic-Right campaign. Regarding the nature of movement, Mohanty argues that many democratic initiatives have been middle-class-led initiatives. The refutation of the government to accept the demand to curb corruption has transformed the movement, attracting people from many sections. The inclusion of lower bureaucracy under the jurisdiction of the Lokpal and other issues was the poor people's requirement. Terming it as Right-wing mobilisation is ignoring the ground reality. However, the campaign is also responsible for not shrugging its middle-class image. They could have formed an alliance with dalit, adivasis, minorities and workers' movements while spelling out the anti-corruption campaign as deliverance of justice to rural and urban people. 'Can a law end corruption?' Mohanty agrees with the criticism against the Anna upsurge that it has reduced the fight to the level of law-enactment. He proposes three approaches to fight against corruption: at the political economy level, at the legal apparatus level and through moral values.

M.P. Singh, in the second chapter, 'Whither the Indian Republic? Representative versus Direct Democracy,' traces the trajectory of the relationship between representative democracy and direct democracy in India. Despite being a significant issue, the literature of politics has not explored this crucial relationship in the theory and practice of democracy. According to him, the nationalist movement all through remained ambivalent between republicanism/representative democracy and direct democracy. Gandhi's own method exhibits the dilemma between the democratic and revolutionary methods of struggle. His intervention in Champaran and the mill workers of Ahmedabad was not a full-scale revolutionary class struggle. However, the 1942 Quit India Movement was probably the only revolutionary struggle that attempted direct seizure of power by the people. In fact, Singh says that Gandhi demanded in 1922 that the Constitution should be framed by the people directly. Conversely, the indirect election to the Constituent Assembly, which came under the British Cabinet Mission Plan, by provincial legislatures in 1946, was based on limited franchise. He argues that 'We the people' as a guiding principle is very close to the American and Swiss constitutions due to some provisions of direct democracy. Unlike the constitutions of the USA and Switzerland which had revolutionary birth (rupture from the erstwhile system), the Indian Constitution has been evolutionary (evolving from the British era); therefore, provisions of direct democracy like a formal people's initiative in law-making, referendum and recall of elected representatives remain absent. The Swiss Constitution does provide all these whereas the USA constitution provides some of these. The Constituent Assembly, though giving very limited importance to the village panchayat, did not ponder over referendum and direct election of the President of India. In the Indian Constitution, provisions of directive democratic devices of initiative, referendum and recall are absent. He states that there have been three occasions, that is, the Jayaprakash Narayan-led movement of the 1970s, the post-Emergency 44th Constitutional amendment (1978) and Anna Hazare and his team-led campaign against corruption (2011), when the issue of direct democratic devices in governance sprang into political discourse. According to him, participatory direct democratic devices should be incorporated in a partial combination and a harmonious construction within the framework of India's parliamentary-federal democracy.

The third chapter, 'Story of an Imaginary Movement: Uncovering the Anna Spectacle', written by Manoj Kumar Jha, analyses the Anna Hazare mobilisation critically. Jha raises several questions before explicating the edifice of the movement. When and why do movements occur? Who joins or supports the movement? How are movements organised? What are the ideological moorings of the movement? What do movements do? How does media influence and shape the movement? What are the symbols and images propagated by the movement? Taking a clue from these questions, according to him, the Anna phenomenon cannot be bracketed as a genuine mass movement in democracy. According to Jha, the sad story is that the government has failed on multiple counts, especially on its basic agenda of governance. The real question is whether the Anna phenomenon meets the challenges of the existing problems? According to him, the Anna phenomenon was never a democratic movement because it harks back on media which does not allow ideological, symbolic and mobilisation based strategies to be debated in the public realm. Metropolitan-centred people are also the fulcrum of this phenomenon. This class has shown a sense of resentment 'against vote politics' and are also responsible for the corruption being a cog in the machine. Jha thinks that at best, the Anna phenomenon can be called a spectacle, a creation of media. Even the Anna phenomenon and Gandhian tactics cannot be compared. He further pointed out that Gandhi was, even critics would accept, a great assimilationist, whereas Anna and his team demonise dissimilar views.

Vivek Kumar in Chapter 3, 'Recognising Structures of Corruption and Understanding the Nature of Mobilisation against It', contends the definition of corruption. He divides the definition of corruption into two categories, that is, broader definition and narrow definition. broader definition of corruption entails the process of denial by minority to large sections of the society to avail human rights for a dignified existence: an equality of the economic, political and social; and liberty of occupation, residence and religious practices. Due to denial, there is a monopolisation of religious, political, economic, educational and judicial institutions by the smaller group. In the Indian context, they are legitimised by dharma and karma. According to the narrow definition, corruption is the misuse of a government office for personal gains. However, to restrict this idea of corruption to the government offices is a mistake. There is a caste dimension to it as the government offices are largely occupied by the upper caste. He suggests that corruption is rooted in the social institution of caste, and the government offices are mirror reflections of the former. The way

Hindu society is socialised from childhood, it augurs the practice of corruption. Gifts on the occasion of the festivals such as Diwali can be cited in this regard. In this backdrop, Kumar locates the 'Kisan Baburao Hazare' mobilisation. He does not call it a movement because movements are based on ideology and organisation where leaders are in command. It also cannot be called a second freedom struggle and no comparison should be made with JP movement (Jayaprakash Narayan Movement). The unrepresentative character of the agitation is exposed since the Scheduled Caste, Scheduled Tribes and minority groups are not represented. This mobilisation against corruption survives on the narrow definition of corruption and it does not take cognisance of corruption by industrial houses. He further claims this mobilisation promotes hero worship by method of civil disobedience, non-cooperation and *satyagaraha* which is nothing but the grammar of anarchy.

Satish Kumar Jha in Chapter 4, 'Democratic Meaning of the Anna Movement: One View', has ask a fundamental question pertaining to the representative character of democracy. The Anna phenomenon has been castigated as middle-class cyber-politics and corporate-sponsored tirade against the political class, and a sabotaging ploy of the silent revolution of dalits and Other Backward Classes (OBCs). However, according to the significant issue raised by the Anna phenomenon that is representational deficit of democracy, is side stepped. In fact, the anti-corruption movement by Anna Hazare has brought up the fault lines in the established framework of political representation in India. Jha finds the similarity between UPA II and the Pre-Emergency Congress government on several accounts, namely, arrogance of power, high-handedness, lack of a pro-people approach, a single agenda of dynastic politics and alliance with corporate houses. The Anna phenomenon provides historic opportunity to both votaries of procedural democracy and the custodians of the state power of self-retrospection. It is important to understand that each passing day, the gap between representatives and constituencies is widening. Therefore, such moments should be utilised to understand the weak links in the representative democracy and cannot be considered as representing 'grammar of anarchy' which was used by Ambedkar in the context of constitutional monarchy. On the other hand, there are some more difficult questions to be answered by civil society with respect to representation of the popular will through a non-electoral channel. He asks the reader to consider the following questions. Why does the state adopt an ostrich-like approach towards the decade-old fast of Irom Sharmila in Manipur? Is it because she has no mass support for the cause that she is espousing? Or, does her demand harm the political class more than the creation of the office of a Lokpal? Or is she being ignored because the middle class of India has not lapped up her movement, the way they have done Anna's? Moreover, certified mass mobilisation by the state is also fraught with danger because of the following questions. Who ultimately should be the adjudicator of the popular will? Does it also reside outside the electoral arena? Should the states' inclination to negotiate and engage with a civil society group be the only proof of the legitimacy of the issues in question? In the end, he suggests that 'accountability and responsiveness are valid in themselves and have to be settled in their own terms'.

In Chapter 5, 'Anna Hazare's Soap Opera', Ajay Gudavarthy compares Anna Hazare's anti-graft movement with the epic predicament wherein the end is known and predictability sustains it. Gudavarthy points out the changing nature of the Indian economy in the reform era had led to the emergence of rent-seeking classes who accrue profit from contracts, thus dominating the state. The state needs them and they need the state. Now, the nature of capital is speculative; therefore long-term planning and industrialisation get avoided by these classes who harp on a quick and speculative mode for making profit. This changing nature of the political economy has led to the cause of corporate and official corruptions. Anna's Lokpal can do little about this structural limit but remains hopeful to fight against corruption. Though Anna's movement is important, its complexity makes it neither to be rejected it nor accepted wholeheartedly. For the Left-of-Centre, progressive and radical forces, it is difficult to be with the Anna side wholeheartedly since corporate corruption is not addressed and the mammoth corruption of the ruling elite is difficult to oppose. Liberal democrats are worried about undermining representative institutions but institutions turning into corrupt practices have left no option with them. The Right-wing is an important beneficiary since the spectacle of Anna contains all elements of Right-wing mobilisation. The success of these mobilisations contributed by mass mobilisation is an insufficient explanation because it got success due to the professionals' and urban-rich/NRIs' dream of a corruption-free India that will not only benefit them but also attract global investment.

Anand Teltumbde's Chapter 6, 'The Neoliberal Revolution', asks whether various legislative reforms can arrest the accumulation in the dominant classes. At the onset, it has to be asked what the game plan of the government is. A government comprised of several individuals of different acumen cannot do so many blunders while dealing with Anna Hazare. It is the act of government to facilitate the germination of public opinion against the government in favour of more free market reform. This government has been marked by a series of scams, untamed inflation, rising movements against land grabbing, growing unemployment et cetera. These were exposing the anti-people character a of neoliberal regime. To overcome the anger of the masses, the government needed support from people so they could push for further reforms. The Anna Movement is a blessing in disguise for the government they seek regulatory mechanisms which are nothing but a prescription of the neoliberal framework to ensure that the free market operates by certain guidelines. The Bhartiya Janata Party (BJP) is the net gainer by way of preparing the general public opinion for further market reform and causing embarrassment to the government. The support base came to Anna mainly from urbane, English-educated, upper-caste, upwardly mobile young people. Caste culture produces doublespeak—in a sense, on the one hand, altruistic concern for the people is expressed and on the other hand, continuation of exploitation remains intact. The remedy is eradication of socio-economic inequality, not the Lokpal prescription which focuses on the symptom while ignoring the diagnosis of the disease. However, the campaign has prevented people from seeing the real rot. Teltumbde suggests that if it is qualified for a revolution, as many votaries would have us believe, it can be called the neoliberal revolution.

Shailaja Menon and N. Sukumar, in Chapter 7, 'The Old Man and the Sea of Troubles', highlight the skewed and selective response vis-à-vis any protest including Irom Sharmila's. They ask several questions. How does one make sense of this hierarchy of protests?

What makes a protest newsworthy? Does the success of a protest revolve around a particular personality dressed in the theatre of Gandhi? Why is there a silence by the same groups of media savvy protestors when confronted by systemic deprivations? The consumer-citizen may be satisfied by some face-saving legislation, however, The concern is to understand why the systemic checks have failed to stem the rot in the system. Team Anna has failed to negotiate with Articles 38 and 39 of the Constitution which are against inequality. The entire episode can be termed as a theatre of the absurd primarily because it sought to establish a patron-client relationship. Kumar and Menon compare Khap Panchayats and Anna, both for their undermining constitutionality and emphasising personal diktats. Another institution will not cleanse the corruption unless brahminical mentality in the body-politics of India has not been cleansed. Unfortunately, Nehru's tryst with destiny and Ambedkar's social democracy have been side-lined for the pursuit of crony capitalism.

Chapter 8, 'Media as Echo Chamber: Cluttering the Public Discourse on Corruption', by Sukumar Muralidharan, exposes the acts of media and its duplicity with reference to the Anna Hazare-led mobilisations. Muralidharan points out that the coverage of Anna's fast was so distinctive in all channels, which suggests the strong linkage between coverage and revenue implications. The concept of a news-hole (news filled in 'holes' after committed advertisement) has been extended from print media to electronic media. In electronic media, it is filled up as time. It means that news is reduced to a secondary position after advertisements. News content is adjusted because ads are a source of money. Moreover, an informed discussion is missed and the corruption faced by the middle and upper strata, like passport delays and non-clearance of business, is highlighted at the expense of other issues such as non-registration of names on daily muster rolls for the rural employment guarantee programme. The trade unions rally in February, 2011 remained indifferent news for most channels or was covered with disdain in comparison to the eulogised coverage of Anna's fast. *The Times of India* (TOI), Delhi Edition, presented it as 'Red Wave Sweeps City' and 'Halts Traffic in Central Delhi'. The language of the same newspaper got changed in case of Anna's coverage. The TOI's local news on 17 August 2011 was 'City Centre Comes

Alive With Marching Throngs' and somewhere else as 'Massive Jams in City but Few Were Complaining'. According to Murlidharan, the corruption issue has been framed as such that other anxieties can be shifted. The desire for single supra authority, in fact, resembles the elite's conviction about the colossal failure of representative democracy. Murlidharan's two questions remain important: would the target then shift from 'corruption' to 'politics' itself and would representative democracy itself fall victim to an awakening Indian middle-class rage?

Harish S. Wankhede, in Chapter 9, 'Understanding the Dalits' Critique of Anna Hazare's Movement', offers a dalit critique of the 'movement'. He argues that the criticism of the bill's technicalities and its mandate that civil society dictate to the parliament are not sufficient. One has to ponder over the political objectives of the movement. Here, the dalit perspective becomes very important. Liberal democracy has a dual role in terms of catering to interests of the majority and the legitimate space to all. There are three important arguments of the dalits against the movement. The first is the absence of issues, concerns and representation of marginalised sections. Independent analysis/articulation and adequate representation have been twin elements of Ambedkarite politics. The second is that the entire gamut of movements has been borrowed by the brahmanical social cultural domain which is antithetical to the project of the dalits. Even modelling along Gandhi's lines is not helpful because he had defended conservative and regressive ideas and had no faith in parliamentary democracy. Gandhian ethics is nothing but the ethics of a Hindu social order. The third is that there is a negation of constitutional authorities like Parliament. Firstly, the movement undermines the fundamental rights of the legislature to discuss and formulate the bill. Secondly, accusation against political representatives is accusation against changed demography, that is, more representation of OBCs is there in place of Brahmins. There is silence over corruption in business houses, NGOs and religious institutions. Three political possibilities are coming out. Firstly, the movement proposes a replacement of party politics and political opposition by a non-political association of middle-class elite. Secondly, this movement is dangerous for a functional democracy. Thirdly, plurality is ignored and this will pave the way for an elite upper caste.

Atul Mishra, in 'Nouveau Claims on Traditional Visions of Indian Democracy', Chapter 10, argues that the idea of apoliticality is being encouraged by the market. The middle class' association with the Anna Hazare movement has attempted to redefine Indian democracy in place of the traditional vision of Indian democracy. Suppressed and exploited groups have been primary constituencies of Indian democracy. The nouveau claim by the movement is a certain rupture which is based on the 'apolitical'. This apolitical is not new. Since Gandhi, there has been a difference between ideologues and executives. Ideologues never assume power but the relationship between both is hierarchical. Politics is associated with dirty, unclean, impure space and activity in contrast to apolitics which are apostles of the tidy, clean and pure. The movement against corruption has a strong spillover of the middle class in the realm of Indian democracy. The political agenda of neoliberalism has been to homogenise the political condition of the world and especially by a global south. Ideology, social justice and global welfare are obfuscations to efficient governance. Under the ambit of the market, the aplotical is a false prioritisation over politics, and governance over politics. Many concerns like justice, equitable distribution of resources and safeguards have been vital constituents of Indian democracy. By claiming that corruption is the only concern, it has employed with a disregard for a traditional vision of Indian democracy which has been for more just. The first major agenda of the middle class is to upset the politics and traditional constituents. This movement will possibly create substantial conflict between the middle class and the traditional constituencies of Indian democracy. The problem is that this middle-class-led movement is entering into politics while claiming apoliticality. For traditional constituents of Indian democracy, it remains exclusionary in nature, exhibited through slogans and symbols. Particularly its brahmanical overtones instil fear in dalits. It has also shown utter disregard to political institutions. A similarity between Western worldviews of democracy by way of market and civil society and this movement can also be noticed.

The last article of Part I is 'Moment and Movement: De-hyphenating the Debate' by Dhananjay Rai. The author distinguishes between two types of questions: needful questions and necessary questions. Needful questions are outcome questions whereas necessary questions are foundational questions. He argues that India, or for that matter any liberal constitution/institution-led country, has been understood from institutional perspectives by way of asking needful questions that are outcomes of institutions. The question will entail as to how democracy is functioning, et cetera. The issue is to ask foundational questions like how democracy and institutions are functioning the way they are. Asking the first question will easily miss the many foundational issues and will remain focused on an institutional arena whereby difficult areas are ignored. He thereafter focuses on mobilisations which have the possibility to become moment and movement. Mobilisation can be of three kinds: anti-constitutional, constitutional and beyond the constitution. The institutional perspective ignores the nature of mobilisation due to their focus on the institutional alone. The author remains focused on constitutional mobilisation and that beyond the constitution. At the outset, any mobilisation which gets originated due to a gap in the practice of the constitution is being termed by the state as anti-Constitution. Thereafter, mobilisation becomes rigorously pro-Constitution because the ruling echelons present themselves as authors of the constitution and people as owners of the constitution. Since they own the constitution, they must not go against. This type of mobilisation can be termed as moment because they are transient in nature and repose faith in the institutions. The state also gives quick response to it because of the issue of legitimacy. The other type of mobilisation is movement, which goes for transforming institutions through scaled accumulation, ascriptive nationalism and creation of the political subject which is absent in the case of moment. It can be called 'beyond the constitution'. He further questions populism because of its emphasis on negotiation, bargains and postponed endeavour. Applyng the moment and movement dichotomy, he suggests that all three important approaches (institutional, possibility of rupture and cause of success) fail to make a distinction between moment and movement in the case of the Anna-led-mobilisation which leads to erroneous conclusion in terms of critiquing, supporting and fathoming the factors. The Anna-led mobilisation reinforces the faith in the intuitions and becomes constitutional: therefore it can be termed as moment. And focusing on only Anna-led mobilisation, or likewise, will be ignoring the nature of the Indian Constitution/Liberal Constitution where maximum concession is the constitutional method which remains silent over scaled accumulation and nationalism which is enmeshed in ascriptivity and in the case of India, suzerainty of brahmanism.

III

The second part of the book contains short and long interviews. Three methods have been adopted while conducting the interviews. Firstly, there would be commonality of questions in most of the interviews to ensure that there should be a certain response on defined questions. Therefore, readers many find overlapping questions in many of the interviews. Secondly, heterogeneity, like the articles in the first section, is an utmost priority to endure divergent opinions and their merits. Thirdly, interviews are quick reflections which bear out from interviewees' rigorous academic engagement in the realm of academics for many years. They have expressed their concern robustly while analysing institutions, democracy and mobilisations.

K.N. Panikkar (Chapter 13) points that Anna Hazare is apolitical only in one sense that he is not a member of a political party; otherwise, his past engagement catapults him as political. His politics emphasises on compromise to tame the internal contradictions of society; therefore the Indian state accords so much importance. The agitation in his name is an extension of reformist politics. The politics of Anna Hazare or the people who run the agitation in his name is to preserve the interest of the rich and affluent. The claim on behalf of the poor is a joke. Moreover, the method adopted by him is anti-democratic and anti-Constitution because Parliament is bypassed and authority cannot lie with certain people however eminent they are. In place of emotional blackmail, people's support to any cause in a democracy being based on mobilisation by means of political education is the preferred way. And without popular consciousness, corruption cannot be done away with. The social and political ideas of Anna and his associates are very conservative and reactionary and their method is based on authoritarianism. According to him the inherent character of the movement is lifted towards Right-wing character. Right wings' (RSS,

VHP and Communal forces) support is not incidental but to unsettle the democratic institution and capture the power. The movement does not reflect popular will because it is laced with the emotion of the middle class while not raising the fundamental problem of Indian polity like marginalisation of dalits, minorities and women. History will rate this movement as another attempt to maintain social equilibrium by the capitalist order.

Randhir Singh (Chapter 14) denies that Anna Hazare has a broader perspective on corruption due to negation of the larger issues like ideology of capitalism and the cause of structural alienation. However, he insists that the left could have intervened in a movement like this. Regarding the effective intervention by civil society, he maintains that the real stage of intervention by civil society is over because the state is the repository of real power. Though civil society gives voice to the people, it also creates the illusion that problem can be solved locally. For him, the state remains important. He does not agree with James Petra's formulation that NGOs are agents of imperialism. According to the questions on role of civil society he suggests that all NGOs cannot be called agents because they perform a variety of functions. As he envisages, old fashioned protest is still important and all protest must be concerted to bring in transformative politics. The real forces of any revolution are workers and farmers. Democracy and democratic credentials are very important; otherwise people will be pushed to dictatorship and capitalism. However, parliamentary methods and extra-parliamentary methods have to be defended because they all reflect the people's aspirations. A significant criticism of the Anna Hazare Movement is that it has allowed the government to criticise any extra-constitutional practices. In Marxist terms, the question is of building socialism.

G. Haragopal (Chapter 15) expounds that the Anna Hazare Movement coincides with the exposition of a series of scams. The Anna movement seeks institutional correction to the political distortion. The system has permitted, patronised and legitimised the movement so that the loss of faith in politics and institutions can be restored. Anna Hazare helped the ruling classes to restore their credibility. This is the politics of the Anna Hazare Movement. On the positive side of the movement, middle classes were activated, politics of movement and mobilisation were brought back in the scene. On the whole, Indian democracy has been benefitted slightly. This movement cannot be termed as anti-Constitution because the constitution is not merely an arrangement of formal institutions. Moreover, they are using the rights of Part III of the constitution to ensure the implementation of Part IV. On the negative side of the movement, it has reposed faith in institutions that are crumbling under heavyweight corruption. It is also important to understand that democracy is a way of life; therefore any demand for greater accountability on the part of members of Parliament or Parliament cannot be stated as a compromise of democracy. Anna Hazare has no formidable worldview or a sense of history; thus such persons eventually end up with Right-wing politics. The inability of Congress to enact a law is also helping the Right-wing forces. The nature of the movement is middle, professional and elite classes and lower castes; deprived classes and disempowered women are not included. The support of the national media gives reason to suspect the forces of global capital behind it. Since this movement does not challenge the existing structures, capitalist framework and development model, movements of this kind are always supported by the process of globalisation.

D.L. Seth (Chapter 16) confirms that the Anna Hazare and India against corruption movement has made the concept of civil society widely accepted. In a democracy, a five-year contract is not only important but the role of the non-electoral is also vital. Civil society has developed in India into three phases, that is, a national movement, the JP Movement and the post globalisation movement. Civil society keeps localised views/problems in a detailed way before the state. Therefore, elected representatives being the only main source of legitimacy is limiting the meaning of democracy because 'by the people' is much beyond that. Similarly, civil society is not against the state because we are referring to the state as a democratic state. The movement broadens participation particularly in the decision making process. In fact, the role of the state is not enough and 'multiple-governance' is a seeming possibility. And the role of civil society is evidence of multi-layered governance due to the complication of state power. However, civil society cannot control and regulate people's movements; they can only give direction. Especially after the JP Movement, the role of civil society has changed in a big way; even today, many contemporary progressive legislations have the imprint of civil society.

Imtiaz Ahmad (Chapter 17) states that the anger generated due to corruption is being exploited by the Anna Hazare Movement (AHM). However, there remains a loud silence over the role of big business houses and corporate roots. Technically, the AHM is not anti-Constitution but cannot be dubbed as a people's movement. It is also not democratic because demands like the Right to Reject and the Right to Recall will weaken the structures of Indian democracy. In fact, the success of the AHM will lead to a compromise of democracy. Anna Hazare belongs to the RSS (Rashtriya Swayamsewak Sangh) which is communal and casteist in its policies. Moreover, it should not be called a movement. The nature of mobilisation suggests the exclusion of the minority, dalits and adivasis. It is located in urban spaces which are led by the upper caste middle class which has a grudge against politics, especially after the second wave of democratisation in which the political rise of rural India has been seen. The root cause of all problems is capitalism, and without its reference, one cannot have any solution. Ingraining social values is important through a democratic movement having the participation of deprived sections. Dalits found distance from this movement as they perceived it as a diversion from the struggle of B.R. Ambedkar. In the case of Muslims, they do not have any hope from the politics and their social psyche is one of statelessness.

Manager Pandey (Chapter 18) avers that only speculation is possible regarding the politics of the Anna Movement. The force behind it, however, is despair and disenchantment of the middle classes. The issue of corruption affects everyone alike from labour to middle class. The root cause of the problem is big capitalist houses and firms. This movement is not a movement of the upper class, yet it remains as middle-class politics confined to the demand for an effective administrative and judicial system and not going for a significant change. Any mass movement cannot be termed as anti-constitutional. Failing to cater to the people's aspirations and hopes is anti-constitutional on the part of the government. Going by the insertion of socialism in the preamble, it is the government which has turned against the constitution. The constitution is not sacrosanct. If the Arab revolution is 'spring', then it is also favourable to democracy. Terming it as Righ-wing politics is a ploy of the ruling class. Herein, the role of the Left could have been decisive. Middle-class centrality has captured the media's attention which is good for the movement. Garnered attention by way of this movement would do good to the culture of protest and popular demands.

Tulsi Ram (Chapter 19) does not like movements of this nature precisely because the issue of corruption is raised but not poverty, education and unemployment. It has the influence of North Africa, Yemen and Tunisia-based movements which are funded by NGOs. These NGOs are hand-in-glove with US foreign policy makers and are used by the USA to dislodge uncomfortable governments. Georgia was the very first country wherein the twice-elected President Eduard Shevardnadze was ousted; this was orchestrated by the USA-based NGO, George Soros Foundation. The replacement was a US citizen, Mikheil Saakashvilli. Soros funds hundreds of NGOs and dislodges governments through them. In fact, Egypt, Tunisia and Libya and other countries are influenced by US-led NGOs. The Anna Hazare Movement is impacted by the North African and Egyptian trend. The problem with Team Anna is that it is developing into an extra-constitutional authority. He thinks NGOs are the biggest source of corruption and populist demands are being catered to by them. The Right-wing politics has cajoled the movement to reap the benefits. The movement is not conscious about communal, gender and class divides. The involvement of communal forces in the movement is against the spirit of democratic or secular systems. Accumulation as an inherent weakness of capitalism has revived the demand for a socialist pattern of development. And of course, corruption is an inherent part of the rigid capitalist system.

Hilal Ahmed (Chapter 20) delineates two phases in the movement. In the first phase, 'apolitical' was an important feature. The figure of Bharat Mata was exhibited as if politics is dirty. So, pious representation was an important endeavour. In the second phase, a picture of M.K. Gandhi was brought in to interpret the politics around corruption. It is important to understand these people vis-à-vis the political and organisational. The epithet 'Team Anna' is a problematic one. The act of movement is important to make observations in place of one's own opinion. Here, Gramsci's distinction between spontaneity and consciousness becomes apt. Unhappiness, genuine anxiety and resentment against the system generate spontaneity. However, spontaneity cannot be considered as conscious, which can throw the system by way of organic intellectuals for counter hegemony. The Anna Movement has harped on resentment but failed to create counter hegemony, precisely because they are intellectually very weak and their demands have been reduced to the Lokpal Bill. An alternative is not proposed. Ahmed suggests an arena of representation in and outside the Constitution. The period of the 1950s and 60s witnessed the idea of representation through an electoral body; this got changed during the JP movement wherein a possibility of alternative politics of representation outside the electoral domain was exhibited. Even the Communists' strategies, as averred by Harikishan Singh Surjeet, rely on struggle in and outside the parliament. The post-globalisation era has seen some departure. After the realisation that a political party is not the only mode of representation, we have the National Advisory Council (NAC). Democracy cannot be reduced to a mere electoral form of democracy. As far as the Right-wing or the omission of certain identities are concerned, it is difficult to accept any movement to acquire secular identity or relinquish identity.

Manindra Nath Thakur (Chapter 21) underlines the significance of the Anna Movement as an important intervention in both theory and practice because due to increased inequality, there exists a situation against democracy, the preamble and directive principle of the state policy of the Indian Constitution. And corruption is the visible explanation of growing inequality and hardship. Various slogans like '*Bharat Mata ke jay*' and '*bande matram*' have been made junior partners in this movement, which is quite symbolic. Moreover, it is difficult to say that Muslims were not there but certainly their leaders were absent. The Dalits' opposition is rested on threat to the Constitution and fear against reservation. The first fear is not substantive because amendments have taken place many times. Regarding the second issue, the movement has to insure that the reservation policy will not be touched. Equal leadership to dalits is to be guaranteed. Calling it a middle-class movement would be erroneous because it has drawn people from across varied sections and people have interpreted connectivity in their own way. Without comparing great leaders, it must be stated that he has proved the appreciation of a Gandhian model of leadership by the people. His simplicity and transparency are important. The need of an alternative model is important because three important modern institutions, namely party, parliament and property, are facing a severe crisis. Parties have become family affairs and are looking for people in place of people making parties. This movement has raised the issue of representation before Parliament and private property. The contradiction between democracy and capitalism has widened and governments are unable to contain the discontent. There are also many challenges before the movement. The leaders of the movement do not seem to have any idea of the nature of capitalism. The treatment of corruption cannot be isolated from capitalism. There has to be an incorporation of more fundamental issues concerning people. The movement is bound to fail if it does not understand the fact that struggle against corruption ultimately has to be struggle for socialism.

This book is a modest attempt towards an exhibition of plurality of different opinions. The Anna-led mobilisation has been a crucial watershed in Indian democracy. A discussion on it is necessary for unravelling of its numerous strands. An attempt towards a discussion is a march towards engagement. Engagement paves way for the arrival of a standpoint. Each standpoint adds significant epistemological contribution. Inclusion and availability of many opinions primarily suggest that the evaluation of this phenomenon is unsettled. Nonetheless, many contentions also indicate the churning process which is going on and the issue is how to grasp it. This book must be treated as a documentation of the standpoint of each author. Each article/interview evaluates the entire phenomenon on the basis of academic recourse and intense engagement with 'active lives'. They provide a vantage point of dialogue. It can be stated, at the end, that the book aims to initiate the process of dialogue from different vantage points which is a hallmark of the creative theory.

Part I

1

People's Movements and the Anna Upsurge

Manoranjan Mohanty

The absence of collaboration between the Anna Hazare campaign and people's movements fighting for democratic rights elsewhere in the country was stark and for that, both the limited nature of the campaign as well as the short-sightedness of the various social movements are to be blamed.

The nationwide upsurge under the leadership of Anna Hazare has put the issue of corruption—both in high places of government as well as in the day-to-day life of common people—at the centre of public consciousness.

Yet, the distance that was very visible between the ongoing people's movements in India and the Anna Hazare campaign remains a troubling issue challenging the latter and asking it to reflect upon it. They must ponder over the fact that all major streams of the dalit and adivasi movements in the country remained outside this campaign, even though some non-governmental organisations (NGOs) did bring some of these groups to take part in the agitations at Ramlila Maidan in Delhi. The minority groups and their leaders, by and large, were either critical or indifferent. Most conspicuously, the banners of most of the movements going on against mega-mining and industrial projects in Orissa, Chhattisgarh, Jharkhand, West Bengal and elsewhere were missing. The forest workers' organisations, which have been on the forefront of the campaign for the Forest Rights Act, and are trying hard to secure its proper implementation, were not only absent but came out with sharp critiques of the Anna-led campaign. And other movements of the workers, especially in the unorganised sector, did not feel enthused to take active interest in the Anna campaign either.

The autonomy and self-determination movements in Kashmir or the north-east could not relate this anti-corruption campaign to the issues they were fighting for. The civil liberties movement including the People's Union for Democratic Rights and the People's Union for Civil Liberties kept out of the Anna campaign. Even the symbolism of having a dalit and a Muslim girl to offer coconut water and honey to Anna to break his fast did not make up for the persisting gap that the campaign has with the people's movements. In contrast, this entire range of people's movements solidly identify with Irom Sharmila's protest in Manipur. Sharmila has been force-fed in a hospital prison for over 10 years in defence of the right to life and liberty of the people of Manipur and has demanded the withdrawal of the Armed Forces Special Powers Act.

At the same time, these groups ought to examine whether they did the right thing by not recognising a clearly democratic element in the Anna upsurge, not considering the corruption issue as a part of their democratic rights campaign and thus missing an opportunity at this historical moment. That 'democratic' element caught the imagination of a vast number of common people who not only were present in Delhi's Ramlila Maidan but also thronged at solidarity rallies in big and small towns all over India. Were they led into a trap by Congress spokespersons who characterised (and later regretted the Act) the Anna campaign—as a move by 'armchair fascists, over-ground Maoists and closet anarchists'—a refrain which some eminent personalities continued to maintain till the very end? Even when the government and the parties in the opposition had come around to respecting the democratic voice of the Anna campaign?

The presence of Medha Patkar, leader of the Narmada Bachao Andolan, in the core group of the Anna campaign did lend some credence to the participation of some social movements. Yet, over the course of the campaign, it was clear that while she was committed to the goals of the Anna campaign and some of her followers were with her in it, the nationwide network of the National Alliance of People's Movements (NAPM) was not mobilised in support of the Anna campaign.

A Middle-Class Campaign?

One of the reactions to the Anna campaign from the left and social movement circles is that it is a middle-class initiative having appeal primarily in urban areas. Firstly, many democratic initiatives have started as middle-class initiatives. The civil liberties movement in India in the wake of the Emergency was a middle-class movement. Even the dalit liberation movement had its origins in the educated middle-class and literary circles and then gradually acquired a wider popular base. Secondly, the Anna campaign may have started as an initiative by a group of middle-class activists to pass an effective law on curbing corruption, but as soon as the government started rejecting their proposals, it incurred the wrath of the common people and the protest spread to wider sections of society. When Anna Hazare moved the location for his fast to Ramlila Maidan, the crowd swelled everyday. It was no longer just a composite of middle-class groups and NGOs and their constituents but also that of ordinary people—rickshaw pullers, vegetable vendors, autorickshaw drivers, students and lower class families with all their members spent time in the maidan. Thirdly, the issues that were seen as the final bone of contention between the government and the protests—including the lower bureaucracy under the jurisdiction of the Lokpal, a mechanism for grievance redressal and Lokayuktas in the states were poor people's issues as well. If indeed, some mechanisms are put in place and the delivery of government services improves, eliminating the phenomenon of bribery, it would bring a great relief to the common people.

It is true that several secular and democratic forces were put off by the arrival of the Rashtriya Swayamsevak Sangh (RSS) cadres and the followers of 'yoga guru' Ramdev and Sri Sri Ravi Shankar in the rallies all over the country. People recalled how the Bharatiya Janata Party (BJP) emerged as a strong force as a result of the JP Narayan led movement in the mid-1970s. However, that was yet another historical occasion when many progressive forces critical of JP left the space for the RSS to fill.

The crowd in the Anna campaign cut across many classes. It soon became clear that the BJP followers were not the main group of people responding to Anna's call. In fact, the BJP had remained ambivalent about several issues in the Jan Lokpal Bill till the very end. Therefore, to describe the Anna campaign as a Right-wing campaign launched by Hindu reactionaries is to ignore the realities on the ground. Fortunately, that criticism died down as the campaign proceeded to achieving its first success.

That some NGOs provided the backbone for the campaign may be true. That some technologically adept young activists and enterprising NGO leaders arranged the basic resources to set up the infrastructure for the rallies and to carry on the campaign may also be true. That is a part of the contemporary reality of the neoliberal economic process in Indian society. During the past two decades, all governments at the centre and the states have associated with NGOs in policymaking and delivery of services. The United Progressive Alliance regime's National Advisory Council headed by Sonia Gandhi formalised this trend, integrating the NGO sector within the state process—a phenomenon promoted by the forces of globalisation and liberalisation. In this case, while some NGOs remained critical of the campaign, others helped the anti-corruption drive. The presence of non-resident Indians made it seem even more elitist as did the solidarity demonstrations abroad—inviting grateful acknowledgement from the Anna campaign activist Arvind Kejriwal in his thanks giving speech. It should be pointed out that while the NGOs took care of the logistics, there were many humble contributions from individuals and small groups of volunteers from all over the country.

However, the campaign defaulted in not doing enough to change its middle-class image. Its original approach was to negotiate with the government just as the National Campaign for People's Right to Information (NCPRI) did and achieved the passing of the Right to Information Act. Only when Anna Hazare turned it into a mass campaign by going on a fast and when the government's unwise and most deplorable decision to arrest Anna created a massive groundswell of support, the dynamics of a mass upsurge began to unfold. Thereafter, the organisers were so preoccupied with the negotiation process with the government that they did not see the need to seek allies among other people's movement groups. There was a great opportunity to spell out how an anti-corruption campaign can deliver justice to the rural and urban poor and the common people in general. They could have formed support groups with dalit, adivasi, minorities' and workers' movements. For example, they could have convinced them that the land rights movements going on in massive scale in many parts of the country may actually be strengthened by the anti-corruption measures being proposed by the campaign. The anti-state perspective of the people's movements could have provided further ammunition to the Anna campaign's effort to expose the hollowness of the official Lokpal Bill. On the other hand, the electronic media emerged as the Anna campaign's major ally. The TV anchors had a sumptuous menu to serve—an avatar of Gandhi with incredible moral appeal, the photogenic, *topi*-headed youth declaring 'I am Anna', minute-by-minute dramatic developments, the government's flip-flops adding midnight melodrama with the uninterrupted sermons and sentimental jibes along expected lines from familiar faces on the TV screen. It is no surprise that in Anna's list of thanks the media figured next only to the people in the maidan who came first.

Can a Law End Corruption?

The Anna campaign has been accused of reducing the fight against corruption to enacting a law that envisaged establishing a gigantic, powerful, independent ombudsman to investigate and punish the corrupt, as if that would eradicate the scourge of corruption at all levels.

On the face of it, it is a valid criticism. The whole debate has focused on alternate bills, the Lokpal Bill of the Government of India and the Anna campaign's Jan Lokpal Bill. Other drafts also came up for comparison. One was the draft of the NCPRI of Aruna Roy, another by the Lok Satta Party leader from Andhra Pradesh, Jayaprakash Narayan, and yet another by the former Chief Election Commissioner, T.N. Sheshan. The media drew so much attention to the comparative provisions of the various drafts that the larger causes of corruption in contemporary India got little space.

Much discussion and thinking has gone on in India and globally on corruption. One of the high points of this discussion was during the JP Movement in 1974. JP gave the call for 'total revolution' to bring about structural changes to achieve a just, egalitarian and a clean democratic society. There were attempts to formulate proposals on electoral reforms to tackle one of the major sources of corrupt practices for getting votes. However, after the onset of economic reforms in 1991, the operation of the liberalised economy has vastly expanded the arena of discretion of the executive—both political and bureaucratic causing an exponential rise in the number and scale of malpractices. This was evident in the 2G scam, the Commonwealth Games scam, the mining scams in Karnataka and Orissa and the light thrown on the politician-corporate-media nexus in the Nira Radia tapes, to mention a few. Thus, the magnitude of corruption has increased vastly during the reform era. Incidentally, the same is true in the case of China where the magnitude is many times more than in India because of the size of the economy and corresponding business deals.

To put it in a nutshell, corruption has to be tackled by a three-pronged approach: at the political economy level, at the legal apparatus level and through moral values. The political economy of poverty and destitution puts the poor at the mercy of the lower bureaucracy and local politicians whose corrupt practices harass the poor on a day-to-day basis. At the same time, the liberalisation of the national economy has facilitated big scams. Structural measures have to be taken to address poverty and provide democratic rights to the common people and policies have to change at the political economy level. The elimination of the discretion of civil servants and ministers, laying down transparent procedures of decision-making and delivery of services are essential together with policy changes. And that is not likely in an unequal society. Next, effective laws and institutions are extremely significant to prevent corrupt practices and to punish the corrupt.

Political parties have so manipulated these institutions to protect their own interests, favour corporate houses and harass their political opponents using institutions of state, that we needed a campaign like Anna's to bring focus on these. In addition to these two dimensions, inculcation of moral values is as central to this endeavour as legal measures. If on the one hand we encourage an acquisitive, consumerist, commercial culture that tempts every person to make more money to satisfy his/her desires and internalise a money-making culture, and on the other hand ask them to be non-corrupt, there would be a contradiction. If a parent has to pay Rs 10 lakh as capitation fee for the admission of his/her child to a professional school, the child is groomed to make additional money to compensate for that investment. The Mahatma Gandhi tradition as also the socialist tradition to treat public property as more sacrosant than private property and account for every paisa that is earned and spent in both public and private transactions is pretty much a dead letter today.

This is where common school education, public universities and colleges with a clear commitment to values of integrity and service to society become relevant. Unfortunately, the Anna campaign narrowed down the anti-corruption discourse to a Jan Lokpal Bill, however strong and effective it may be, and did not touch wider political, economic and moral issues even to put the the law campaign in perspective. Particularly noteworthy was the near silence on corporate dimensions of corruption. Kejriwal administered a pledge, at the time of the ending of Anna's fast, asking people not to give or take bribes. However, value inculcation involves more than that form of symbolism or tokenism.

The Anna-led campaign may have a reason for focusing on a law. Rather than broad talk on the subject which has failed to enact a Lokpal law despite eight attempts over the last 43 years during which corruption has risen to unbearable proportions at every level, it may be worthwhile to zero in on an effective bill and pursue with determination a non-violent mass protest. The Anna-led campaign was a *satyagraha* in the classic Gandhian mode, though it did not use the term for some reason to get a strong law enacted. Anna Hazare, a crusader with mass appeal, emerged in the public arena to carry it forward with a carefully worked out strategy. And in a liberal democracy, when the governing parties refuse to formulate an effective law, any citizen, any group has a right to mobilise public opinion and try to put its proposal before the government or an appropriate committee to place it before Parliament. It is a pity that the people's movements and many progressive forces failed to appreciate this as did the political parties until they saw a massive popular will backing the initiative.

Hopefully, the Anna campaign will grow into an even more effective mobilisation for achieving the actual Lokpal law in the course of which there will be greater understanding between the people's movements and the anti-corruption campaign and it will become a part of the process of systemic transformation of Indian society.

2

Whither the Indian Republic? Representative versus Direct Democracy

Mahendra Prasad Singh

The problematique of this paper is to explore a crucial aspect of Indian democracy in terms of the original design as well as its subsequent evolutionary trajectory bearing on the relationship between representative democracy and direct democracy. This relationship appears to be central to the making of the Indian Constitution and the working of the Indian political system for over six decades since the commencement of the constitution in 1950. Yet, despite its foundational and developmental centrality, this crucial relationship in the theory and practice of Indian democracy has not been systematically explored and analysed in the literature on politics in India. This paper seeks to fill this gap in the study of the Indian political system.

Anti-colonial freedom struggle in India led predominantly by the Indian National Congress in the first half of the twentieth century was deeply ambivalent between republicanism or representative democracy on the one hand, and ideas of direct participatory democracy and direct action or militant nonviolent political agitations, on the other. This ambivalence recurs throughout the nationalist movement. This is evident in the debates between the Congress moderates like Dadabhai Naoroji, M.G. Ranade, and G.K. Gokhale and extremists like Balgangadhar Tilak, Lala Lajpat Rai and Bipin

Chandra Pal. The Congress leaders were also divided on the issue of whether the Congress should enter the Legislative Councils set up under the Government of India Act, 1919, or boycott them. The successful *Swadeshi* Movement in Bengal against the partition of the province between a Hindu-majority West Bengal and a Muslim-majority East Bengal by Lord Curzon in the first decade of the twentieth century was also a limited struggle within the overall imperial-colonial framework for the annulment of a specific divisive decision of the British government in India. Gandhi's Non-cooperation Movement of the early 1920s, its withdrawal after the outbreak of violence in Chaurichaura in UP his Civil Disobedience Movement in the early 1930s and his subsequent withdrawal into what he called 'constructive politics', clearly reflect a valiant attempt to resolve the dilemma between democratic and revolutionary methods of struggle. The two local struggles that Gandhi waged in the second decade of the twentieth century on behalf of the peasants in Champaran in Bihar and mill workers in Ahmedabad in Gujarat were also a tightrope walk between the poles of conflict and cooperation with the existing system rather than a full-scale revolutionary class struggle. The Motilal Nehru Committee Report, 1928, commissioned by an all-party conference in colonial India, presented a blueprint of parliamentary federal government with a bill of rights for the Indian subjects within the overall framework of dominion status under the British Crown. It was superseded by the Lahore Resolution of the Indian National Congress presided over by Jawaharlal Nehru for complete independence from British rule in 1930. It was followed by the Karachi Resolution of the Congress in 1931 that contained a comprehensive charter of political and economic rights that presage the fundamental rights and directive principles of state policy enshrined in the constitution of independent India enforced in 1950. Yet, when the imperial government introduced the next round of constitutional reforms under the Government of India Act, 1935, offering limited federal autonomy to the provinces and princely states and a diarchy of bureaucratic and representative governance at the centre, the Indian National Congress first decried it but subsequently formed ministries in the Congress-majority provinces. It is another matter that the federal component of the 1935 constitution could never be operationalised due to the reluctance of the princely Indian states to join the proposed federation, and the Congress ministries in the provinces later resigned protesting against the British decision to get India involved in the Second World War without consulting the Congress. The 1942 Quit India Movement, backed by Gandhi's call for 'Do or Die' and led by Jayaprakash Narayan from the underground when the entire top Congress leadership was jailed, was probably the only revolutionary struggle that resulted in direct seizure of power by the people in some local areas. However, it was soon suppressed and contained and the Congress leadership was back to the negotiation table to discuss with the British rulers the British Cabinet Mission Plan, 1946, for the independence of united India under a confederal constitution. The Constituent Assembly of India, elected under the Cabinet Mission Plan, even endorsed the Objectives Resolution moved by Jawaharlal Nehru, anticipating that the Muslim League would also subsequently accept the confederation option and join the process of making such a constitution. However, that was not to be, ând the Cabinet Mission plan was superseded by the Mountbatten Plan, 1946, for Independence based on the partition between the two post-colonial states of India and Pakistan, following the British withdrawal in the wake of the Second World War.

It is evident from the foregoing that, unlike the modern USA, France, and Switzerland that were born in wars of independence or revolution, Indian independence was gained through a legal transfer of power from the British Parliament to the Constituent Assembly of India under the Independence of India Act, 1947. Unlike those countries where the established governments were overthrown and the people took power in their own hands and established new regimes, India experienced a constitutional change of regime at the time of Independence. Gandhi had demanded as early as in 1922 that the constitution of India would be framed by a Constituent Assembly directly elected by the people. Instead, under the British Cabinet Mission Plan the Constituent Assembly came to be indirectly elected in 1946 by the provincial legislatures, which were themselves elected by a limited franchise based on educational qualifications and property ownership extended to only 38.5 per cent of the Indian adult population under the Government of India Act, 1935. The Preambles of the constitutions of both the USA and India begin with the ringing declaration of popular sovereignty proclaiming 'We the people ...' as the source of all political power. Yet, it has a greater ring of authenticity in US constitutionalism than in the Indian, for the following reasons. The differences between the revolutionary birth of the US and Swiss constitutions, for example, and the evolutionary birth of the Indian constitution have left their imprints on their respective constitutional principles, practices and laws. For example, the constitution and laws of India do not give any quarters to institutions of direct democracy such as a formal people's initiative in law-making, referendum, and recall of elected representatives. The constitution of Switzerland provides for all of these, and the constitutions of the USA—federal and those of some states in the western USA—provide for some of these. In Canada, too, direct democracy has been a part of the political experience, especially in the western provinces contiguous to the western USA, and to an extent in the French Canadian province of Quebec. Australia, too, uses referendum for ratification of constitutional amendments after their passage by the two houses of the Parliament. Referendums are also used at the state level in Australia, the only British Commonwealth country that has also adopted some daring features of American federalism such as a directly elected Senate and residuary powers to the states. These 'wayward' ways of Australians may perhaps be understood in terms of their continental size and distance from the mother parliament in Westminster. France also employs some of these devices of direct democracy. All these political systems combine representative democracy with certain measures of direct democracy in varying degrees, Switzerland exceeding and excelling all.[1]

Ancient Athens and some other Greek city-states of the time as well as the Roman Republic of yore practised direct democracy in which citizens deliberated and made laws and elected their officials. Most of these early experiments in direct democracy degenerated into mob rule that later gave rise to dictatorships or rule by aristocrats.

In the trail of the American War of Independence, a strong strain of plebiscitary democracy persisted, but one of the founding fathers of the American Republic, James Madison, reflected the sober view of many of the framers of the United States constitution when he wrote in 1787: 'Such democracies [as those of ancient Greece and Rome] ... have ever been found incompatible with personal security, or the rights of property; and have in general been as short in their lives, as they have been violent in their deaths' (*The Federalist*, paper no. x).[2] Madison was apprehensive that direct democracy might be dangerous to freedom, minorities and property, and breed violence by one group against another.

The Indian constitution basically contains a scheme of republican or representative democracy with a periodic renewal of the electoral mandate at a normal interval of five years. This is despite the fact that the interim President of the Constituent Assembly and a leading light of the Patna Bar, Dr Sachchidanand Sinha, in his inaugural address had broached all the leading models of comparative constitutionalism including the Swiss model to the attention of the makers. However, the Legal Advisor to the Assembly, Sir B.N. Rao and the Chairman of the Drafting Committee, Dr B.R. Ambedkar, had in their notes and addresses, focused mainly on the Anglo-American and the White Commonwealth models in Canada and Australia. The Constituent Assembly clearly rejected any major or formal concession to direct democracy beyond its limited acceptance at the level of the village panchayat under the towering structure of parliamentary federal governments at the Union and State levels in the representative mode. The Constituent Assembly debates do not have anything great and exciting on the panchayats of Gandhi's imagination. The idea of *gram swaraj* as a bottom-up scheme of power *from* the people (rather than the rhetorical power *to* the people), was simply buried without much wide lament. The debate on article 31A of the draft constitution—which ended up being article 40 of the constitution in Part IV of the constitution—on the directive principles of state policy, was marked by a profusion of rhetorics and naivety by a few Gandhians like T. Prakasham (Madras, General Seat) and Surendra Mohan Ghose (West Bengal, General Seat). Even the shrewd K. Santhanam appears to have paid some clever lip service and indulged in platitudes at best. Praksham made reference to President Rajendra Prasad's remark at some point in the debates that the panchayats should be the 'basis' of the constitution and the Legal Advisor, B.N. Rao, commented that while he sympathised with the idea, it was too late to make changes on the basis of the constitution; yet, in the next breath, Prakasham thanked Ambedkar, the Chairman of the drafting committee, for including, albeit belatedly, the article on panchayats as one of the directive principles of state policy! Everyone knows that this article itself is no more than a euphemism. Someone also made a reference to the very negative opinion of Ambedkar, expressed about the village communities while presenting the draft constitution for debate in the Assembly. Even K. Santhanam, who moved the amendment with an overwhelming support of the House to add the article under the debate to the constitution that was adopted, seemingly agreed with those who disapproved of the almost mystical idea of self-sufficiency of the village community. L. Krishnaswamy Bharathi (Madras, General Seat) reads as the only realist among those who participated in this debate, including Ambedkar who quickly accepted the amended article that became article 40 at the end of the day in the final text of the constitution. Bharathi said, 'I must confess that I am not fully satisfied with this amendment, for the simple reason that even today under the present constitution, I think the Provincial Governments have enough powers to form village panchayats and operating them as self-governing units. But to the extent it goes I must express my satisfaction.' Ultimately what boils down to the conclusion, according to Bharathi, is what Gandhi said on the occasion of the Asian Relations Conference convened by Nehru in New Delhi as the head of the interim government of India : 'Non-violence with its technique of Satyagraha and non-cooperation will be the sanction of the village community.'[3]

There is another instance in which the Constituent Assembly turned its back to the direct democratic device of referendum. The rejection of the idea of having a directly elected President of India is a case in point. The matter was settled in favour of a president indirectly elected by the elected members of Parliament and of the State Legislatures by proportional representation by means of a single transferable vote. This also happened during the debate on the power and process of amending the constitution (article 304 in the draft constitution, which became article 368 in the final text). In the context of ratification of federally relevant amendments by states, Brajeshwar Prasad (Bihar, General Seat) proposed the idea of ratification in a referendum by the people in various states of the Indian Union. This was rejected and the Assembly settled for ratification by state legislatures to the tune of 50 per cent of the total number of states.[4]

So, as it happens, neither the constitution of India nor any law in the country make any provision for direct democratic devices of initiative, referendum and recall. There are, of course, elaborate provisions for periodic elections at Union, state and local levels and for the Election Commission of India for the conduct of polls for the offices of the President and Vice-President of India and Parliament and State Legislatures. The 73rd and 74th constitutional amendments (1992) also prescribe for the enactment of panchayat and municipal laws for local government and the appointment of State Election Commissions to conduct elections at local levels. Part III of the constitution on fundamental rights of the citizens guarantees fundamental freedoms of speech and expression, to assemble peacefully and without arms, to form associations and unions, to move freely throughout the territory of India, to reside and settle in any part of India and to practice any profession or to carry out any occupation, trade or business. These rights are only subject to any law imposing reasonable restrictions in the interest of sovereignty and integrity of India or public order or morality (article 19). Add to these the right to equality (article 14) and right to life and personal liberty that cannot be taken away 'except according to procedure established by law' (article 21). This starry triangle forms a most formidable and strong bill of rights in the realm of comparative constitutional law. And judicial interpretations have expanded them beyond the apparent intents of the makers of the constitution. This is illustrated by the virtual replacement in case law of the 'procedure established by law' clause by the American constitutional doctrine of the 'due process of law' rooted in the theory of natural law. Yet, the fact remains that these rights cannot be stretched to the extent of direct democratic rights of initiative, referendum and recall in terms of constitutional and positive laws of the land. Indeed, even the right to vote has been rather conservatively interpreted by the Supreme Court of India to be a legal right; it is neither a customary nor a fundamental right in its judgement.

The construction of participatory democratic and protest rights in Gandhian ideology and/or political theory is, of course, a different proposition. And I do concede that the Gandhian technique of non-violent satyagraha has become a part of the national ideological heritage of India. It has also found a receptive echo is several other countries of the world. Nevertheless, it is important to recall what Ambedkar said in his last major speech in the Constituent Assembly towards the end of the deliberations. He said:

> If we wish to maintain democracy not merely in form, but also in fact, what must we do? The first thing in my judgement we must do is to hold fast to constitutional methods of achieving our social and economic objectives. It means we must abandon the disobedience, non-cooperation and satyagraha. When there was no way left for constitutional methods for achieving economic and social objectives, there was a great deal of justification for unconstitutional methods. But where constitutional methods are open, there can be no justification for these unconstitutional methods. These methods are nothing but the Grammar of Anarchy and the sooner they are abandoned, the better for us.[5]

In the post-Independence politics of India, there have been at least three major occasions when the issue of direct democratic devices of popular participation in governance has prominently figured in the political discourse. These are the extra-parliamentary movement against corruption and authoritarianism in the government led by Jayaprakash Narayan (JP) in the first half of the 1970s, the post-Emergency 44th Constitutional amendment (1978), and the India Against Corruption (IAC) campaign launched by Anna Hazare and his team in the wake of the Arab Democratic Spring of 2011. In the first half of the 1970s, India was rocked by a chain of extra-parliamentary mass protests—in Gujarat, led by Morarji Desai and in Bihar initiated by students and non-Congress and non-Communist opposition parties that came finally to be led by JP (the Gandhian socialist leader who was drawn out of virtual political retirement)—that spread like a prairie fire across north India down to Bangalore. These movements demanded the resignation of the Congress governments of Indira Gandhi at the Centre and in the states and pressed for the dissolution of the Lok Sabha and Vidhan Sabhas for a fresh electoral mandate on the plea that the people had lost trust in these corrupt and authoritarian governments. JP rhetorically advocated his vision of what he called the Total Revolution which included the popular right to recall the elected representatives mid-term in a genuine participatory democracy. While the Gujarat Movement succeeded in getting the State Assembly dissolved under the pressure of a fast-unto-death by the rebel Congress Gandhian, Morarji Desai, the JP Movement was superseded by the imposition of internal Emergency by Prime Minister Indira Gandhi of the Indian National Congress in June 1975, under article 352 of the constitution, pleading that Congress governments, as duly elected representatives of the people, had the valid democratic mandate to rule for the five-year term. The Emergency as well as the JP Movement appeared to be fraught with the danger of lapsing into authoritarianism of the elite or the masses, but they were fortuitously checked in their tracks.[6]

The post-Emergency Janata Party Government born out of the JP Movement did not institute a recall in the representative-legislative system of the country. It did, however, seek to introduce referendum through the 44th Amendment (1978) to be held prior to a 'Change in the Constitution which would have the effect of impairing its secular or democratic character, abridging or taking away fundamental rights, prejudicing or impeding free and fair elections on the basis of adult suffrage, and compromising the independence of judiciary'... According to the Statement of Objects and Reasons of the 44th Amendment, such changes 'can be made only if they are approved by the people of India by a majority of votes at a referendum in which at least fifty-one percent the electorate participate.' It also said 'Article 368 is being amended to ensure this.' Paradoxically however, article 368 was left untouched by the amendment. The Statement of Objects and Reasons also remains unaltered in the constitution (44th Amendment) Act, 1978.[7] This was probably because of the fact that the Janata Party Government's majority in the Lok Sabha was counterveiled by the majority of the Congress Party in opposition in the Rajya Sabha. Thus, apparently, the Congress opposition did not agree to any alteration in article 368 but allowed the Statement of Objects and Reasons to stand as it was. However, it does not have any effect in law, but only as an ideological function of some sort.

In the wake of the heady Arab Democratic Spring of 2011, the India Against Corruption (IAC) campaign led by Anna Hazare and his team that includes Aravind Kejariwal, Kiran Bedi, Shanti Bhushan,

Prashant Bhushan and Manish Sishodia have again made a pitch for direct democratic devices like the right to recall, besides the right of the voters to reject all candidates if they so like in an election for representative institutions, and an unusually powerful institution of Lokpal at the central level and Lokayuktas at the state level (ombudsmen) to deal with cases of corruption involving political and administrative classes from the top to the bottom. Anna Hazare has also given expression to his vision of participatory direct democracy in India in which law-making would be a joint endeavour between the legislatures and the Gram Sabhas premised on a relationship of parity. The movement, conducted through direct public meetings in metro cities and internet social networking sites and backed by Anna Hazare's public fast unto death on the issue of a strong ombudsman law in the midst of a great media hype in New Delhi, presented a big spectacle of public protest. The Congress-led United Progressive Alliance Government incrementally yielded under its pressure. There was an unprecedented instance of the direct participation of the civil society in drafting a Lokpal-Lokayukta Bill by a government-appointed joint panel co-chaired by a Union minister and a civil society nominee. When the process was stalemated, the government and Team Anna proceeded to draft their respective bills unilaterally, but the government was pressurised to refer both the bills to a parliamentary standing committee. The reconciled constitutional amendment bill failed to muster the requisite two-thirds majority in the Lok Sabha and was roundly thrashed in the Rajya Sabha before it was abruptly adjourned *sine die* at the midnight on December 31 on the last day of the winter session of 2011. The government has gone on record saying it was an one-time-off instance, but then a precedent is set which may not of course settle into a convention.

Summing up, strongly pervasive or partially incorporated institutions of direct democracy are a feature of republics born out of moderate revolutions or wars like Switzerland and the USA. In the Indian case, the transfer of power from the colonial rulers to the nationalists was legal, but Independence was won after a long freedom struggle in which extra-constitutional methods of political agitation were used. Reflecting this dual legacy, India has been ambivalent between representative democracy and direct democracy. There is some tension between the Constitution of India and its national political heritage of the Gandhian vision of *gram swaraj* and political methods of non-violent *satyagraha.* This tension is also reflected in the Preamble to the Indian Constitution which invokes the doctrine of popular sovereignty that proclaims 'We, the people of India...' as the source of all power and the rest the constitution that outlines an essentially representative or republican version of democracy. And the structure of governments in India, despite repeated attempts to incorporate measures of direct democracy, remains rooted in representative democracy. This is not to say, however, that the yearning for a participatory direct democracy in cohabitation with representative democracy is not valid. Nor can it be said to be destined to fail. Within the overall framework of India's parliamentary-federal democracy, participatory direct democratic devices can and ideally should be incorporated in a partial combination and a harmonious construction. This is especially called for in the backdrop of endemic corruption and criminalisation of the political process over the decades since India's independence.

NOTES

1. Steinberg, Jonathan (1996) *Why Switzerland?* 2nd edition, chapters 2 and 3; Cambridge University Press, Bogdanor, Vernon (ed.), *The Blackwell Encyclopedia of Political Institutions*, p.177, Oxford: Blackwell Reference.
2. Hamilton, Alexander, James Madison, & John Jay, *The Federalist,* edited with an Introduction and Notes by Max Beloff, Oxford: Basil Blackwell, 1987, 2nd edition, p. 45. *The Federalist* was originally published in the USA in 1787.
3. India Republic, *Constituent Assembly Debates, Official Report*, 2003, Book No. 2, p. 520, New Delhi: Lok Sabha Secretariat, 4th reprint.
4. Ibid., Book No. 4, pp. 1648–1667.
5. Ibid., Book No. 5, p. 978.
6. Chandra, Bipan (2003). *In the Name of Democracy: JP Movement and the Emergency*, New Delhi: Penguin Books.
7. See the text of the 44th Constitutional amendment reproduced in M.V. Pylee, *Constitutional Amendments in India*, Delhi: Universal Law Publishing Co. Pvt. Ltd., (2003). pp. 206–22, read with the text of the constitution with notes and comments in Bakshi, P.M. 2011. *The Constitution of India*, pp. 334–6. Delhi: Universal Law Publishing Co. Pvt. Ltd., 11th edition .

3

Story of an Imaginary Movement: Uncovering the Anna Spectacle!

Manoj K. Jha

Introduction

As students of movements, we learnt to appreciate that defining movements is one of the most difficult propositions in making sense of any movement. We also realised that lack of an apparently coherent definition or consensus on *the* definition does not harm the cause of the movement. The diversity of approaches notwithstanding, a movement is loosely perceived as a form of collective behaviour when a fairly large number of people asssemble together to raise some pressing grievances against a particular social-political order. It is a collective, organised, sustained, and non-institutional challenge to authorities, power holders, or cultural beliefs and practices (Goodwin & Jasper, 2003). We must also reiterate that movements in a democracy are conscious, concerted, and sustain efforts by ordinary people to look for supposedly extraordinary changes in the institutions governing their lives and times. Still further, *unlike the scholars of the 1960s who studied movements only to get scared and scare their audience, we no more see movements in a democracy as terrifying crowds blindly following the dictates and directions of the demagogues.* There is no hurry, none whatsoever, to portray movements as deindividuated behaviour of unthinking automatons because matured democracies have realised that movements as collective expressions of people are as normal and and desirable as participation in any other democratic processes. However, there are certain important parameters nay preconditions required which distinguish and differentiate between any collective behaviour vis-à-vis movements in democracy. Some of these are as follows: When and why do movements occur? Who joins or supports the movement? How are movements organised? What are the ideological moorings of the movement? What do movements do? How does media influence and shapes the movement? What are the symbols and images propagated by the movement?

While looking for answers to some of these questions, one finds it impossible to bracket the *Anna phenomenon with genuine mass movements in democracy.* The task gets complicated further when one attempts to place the upsurge by team Anna within the constitutional framework governing the nation and its people. However, *in the absence of any other category which could describe this supposed upsurge by 'great masses', I shall be using the term 'movement', albeit reluctantly, and will make an effort to find out some of the little known aspects of the imaginary national movement led by Anna.*

Most movements have inconspicuous beginnings. The significant elements of their origins are usually forgotten or distorted, but in the case of the Anna's movement, we feel that it had an evident beginning almost as predictable as assembly line production. It is rather incongruous to note that the movement led by Anna Hazare and his team, which began to seek answers from the government on issues relating to corruption, has in reality left a wide spectrum of questions unanswered; a few of these questions unswervingly connect to the agencies involved in manufacturing this movement. *A 'sanitised political correctness campaign' on the Anna phenomenon is still aggressively being launched in the media.* Unfortunately, in abiding by the rigid binary of 'for' or 'against', the setting has become grossly inappropriate for a genuine deliberation on a cause that seems to have captured the attention of the nation. The political churning that the country has experienced in recent times demands foremost, an informed and an inspiring discussion on a range of issues, necessitated by the fact that certain crucial concerns are at stake.

It is sad commentary to state that with each passing day, the present government at the centre has been brazenly displaying absolute inadequacy in carrying out the basic agenda of governance, a thing it was fundamentally elected for. It goes without saying that no government is justified to use the plank of 'peoples' verdict only through the general election' as a buffer, for this goes against the very grain of democracy and the sovereignty of people, which all of us would like to preserve and protect. It also slaughters the possibility of immense political innovations people can make for strengthening the same democracy and constitution on which the governments swear. It is in this backdrop that one must dispassionately see whether the 'Anna Movement' has the will or the capacity to meet this challenge emanating out of multiplicity of genuine grievances people have with the political establishment. It also needs to be iterated that the timing of this mobilisation has provided a convenient cathartic outlet to the broad sense of failing that people are tending to experience with the incumbent regime, and which may partly explain the 'misplaced' sense of association that many may have felt towards this Anna phenomenon. It is essential to also understand that these are by far much more integral and important than the either the fate of team Anna or of the UPA regime itself.

This Never Was a Democratic Movement

I am certainly part of the thousands of others who strongly believe that the media has, in a sense, hijacked this event and has played a monumental role in projecting Anna Hazare and his movement as something which it is not, and which it never even claimed to have been. *In more ways than one, the media brazenly indulged in projecting an 'imagined reality' to its viewers and listeners.* By enacting it repetitively, using high voltage theatrical effects, it was indeed able to alter the way reality was perceived, acknowledged and even remembered. These counterfactual narratives manufactured by the media and built around the image and persona of Anna and his highly professional team deliberately terminated the possibility of any 'alternative views' permeating therein. It would not be impertinent to state that the dominant view emanating from the endless mesmerisation by the media hid within its folds the greater reality itself. *What was this movement all about? Was this a movement in the first place?* As stated above, were the parameters met that qualified it to be referred to as a national movement? Did it really represent the diversity of India, which is core to the very idea of India? Except for the shaft of corruption, *why were other important components of a movement such as ideology, symbols and mobilisation strategies never allowed to reach the debate in the public domain?* Most importantly, how could a movement with discernable authoritarian streaks go on to raise doubts about peoples' sovereignty and yet how was every byte ridiculing peoples' ability was cherished by the media?

The queries listed above are just a few out of scores of pertinent others, that should be engaged with, in order to arrive at the inner layers of the innate meaning of this movement. Viewed in context of the limited confines of the 'aired' discussion on the Anna movement, certain critical issues pertaining to the movement have remained cloaked under the mystique of 'expression of national sentiment'. Such an extensive expurgation of those alternat views and opinions by the corporate media houses remind us of the horrifying images of the *Ram-mandir* and *anti-Mandal* agitations and one shudders to think of the eventuality of something like that repeating itself ever. Any critical posture vis-à-vis the Anna movement has been expunged from the public domain and subsequently from the popular memory. Boosted by the unprecedented role of the media as the hyperactive collaborator, the movement and its agency took on the responsibility of defining and delineating 'others' as nothing less than traitors, not only to the cause of corruption but to the cause of the nation itself. As a result, it becomes especially critical to see beyond those exquisite images of 'thousands of beautiful tricolours' and 'chants of *vande matram*'; as also to interpret the texts writ large on the faces of thousands of angry people who appeared keen to have their political presence felt and acknowledged, probably for the first time in the age of 24X7 television.

Apart from the media houses, due credit must also be bestowed on the gladiators of the Anna movement for having sensed that a relatively large section of people, particularly in the *metropolitan centres,* had an appalling unease on matters relating to corruption. It is this section, which in the last twenty years or so, has constituted the second set of recipients of the trickling down of the economic growth, the first being the corporate and business houses. It is the same group which has continued to believe that India is actually shining and this conviction has resulted in the overriding desire that India should not be showcased to the world through the images of slums, ghettos and perpetual poverty anymore. This class has nothing specifically against the poor or the ones who live in the slums and the ghettos, as can be validated by their enthusiastic contribution in the shape of doles to the people who house these sites, particularly during the times of festivals, possibly also thinking of the *grade points* such acts of generosity might entail. Yet, this class has been very keen to showcase an identity of an upwardly mobile India, which invariably clashes with the image of the real India.... on ground—aloof and far away from the success stories of Indian economics. This also happens to be the class whose contemporary hyperactivity on the social networking sites has generally not found a resonance in their political behaviour through the democratic process. *This class has also shown a sense of resentment towards 'vote bank politics' and the enormous votes that the slums, the ghettos and the poor in general possess.*

At the same time, it is this class which has also been an important cog in the machine of corruption, albeit reluctantly but nevertheless so. Hence, the stories of scams unfolding on a daily basis have led to a deep sense of anguish in them. They remain indisputably angry with corruption; and perhaps angrier on account of the fact that they, too, have played a part in nourishing it and making it as rampant and common place as it is in the contemporary frame. In all probability, what is therefore being manifested in the guise of this movement seems to be a curious mix of an exceptional anger against a regime whose credibility quotient is at an all time low and an inwardly directed resentment against one's own self. This angry class can genuinely identify with Bede Jarett, the English priest, when he says that, '*the world needs anger. The world often continues to allow evil because it is not angry enough.*' Anger seems to have suddenly become the most potent, and the most visible symbol as well as the most desirable of human emotions in the prevailing circumstances. Being angry can be attributed to being true to one's salt; and therefore it may have been interpreted as being one with Anna and consequently cementing the edifice of 'Anna is India'. A sincere scrutiny of this 'spectacle of the movement of Anna' necessitates asking as to how a relatively small and motley crowd of angry people have managed to appear so much bigger in size on our television screens and in the frozen frames of newspapers. The collectivisation of distinct experiences into a single whole and the manufacturing of anger through highly sophisticated media techniques, such as chosen camera positions, top-angle shots, crafted frames and simulation have indeed played some role, but there was certainly more to it than that.

As the stories unfold every day, one arrives at the firm opinion that it is LeBon's *contagion* that has been at work, and that this is largely attributable to the highly specialised management of the *Team Anna*. Moving ahead, the agency involved behind Anna has also drawn from Gladwell's *The Tipping Point* (Gladwell, 2000) with a clinical precision, and has aggressively advertised the idea of 'an exclusive national movement', and 'the second freedom struggle' akin to a virus approaching the threshold, only to cross it and increase at an exponential rate. Unlike the abandoned French social psychologist, LeBon, Gladwell's epidemic theory places a high premium on the multiplicity of roles being performed by numerous actors through a predefined set of social networks. There were the 'connectors' from *Team Anna*, who fervently spread the message of 'the second freedom struggle' through a wide spectrum of social networks, both conventional and the not so conventional. The connectors were able to establish a causal relationship between the seething discontents of a class with an antidote of their own. Then came the role of 'mavens', that is, the experts who were overtly impatient to convey that this '*Anna trend*' was the only available option to address what people so intensely seem to desire. The third set of roles was executed by the 'salesmen', the hysterical persuaders from the team as well as the extended teammates from the media, particularly the electronic media. As flawless salesmen, some of the television anchors wore lots of anger on their sleeves and that further enhanced the credibility of the trend in a time when anger is indicative of being with Anna, nay, with the nation itself. As a result, a relatively large section of people in metropolitan India were pre-disposed to letting the 'virus' set in them, thus making the 'well-marketed' epidemic appear as a national epidemic. LeBon's 'hypnosis', too, was brought into the highly dramatic production in a curiously high pitch, whereby the central icon, that is, Anna Hazare himself was 'hypnotised' by the idea that he was leading a national movement.

However, it is imperative to see through the counter-factual posturing of the media vis-à-vis the issues and concerns against the political establishment. Until now, *Team Anna* and the media have been fusing reality and fantasy at one level, and truth and duplicity at another, only a mishmash of connotations become readily available for the common masses.

What Is Anna, If Not the Spectacle?

At the cost of eliciting ridicule from hundreds and thousands of my fellow countrymen who have been rather hyperactive on social networking sites such as Facebook and Twitter, *one finds that this Anna movement is almost a perfect textbook example of a spectacle.* The agencies involved in the making of the spectacle must have drawn from Feuerbach (in his preface to *The Essence of Christianity*) who said, 'But certainly for the present age, which prefers the sign to the thing signified, the copy to the original, fancy to reality, the appearance to the essence ... illusion only is sacred, truth profane.' And further, Jean Baudrillard also points to the 'image replacing the reality' (Baudrillard, 1994). Just like Che on T-shirts, coffee mugs and key chains, Gandhi *topi* (now Anna *topi*) and Gandhi's image seem to serve the same purpose.

The spectacle required a crafted production of a semblance of clarity and unity of purpose of the 'nation' and that meant doing away with anything that distinguished the appearance from the essence. While the agencies involved were looking forward to having the most essential ingredients of the proposed spectacle, the shaky government of the UPA-II obliged by throwing up murkier images of corruption almost on a daily basis. However, the earnestness of the need and the urgent necessity of packaging corruption was brutally captured by the agencies involved in the making of the spectacle and this reflected another important feature of spectacle, which has been substantiated by Guy Deobard, '...to the extent that necessity is socially dreamed, the dream becomes necessary' (Debord, 1983).

Many views have surfaced as to how this spectacle was co-authored and co-produced by the media, which apparently had exhausted all conventional mechanisms to capture and retain the eyeballs, which it necessarily required to remain relevant in the highly competitive market. The media barons also perceived beforehand that 'Anna as a Spectacle' could only be maintained, if the planned spectacle was not merely a collection of images but also managed to build a social relation among people mediated by those images. A cursory glance at the signs, symbols, texts and sound bytes which emerged as the essential constituents of the Anna spectacle through this movement against corruption reveal the extent to which self-fulfilling prophesies surface in the times of 24X7 television. The media did not have to undertake any significant innovation, but only to dig out the available archival materials on an assortment of issues ranging from rabid Right-wing congregations of previous years to *sas-bahu* soap operas and of course, add to it the liberal spray of the genre of *Rang De Basanti* and *Peepli Live*. And lo and behold! *The Anna Spectacle* was ready to roll!

The Anna spectacle came with the prefix-*first* for a variety of things claiming to be the *first* peoples' movement, the *first* assertion of peoples' power against an unrelenting parliament, the *first* expression of national sentiment etcetera. The only time the spectacle used the prefix-*second* was when it albeit grudgingly proclaimed itself as the second freedom struggle. A major component in this is also, it must be said, that the Anna team was well empowered with its own media spin-doctors. Notice that they never did anything during the time-slots when TV channels have sports shows—Sachin's impending hundredth ton kept them on tenterhooks. They created photo-ops such as Anna meditating at Rajghat. They kept supplying statements so that news channels had fresh things to say hour-on-hour. Anna's pre-recorded message was tailor-made by the team for media consumption. One gets reminded of the media attention Osama's pre-recorded messages received. Besides, through the uninterrupted promotional coverage of the spectacle, the biggest ever and the largest watched reality show of the country, the notion of limits of subjectivity in reporting and coverage, was buried. The sign became both the signifier and the signified.

Before the spectacle was launched on a grand scale, it was preceded by beautiful promos and a mixing of the best of music and drama. Thus, while in one moment *Team Anna* was interacting with the family of a martyr in one TV studio, the next moment showed them acting as judges for a singing competition for kids in another studio. As the days unfolded and as the political class made its operative frame look like a 'pathetic comedy of errors', the media gloated over its manufactured spectacle and its potential mass (read class!) appeal. Debates followed in the public domain (read essentially *private* domain of the TV channels!!) and the over enthusiastic anchors of some of these TV channels began using a range of techniques from hard persuasion to cajoling and lampooning of any view which even remotely dared to be critical of this spectacle. Needless to mention that any supposedly national movement necessitates critical and complex arguments, but to be dealt with harangues such as, 'gentlemen, gentlemen it is getting too complex ... let us be clear ... are you for or against...' relegated the whole issue to the mercy of the predisposed wisdom of the anchors. The anchors of this spectacle just needed to know whether the analyst in the TV studio *was* Anna or not (not even *for* or *against* Anna!).

The manufacturers remained sure and certain that one was supposed to amalgamate oneself with Anna; for the person had become the spectacle ... the man was the mission now and it was a mission made possible by the media. Paradoxically, *the medium became the message as McLuhan would have termed it* (McLuhan, 1986). *One lost the locus standii whatsoever in raising queries regarding the class character, the composition of the crowd, about the funding of such a good-looking protest movement and of course about the overtly divisive symbols on display. More than a loss to the political class of the day, it was a greater loss to the cause of the peoples' movements which have eternally lacked the privilege of the OB vans and cameras mounted on buses and cranes to record and transmit their protests.* The genuine peoples' protest in a Manipur or a Jehanabad or a Bastar has to negotiate their protest against an insensitive state and an anaesthetised media, but why should the spectacle care about all this? It may sound bizarre in these euphoric times of the spectacle but this is how the memory of the common masses shall record the Anna movement once the manufactured commotion settles and the media gaze moves on to another spectacle.

When the spectacle entered the *age of maturity*, the media torrent within and around was unambiguous; the technology was at work to showcase it as one of the most historic moments of Independent India. The carefully crafted images of Anna (bringing him in the closest possible physical resemblance to the great Mahatma), top angle shots of people surging to have a glimpse of the central icon, together with waving of hundreds of national flags and high pitch patriotic songs in the background transmitted the frenzy to an exalted level. These techniques were perfected by Nazi filmmaker, Leni Riefenstahl who, using multiple cameras, shot Hitler from low angles thus making him look larger than life) and the crowds from the top hence making them look small (Trimborn, 2007). Subsequently, the images thickened, the soundscape grew noisier and the montage was highly frenetic. It transcended the conventional polarities visible in politics and the democratic movements and the fantasy about the reality of the spectacle posed as reality itself. *There were several overt acts of subversion by the media by way of redefinition.* To name just a few, *we came to know that a movement passes on as a national movement only when some of the television anchors decide so.* For them, 'we the people of India' means, Anna's people or the ones who were at Ramlila maidan or a freedom park and who remained on the one side of the digital divide celebrating the signs, symbols and the slogans of the Anna spectacle. *We were also told in most unambiguous fashion about what constitutes 'national sentiment' and why some people have a more liberal dose of it than the others. It certainly left us to introspect and identify our inadequacies which failed us to be part of the revolutionary spectacle.* It is, nevertheless, a different story that this movement not only mockingly questioned the legislative supremacy of the parliament but in more ways than one, 'democracy' itself. 'We the people', the opening lines to the preamble of the Indian constitution was invariably shown in the backdrop of 'Annas' on the television screen; the fantasy was real again, for Annas at the Ramlila Maidan or Azad Maidan were the only *bona fide* 'we the people' and rest of the others were the '*apologetic others*'. The spectacle in this case went ahead and rather blatantly puffed up the numbers and the will of the 'contagious crowd' of LeBon appeared as the de facto voice of the nation (LeBon, 1896). One could dispute the 'number game', and one could also argue with Team Anna that vibrant democracies need to be little cautious with showcased numbers.

Alas! The Anna Spectacle Tries the Having Gandhi Tag

There have been several appalling outcomes of the orchestrated Anna movement and a few of them have been shared above, but not many of us have been able to perceive the kind of impairment it has caused to the psycho-social and political health of the nation in entirety. *A hyperactive media has only facilitated the movement to generate a collective sense of being under siege, wherein one is literally being coerced to feel that the rest of the world is a cheat, a crook and inherently hostile.* This 'siege mentality' has engulfed a large tract of the public sphere which has only been helped by the incessant follies committed by the political class. This siege is being increasingly intensified with each passing day by a group of megalomaniacs who regrettably call their theatrics as Gandhian. *While the rhetorical warfare by Anna goes on, we sadly remain as silent bystanders to one of the most perilous language manipulations in the public sphere which has resulted in the daylight robbery of the peoples' ability to debate and dissent, and most regrettably, it is being done in the name of Gandhi. Even a cursory glance over some of the works of Gandhi, his method and strategy to deal with the political problems of the day, informs us that any comparison of Anna with Gandhi is not only delusionary but also repulsive to even contemplate such a dangerous association.*

It is to be noted that even the worst detractors and critics of Gandhi maintain that in his political philosophy and through his worldview, he was a great assimilationist; a master craftsman who engaged with the diversity of views and opinion even under most difficult circumstances. He also took the vows of silence but they were meant largely for self-purification and never intended to shut out the opinion contrary to his. On the other hand, Anna and his team have further advanced in building the strategies of *demonising* views and opinion dissimilar to them. In fact, the sound bytes coming from Ralegan Siddhi, or Hissar or from a distant Gorakhpur underscore the extensive resemblance of their politics not with Gandhi but with *eliminationist* anti-Semitism and that is frightening.

It is indisputable that the ordinary Indians have thousands of reasons to have an acute sense of alienation from the political class and their misdeeds, but in spite of the media hubbub, the common masses certainly did not speak from the ramparts of the Ramlila Maidan. It certainly was not a mass movement and being democratic was possibly not in the grain of the people who crafted this movement, nay spectacle.

REFERENCES

Baudrillard, J. (1994). *Simulacra and Simulation* (1981 ed.). (S. Faria, Trans.) Ann Arbor: University of Michigan Press.

Debord, G. (1983). *Society of the Spectacle.* Detroit: Black & Red.

Gladwell, M. (2000). *The Tipping Point: How Little Things Can Make a Big Difference.* London: Little Brown.

Goodwin, J. and Jasper, J.M. (2003). Introduction. In J. Goodwin and J.M. Jasper, *The Social Movements Reader: Cases and Concepts* (pp. 3–8). Malden: Blackwell Publishing.

LeBon, G. (1896). *The Crowd: A Study of the Popular Mind.* New York: The Macmillan Co.

McLuhan, M. (1986). *Travels in Hyperreality.* (W. Weaver, Trans.) New York: Harcourt Brace.

Trimborn, J. (2007). *Leni Riefenstahl: A Life.* (E. McCown, Trans.) Berlin: Faber and Faber.

4

Recognising Structures of Corruption and Understanding the Nature of Mobilisation Against It

Vivek Kumar

The recent debate on corruption and agitation against it has raised a larger debate without defining the contours of 'corruption' and its structural location in the Indian society. It has also brought the theoretical debate on what is a movement and the nature of democratic assertion into the centre stage. The clandestine support of the media and political parties to a movement led by so-called 'civil society' raises the issue of legitimacy of the 'civil society' in the context of the Indian society. Therefore it is pertinent to understand and analyse these aforesaid issues. This paper is an humble attempt from perspective below. Before we come to analyse the nature of the agitation led by Kishan Rao Hazare in New Delhi, we will analyse the nature and structure of corruption in Indian society. Corruption can be defined both in a generic and narrow terms. Let us begin with the first one.

Defining Corruption: Broader Definition in the Indian Context

In a generic sense, corruption can be defined as a mechanism by which, a numerically small section of society collectively or individually denies the majority of its people a plethora of rights and privileges whether it is 'Human Rights for a dignified existence', 'equality that is economic, political and social', or 'liberty of occupation, residence and religious practices, fraternity', et cetra. By doing this, the numerically smaller group monopolises religious, political, economic, educational and judicial institutions et cetra. Historically, this mechanism is created, at the inception of the society, through religious texts and sanctions. Later they are legitimatised socially by theories of dharma and karma. The traditional structures are created in this fashion; they do not die in modern times. However, they remain alive, changing their form and style of functioning and influence keeping the monopoly of the numerically small section of the society intact. The existing dominance in and composition of modern institutions of governance, production, and education in India amply prove the point.

Corruption: The Narrow Definition

However, in contemporary times in India, the so-called leaders against corruption have promulgated a very narrow definition of 'corruption.' According to this definition, 'corruption can be defined as misuse of a government or public office for personal gains'. In other words, how a government servant or a politically elected member, or a judge misuses his office is called corruption. This is a very reductionist and sweeping definition because of different reasons. One, this definition has taken cognizance of corruption in government offices only. That means this assumes that, by nature, people are honest but that they become corrupt when they join the government institutions. However, the fact is that individuals are not born in the parliament, bureaucracy, or the judiciary. They are born in society which socialises them before they join institutions of governance or public life. That means we can argue that the institutions by nature are not corrupt; rather, there is something wrong with the people who man them or run them.

In this context, it is important to note that this definition does not take note of corruption induced by the social sector. This is the second lacuna of the narrow definition of corruption. For instance, every year, numbers of women are burnt alive because of dowry. After burning their bride, the groom's parents bribe the police so they are not caught. One can call it a crime. However, I will call it social corruption: because of greed, certain people commit this act and then indulge in corrupt practices. Similarly, a corrupt practice comes to the fore when huge offerings of gold and silver are made to temples without any transparency? Nobody gives a receipt for the donation; neither does one know whether a person has paid income tax on that gold. Further, temple income is also not taxed even though temples have gold worth trillions of rupees. Thirdly, the narrow definition does not take into account corruption that exists in and because of private sector and civil society organisations. Again, the fact is that the corporate sector and big industrial houses have lobbyist to get them government contracts and bribe the government employees to grant them concessions in the tax, excise and import duty by making laws for legitimising their act. Industrial houses do not pay their labourers even their minimum wages. They now have hire and fire policies as well. Is this not corruption? Yet, the narrow definition of corruption does not take all this into account. However, the narrow definition of corruption reveals certain important facts. Most importantly, this definition reveals that corruption is a caste phenomenon.

Is Corruption a Caste Phenomenon?

Generally, it is propagated that corruption is a faceless enemy. However, according to the analysis of both the broader and narrow definition of corruption we can argue that corruption is not a faceless enemy but has an identity of caste. According to broader definition of corruption, corruption can be defined as,

> a mechanism by which, a numerically small section of society denies majority of its people a plethora of rights and privileges whether it is 'Human rights for dignified existence', 'equality: economic, political and social', 'liberty of occupation, residence and religious practices, fraternity etc. By doing this numerically smaller group monopolizes religious, political, economic, educational and judicial institutions etc. (Kumar, 2011)

Going by the aforesaid definition of corruption, who are the people who have made such structures in the ancient period which have denied a majority of people a plethora of rights for thousands of years? Who were the people who monopolised the institutions of governance, education, and production? Of course, the so-called 'upper-castes'! They could do this because they misused their ritual and social position in the society. And hence, they were responsible for a corrupt social order from its inception which was unequal and devoid of equality, liberty and fraternity (Ambedkar 1994).

If that was the case in the ancient period when there were no modern institutions of governance, what was the condition in the colonial period during the British? In this context, Phooley had written long ago in 1873 that,

> The Brahmin despoiled the lower classes not only in his capacity as a priest, but also in the capacity of a Government officer, as the Brahmins had monopolized all higher places of emoluments, the village police Patil being a tool in his hands. He was the temporal and spiritual adviser of the *ryots*, the money-lender in their difficulties...In the capacity of a *Mamlatdar*, a supervisor exploit him, in the Engineering Department, an officer in the Revenue and Public Works Departments he was there to exploit him, league with the Kulkarni, or the lawyer or the money – lender who were Brahmins. So there was nepotism, bribery and jobbery because of the domination of one caste in the administration (Keer 1974: 116).

In the same vein, Ambedkar had also highlighted the relationship between caste and corruption. According to him,

> The Police and the Magistrate are sometimes corrupt. If they were only corrupt, things would not perhaps be so bad because an officer who is corrupt is open to purchase by either party. But the misfortune is that the police and Magistrate are often more partial than corrupt. It is this partiality to the Hindus and his antipathy to the untouchables, which results in the denial of protection and justice to the untouchables (Ambedkar 1982: 105).

In contemporary times, even if we consider the narrow definition of corruption, then what picture emerges? According to the narrow definition of corruption, corruption can be defined as, 'misuse of public office for personal gains'. In this context, let us analyse who are the people who dominate and monopolise the modern and secular institutions, namely, polity, judiciary, bureaucracy, industry, university and media? Again, the answer is the so-called upper-castes! This can be proved on the basis of the composition of the three institutions namely, the judiciary, bureaucracy, and media. The available data clearly shows that these institutions are totally monopolised by the so called upper-castes (for the judiciary and the bureaucracy, see *4th National Commission for Scheduled Caste and Scheduled Tribe Report 1996–7 and 1998–9*, pp. 20–2). According to this report, there are only 3 per cent of SC and ST appointments in the High Courts as judges and Additional judges. Now there is no more additional SC and ST judges in the Supreme Court of India. Further, this report says that Brahmins, Rajputs, Kayasthas, and Banyas constitute approximately 83 per cent of Class I government and non-government services. SCs, STs, OBCs and Minorities roughly constituted only 13 per cent and rest were other castes. That means that in these institutions again the so-called upper castes are directly responsible for corruption.

Corruption and Socialisation

True individuals do not become corrupt in a day or two. Rather there is a long drawn direct and indirect process of socialisation for the same in the society and culture where they live. If we take the Hindu society in particular, we can find institutions, ways and means in which people are socialised from the childhood which facilitate the practice of corruption in the society. The individual and groups are not only socialised into the institutions which give them legitimacy to exploit the others but the individuals are socialised in such a way that they willingly pay without making any fuss. For instance, the young ones are socialised by observing their parents willingly making an offer in cash or kind to priests at the time of multiple rituals performed in the home or in the temples. Children are also told to offer to gods and goddesses whenever there is an exam or some result of a competitive exam about to be declared. For instance, Phooley in his book, *Cultivator's Whipcord* (1883) has described,

> ...how a Brahmin priest persecuted a Shudra farmer all the year round from cradle to cremation, from pregnancy to pilgrimage, and how all this exploitation was done under the cloak of religion and its unending rites and rituals (Keer 1974: 183).

In their youth, they are socialised to demand dowry in marriage and keep demanding from the bride's family for all their lives. And parents of girls are socialised to pay dowry helplessly. It is not only that the individuals are trained to offer and demand but they are also trained for not giving what is due to someone. For instance, in the villages the so-called upper castes have a habit of not paying for the labour of the dalits and other artisan classes. Landlords do not pay minimum wages to landless labourers. The priests are not supposed to work and produce; instead, they are socialised to survive on the hard labour of others and accumulate capital in the temple as their private property without using it for the public good. That is why Indian temples have been found to possess gold and silver worth trillions of dollars apart from ready cash. The moneylenders, specifically the Vaishyas, are trained to lend loans to villagers at an exorbitant rate of interest. They exploit the masses by manipulating their records as the masses are illiterate and powerless. Even dacoits make offerings to the Goddess Kali for a big haul. Above all, the Hindus are also socialised to find their the way out of sin or these corrupt practices. The way is simple. Keep your gods/goddess happy by offerings or keeping fasts, chanting mantras and by taking dips in holy rivers like the Ganges. In the medieval ages, *nazrana* (trailer), *shukrana* (thanks giving), and *zurmana* (fine) continued to socialise people in illegal practices. In modern times, the huge gifts the elite exchanged on the eve of the different Hindu festivals, especially on Diwali, is akin to socialisation and initiation into corruption. In this way, we can argue that Indians have many structures and processes which train individuals to indulge in corrupt practices later in the life. And they do not hesitate to give or take bribes.

Having defined the structures and phenomenon of corruption, let us analyse the nature of mobilisation against the corruption that took place in August 2011.

II

An Un-representative and Un-informed '*Anshan*' (Sit-up): A Sociological Perspective

To begin with, the agitation *(anshan)* on the single point agenda of Kisan Baburao Hazre ('He is not Anna to me') caught the imagination of many for different reasons in mid-August of 2011. Some called it a movement; some named it as '*doosari aazadi ki ladai*', ('second freedom struggle'). Yet another group compared it with Jayaprakash Narayan's movement of '*sampoorn kranti*' (total revolution). There was huge support from people in Delhi and different parts of the country. Apart from the real world support, people were supporting the movement through the virtual world websites, facebook, Twitter and SMS also. The visual media with its power of construction of history, projected that it was a nationwide phenomenon by showing coverage from different parts of the country simultaneously on the same screen. However, the media gave very little or no space to alternative and dissenting voices. There has been a one-sided projection of the sit-up, at least from the private channels.

Anshan or Andolan (Agitation or a Movement)

Hence, there is an immediate need to highlight facts about these dissenting voices. First of all this *anshan* (sit up) cannot be called an *aandolan* (movement), because a movement is an organised effort of a large group of people based on an ideology and organisation, with leaders in command, to change or sustain a system (Rao ed.1979). This is not an organised effort of people; this is a self-driven and self-motivated population with different ideologies on which Kisan Baburao Hazare does not have any control. This was evident by the fact that different groups were having their own ideological slogans and symbols. For instance, members of the 'Youth for Equality' were shouting slogans against reservation which had nothing to do with corruption. When asked, a leader said they could not stop such frivolous groups. The lack of ideology of the participants came to the fore as the agitation progressed. And it was exposed fully when the individuals who were at the forefront of the movement started making frivolous comments about their concerns. One person asked for the plebiscite on Kashmir, another misused his office for his personal gains and yet another used the national medal for the so-called public good. The zenith of the lack of ideology came to the fore when one of the participants was thrown out of the team because he was allegedly spying for the government. The same member later, after mailing the whole mobilisation at the Ramlila ground with misuse of donation, went to join the popular show *Big Boss*. A number of other credible members resigned from the group because the few leaders of the agitation decided to participate in the political campaign against a political party on their own. Can we really call such a gathering of people a movement?

Not the Second Freedom Struggle

We should not trivialise our 'Freedom Struggle' as well by calling this agitation the 'Second Freedom Struggle'. A plethora of writing exists on freedom movements, highlighting its nature, meaning and significance in the history of our nation. Even then we can highlight some points which will sensitise us about our freedom movement in the context of the on-going sit up. By a conservative assessment the 'Freedom-Struggle' was a long drawn out struggle for approximately one century if we take 1857 as first war of independence. It is impossible to even give an approximate figure of the people who sacrificed their lives and contingent comfort. The oppression and exploitation during colonialism which Indians suffered is second only to that endowed by the black slaves of Africa and America. The string of movements during this struggle which gave us political independence cannot be counted. The gift of the freedom movement being assertion of sovereign existence of the republic with a democratic constitution, took almost three years to be completed with representatives of different ideologies, castes, religions and classes being present and debating.

No Comparison with JP Movement

In the same vein, this, *anshan* cannot be equated with JP Movement either. Because that was not an *anshan*; rather it was an out and out political movement against a government which was centralising power and was abrogating the democratic rights of the people by arresting people. Further, it succeeded in preserving and renewing the constitutional structure which the government of the day seemed to be destroying. After a long drawn political movement which trained a number of future political leaders, a new age of politics was born in India. However, in this present mobilisation, the government is giving space and permission for a *dharna*, on its own, after just one arrest. Secondly, there is no hope that a political party will be formed after victory in the *anshan*.

Unrepresentative Character of the Agitation

The claim that this *anshan* (sit-up) represents the aspiration of the whole nation is also a farce. We should recognise that sociologically, the nation is comprised of a number of social and religious groups. How, can this *anshan* be national in character if it did not represent the diversity existing in the country? Initially, when the *anshan* was launched to negotiate with the government, all the five members of the core group were male. And two members belonged to the same family. There was no representation of women, Scheduled Castes, Scheduled Tribes, and religious minorities. Today, the omission of Scheduled Castes and Scheduled Tribes cannot be done on the basis of merit because, at this point in time, many qualified individuals are available among these sections. That means the core committee of Team Hazare is self-appointed. Neither have they been democratically elected nor have the people appointed them. Neither have they represented civil society. On a national TV channel debate, Kejriwal had replied to my query that they do not represent civil society. The height of absurdity was reached when in the same show, on my query, Kiran Bedi had told the meaning of civil society as being *sabhya samaj*, as if the political class is uncivilised. This is the level of understanding of the leaders of this *anshan*.

People's Support and Question of Legitimacy to Social Action

Now one can ask that when it is not a national movement, then why did so many people come to participate in it? The answer is, corruption is a faceless enemy. Nobody knows the identity of a corrupt person. Even those who have been deeply involved in corrupt practices get legitimacy by protesting in the first row. Therefore, it is easy to come and protest against the state. If you call the same crowd for a movement of social justice, against the atrocities on dalits, for the distribution of resources in the society, et cetra, they will all run away. Why? Because then the enemy has a face and identity. The face may be one's own community, one's own caste or even one's religion. So this crowd is a hypocrite. They are mere spectators who are not conscious; rather they are driven by fashion. Secondly, numbers do not necessarily imply that an act is legitimate and patriotic. Can the demolition of the Babri Masjid be justified because it was demolished by a large crowd? Can we justify the casteist protests against the 'Mandal Commission Recommendations' on both the occasions in 1990 and 2006? Or can we call lakhs of spectators in and outside Eden Garden for an India and Pakistan cricket match as patriotic? Above all, how can we call a crowd of a few lakhs of people in a population of 1200 million, as representative of national aspiration?

Narrow Definition of Corruption

Another flaw of Hazare's *anshan* is that he and his team have a very narrow definition of corruption which should be brought under the proposed bill: the corruption of the government sector which emanates from the misuse of public office is alone to be checked. The team does not take cognizance of rampant corruption in the day-to-day life of the society. Starting from the denial of human rights to a number of groups to the access to institutions of governance and resources, et cetra, all amount to corruption. Then the corruption in the corporate sector, the media and above all the corruption of international and national non-governmental and civil society organisations has been left by alone by Team Hazare in the proposed Lokpal Bill. This raises a serious debate. Specifically, the deprived sections are asserting that the present *anshan* is deliberating targeting only those institutions where a little caste and religious diversity is reflected. They are not taking note of industrial houses where the monopoly of a few families still exploit the natural resources of the country and lobby to influence the government to launch favourable polices to benefit them.

Hero Worship: Danger to Democracy

The irony of this *anshan* is that it is based on a personality. A larger than life image of Hazare is being presented to the masses by the media professionals and event managers involved in the *anshan*. The way the whole stage of the *anshan* site has been designed and managed is testimony to the aforesaid fact. The giant poster of Gandhi and then Hazare in the Gandhi cap, sitting all alone at the top of the stage is not a coincidence. It is a well thought out strategy to project Hazare as the brand of *anshan* Jan Lokpal bill. Further, to popularise the idea from day one of the *anshan,* T-shirts with Hazare's photograph, Gandhi caps with 'I am Anna' written and printed posters of Hazare were distributed across the big cites—Delhi, Mumbai, Chennai, Bangalore et cetra. The lacuna in this type of mobilisation is that this process leads to 'hero worship or bhakti'. In this way, a 'great man's' image is constructed and all of us lay our freedom at his feet. That is why John Stuart Mills has cautioned that those who want to maintain their democracy must not, 'lay their liberties at the feet of even a great man or to trust him with powers which enable him, to subvert their institutions'. Taking cue from him Ambedkar cautioned the Parliament while presenting the Constitution that, '*bhakti* in religion may be a road to the salvation of the soul. However, in politics, *bhakti* or hero-worship is a sure road to degradation and to eventual dictatorship' (Ambedkar 1994: 1215–16). That is why Hazare's *anshan* is based on mistrust. Mistrust of Parliament, mistrust of government and mistrust of the judiciary. He is so adamant that he wants the whole nation to trust him although he is not ready to trust parliament with 543 duly elected members of Lok Sabha and 242 in the Rajya Sabha. This means, in turn, that he does not trust millions of voters who have elected their leaders according to constitutional provision? The most crucial aspect of this election is that if these elected representatives do not perform, they can be removed by simply casting a vote at least once in every five years. How can we remove Hazare who has not even passed the test of democracy by going to the people in the manner in which the constitution of India desires?

Constitutional Mechanism and Maintenance of Democracy

That is why Babasaheb Ambedkar said that if we want to maintain democracy not merely in form, but also in fact, we have to hold on to constitutional methods. It means we have to abandon the bloody methods of revolution. It means that we must abandon the method of civil disobedience, non-cooperation and *satyagraha*. These methods are nothing but the grammar of anarchy. How can we undermine an established democratic institution of our nation which is the only hope for the world's largest democracy?

Conclusions

So what are the conclusions we can draw from the above analysis of structures and mechanisms of corruption? Firstly, there has to be a broad definition of corruption in Indian society which can highlight the structures and mechanisms of corruption. This definition should include corrupt practices in every sphere of society. The narrow definition does not explain the evolution, development and processes of initiation in the phenomenon of corruption. Neither does it give a picture of the corruption existing in different spheres of society. From the above analysis, we can also conclude that corruption is not a faceless entity; rather it can be identified in Indian society with the institution of caste. It can easily be called a process associated with the castes which dominated and monopolised the institutions like political, economic, religious, educational, production etc. These castes deny the so-called lower castes access to these institutions. Even if they are inducted, they remain in minority and at peripheries in the institutions of governance. Corruption does not have legitimate structures and caste only; there is a process of initiation in a particular act of corruption in India. Hence, individuals do not hesitate in indulging in the real act of corruption when they begin to perform their roles in public life. On the other hand, the ongoing campaign against corruption is not a movement, rather only an agitation which, with its narrow definition of corruption, is only trying to delegitimise the democratic institutions which have shown diversity in inducting the diverse groups. The agitation was the product of the government creation as it gave legitimacy to the group without verifying its credentials and its organisational strength. The agitation was given boost by the traditional and new-media (Internet and SMs). The media constructed its image as national with the power of its reach. It also rationalised its terms and condition by highlighting the suitable terms in the channel-room discussions. Some of the television anchors played the role of an aggrieved party by scuffling the voice of any type of dessent. They telecast the agitation round the clock without the voice of dissent, making it look as if the whole country was supporting it. Another element which should be kept in mind is that all these mechanisms under the garb of the 'civil society' movement are other mechanisms to create a new-elite from the erstwhile dominant castes of the society. Last but not the least, it is a forgone conclusion the Lokpal cannot remove corruption from Indian society unless we treat the exploitative nature of our society which is caste-ridden and hierarchical.

REFERENCES

Ambedkar, B.R. (1982). *Dr Babasaheb Ambedkar Writings and Speeches*, Vol. 2, Education Department, Government of Maharashtra, Mumbai.

——, (1994), *Dr Babasaheb Ambedkar Writings and Speeches*, Vol. 13, Education Department, Government of Maharashtra, Mumbai.

Keer, Dhananjay (1974). *Mahatma Jotirao Phooley: Father of Indian Revolution*, Popular Prakashan, Bombay.

Kumar, Vivek (2011). Recognizing Structures of Corruption: Indian Context, *Counter Currents.org*, August 31.

Rao, M.S.A. (ed.) (1979). *Social Movements in India: Studies in Peasants, Backward Classes, Sectarian, Tribal and Women's Movements*, Manohar Publications, New Delhi.

5

Democratic Meaning of the Anna Movement: One View

Satish K. Jha

The true meaning of the Anna phenomenon will be known only in due course of time. In the meantime, the debate surrounding the Anna Movement has got so charged up that it is becoming difficult to make a political judgment on it. The whole spectrum of the debate is so diverse and polarised that the characterisations of the movement have acquired mind-boggling proportions. It starts at one end by declaring it as middle-class cyber-politics and a corporate-sponsored tirade against the political class, in which the erstwhile beneficiaries of corruption are jockeying to foreclose 'the level playing field' from the reach of the new entrants to the state sector. At the other end of the debate, one finds a position that castigates it as a camouflaged attempt of the neoliberal elite to discredit the state institutions in order to get a freehold lease of societal resources. Because of the apprehensions galore, it is alleged that this movement, with Anna as a mascot, is a clandestine move of the entrenched classes and castes to neutralise people's power (Parliament) by foisting a non-representative body like the Lokpal for its superintendence and thereby sabotaging the so called 'silent revolution' of the deprived people like dalits and OBCs in India, who have started calling the shots through their increased presence in the elective political institutions for the first time in post-independent India. In support of such a contention,

Anna's selection of *hindutwa* symbols like *vande matram, Bharat Mata ki jai,* and the exclusion of dalits and OBCs from the Team Anna are cited.The debate, however, is gradually becoming so passionate and overcharged that other meanings, which the movement also transmits, are getting blurred. In the event, one vital issue, which was simmering for some time and has found expression in the Anna phenomenon, is being conveniently side stepped. This pertains to the representational deficit in Indian democracy.

It cannot be mere coincidence that whenever a movement against corruption has started in India, be it Jayprakash Narayan's or Anna's, it invariably rakes up the question of a betrayal of the trust and mandate by the elected representatives of the people. Though it may not be difficult to see the linkage between the two, the essential premise of parliamentary democracy is rooted in the principle that the parliament would render effective control on the administration by subjecting the executive to its rigorous auditing and accounting and thereby could keep vigil on the incident of corruption as well. Hence, whenever the parliament has been found wanting in this role, the nations practicing parliamentary democracy embark on devising mechanisms to complement it. Thus, where ever the institution of ombudsman (Lokpal) has been institutionalised in a practicing parliamentary system—be it Sweden, New Zealand or England—it has been conceived as a helping arm of the parliament; so much so that it is called 'parliamentary commissioner' in New Zealand. Hence the raison d'être of this institution is in the failure of the legislature to render effective control on its own, for whatever reason, upon the administration. It is, therefore, natural that whenever a movement against corruption materialises in India, it is the legislature and the elected representatives of the people who face the ire of the people. The Anna Movement is no exception.

However, what is disturbing in the whole Anna episode is that in the heat of the moment, the crucial question of the representational deficit in Indian democracy has been forgotten. No one would deny that the movement of Anna is on the question of corruption and the institution of Lokpal. However, the larger question it puts before the political class also needs to be addressed and understood before it is too late to wake up! The nationwide protests witnessed in the recent months have amply proved that the legitimacy of electoral representation has nosedived to a all time low in India and there seems to be few takers of the Prime Minister's argument that the civil society is at the parliament's neck and if the parties did not close ranks and understand its implication, it might jeopardise the constitutional edifice of the country. On the contrary, the general perception which has gained ground is that the congressled government as well as the political classes in India are skirting the key issues in the turmoil.

The anti-corruption movement led by Anna Hazare has highlighted, consciously or unconsciously, the fault-lines in the established framework of political representation in India, which keeps surfacing off and on in Indian politics. In post-colonial India, if Jayaprakash Narayan became the tallest figure to voice the legitimacy-deficit of the elected leaders to speak for the masses, the current Anna movement might become a decisive interrogation of the representative democracy based on periodic election in India! The outpourings of public support for Anna's fast and the way the Indian middle class got incensed on the issue of corruption have brought some startling similarities with the JP Movement of 1974, which had been kicked off on the similar plank of corruption in Gujrat and Bihar and only later acquired an all-India stature in which many issues of society and polity got converged. The JP Movement, like the recent Anna Hazare event, had highlighted the maladies of governance in post-colonial democratic India and had found itself pitted against a duly elected congress government led by Mrs Indira Gandhi, who in her second stint in the office, after getting a landslide victory in the general elections of 1971, had turned arrogant and apathetic to the concerns of the people and was brooking the incidents of corruption in high places! However, since at that time the electronic media was not as omnipresent and vigilant as today, the Right to Information Act had not been enacted and the judiciary was yet to fully embrace the role of an activist, the scams of that period remained covered and could not reach the public domain for scrutiny. However, the people's disgust with corruption could be gauged from the fact that as soon as JP came out from his political sanyas and took the matter to the streets, people lost no time in grabbing the opportunity and extending full support to the anti-corruption platform of the movement.

Nevertheless, interestingly, there seems to be a big similarity between Indira Gandhi's storming back to power in 1971 and the UPA'S second inning in the office. If Mrs Gandhi was rewarded at the hustings for her deft handling of the Indo-Pak war and her call to eradicate poverty, the UPA-2 romped home with comfortable majority due to its socio-economic agenda like NREGA and its slogan for good governance. The similarity does not break here—it appears that many negative features of the then Indira team are being copied by the present government! There is no exaggeration in saying that the UPA-2 is moving in the footprints of the Congress government of the pre-Emergency period in more than one way. Arrogance of power, highhandedness of the high and mighty in the government, intransigence towards the plight of the people and above all, the one point programme of the managers of the government to keep the chair safe for the scion of the Nehru-Gandhi dynasty, besides promoting the unholy alliance between the corporate world and the government, are some other instances which put the Manmohan Singh government in an ugly historical league with the Congress government of 1971–7. It has been rightly said by Marx that 'history does not repeat itself and if it repeats then first time it comes as tragedy and second time as farce'. I hope the strategists of the present ruling dispensation are aware of this dictum!

Whatever may be the similarity and difference in the craft of governance and the art of politics in the two crucial moments of Indian democracy, no one can deny that the Anna episode has given a historic opportunity to both—the votaries of procedural democracy, who scoff at the very idea that popular sovereignty could also reside outside the electoral politics, and the custodians of the state power, for whom any attempt by the civil society to take account from the elected representatives before the end of the term in the office is to devalue constitutional governance—to do a self-introspection! It is high time that they, in their own interest, revisit some of the conceptual premises of the represented democracy which seem to be losing their sign with each passing day, particularly when the gap between the representatives and their constituency is widening at a rapid speed. Although, the growing distrust for the elected representatives may not augur well for the overall health of electoral democracy, the salience of the message, it transmits to the political class about the depth of the discontent which has set in to the society, cannot be minimised. Yet, surprisingly the response of the political class is so banal that any imaginative engagement with the issue appears a remote possibility. The elected representatives, we are told, are the only legitimate voice of the people in a parliamentary democracy and any attempt to question their actions would amount to a crime against the constitution.

However, if that is the case, then one wonders as to why so many democratic actions and aspirations in today's India are materialising outside the framework of electoral democracy? The present Anna episode, even if we ignore similar churnings from the recent past, brings out sharply a latent tension which is brewing within the conceptual matrix of democratic representation which the political class as a whole is yet to realise. The Anna Movement has refreshed some of the questions which Jayaprakash Narayan tried to raise in the 1970s through the grid of legitimacy and accountability in democratic governance. And since some of these questions have re-surfaced in the form of a face-off between the government and the civil society on the issue of enacting a Lokpal Bill, such moments should be utilised to reflect on the weak links in the representative democracy like ours, rather than debunking them as the 'grammar of anarchy'. When Anna's movement questions the legitimacy of the government to be the true representative of the people and casts doubts on their sincerity to create a strong and effective Lokpal, it only echoes JP when he called upon the people to disobey the elected representatives for the betrayal of the trust reposed in them at the time of elections.

There is no denying the fact that there are very few mechanisms available, practically none, through which the popular will of the people could be ascertained on a continuous basis in a democracy like ours. Hence, sometimes it adds strength to the argument on that side of the political divide which argues that only the elected leaders have the locus standis to transact on behalf of the people! Not only this, the purists of parliamentary democracy even say that any attempt to question the authority and legitimacy of the elected members of legislature before the expiry of the term, except through the constitutionally mandated procedure of no-confidence and no-trust, is tantamount to spreading the 'grammar of anarchy', a phrase interestingly used by Ambedkar in his last speech on the floor of the constituent assembly while winding up the debate on the draft constitution. Nevertheless, while invoking Ambedkar's phraseology in defense of such a position, one should remember the broad contours of this argument, which he presented in his earlier speech in the same assembly while moving the draft constitution. In the said speech, Ambedkar, quoting Greek historian Grote, had extensively dwelt on the importance of 'constitutional morality' in the representative democracy due to the possibility of a distance between the people and their representatives. He said 'constitutional morality is not a natural sentiment. It has to be cultivated. We must realise that our people have yet to learn it. Democracy in India is only a top-dressing on an Indian soil, which is essentially undemocratic'. The upshot of his statement is quite clear—the spectre of the 'grammar of anarchy' is the speed-governor in institutional democracy whereas 'constitutional morality' as self-restraint should constitute the ground rule for free play of democratic politics. However, the moot point is whether the political class in today's India can claim adherence to it? Does not this appropriation of Ambedkar's argument from the constituent assembly debates by all and sundry today look insincere, selective and insensitive to the larger context in which it was presented, with the obvious intention of just running away from a more nuanced and reasoned debate on the issues in question?

However, the question of whether the representative is a trustee of the people's will or a mere delegate who is to be continuously commanded by the constituents, is itself an open and unresolved issue in the annals of represented democracy since the time of Burke and Mill, who had strained their nerves to come to a definite answer to this dilemma. The present turmoil on the question of enacting a Lokpal bill seems to have further aggravated this unresolved riddle of democratic politics, which has been smoldering since the time the direct democracy of a participatory mode made way for the indirect one along with the resultant questions as to whether authorisation through election implies giving carte blanche to the representatives till the next election to do whatever they may consider and construe to be in the constituents' interests? Or, are the representatives only delegates, who have to take directive and command from the people, whom they represent, from time to time and at different stages of political transactions? Not only this ... would the represented, when they feel that their mandate has been betrayed, be within their democratic right to demand an account from their representatives and foist their will on them through the democratic means, even before the expiry of their electoral term?

Though, what constitutes democratic means in a democratic polity is itself an unsettled matter in today's context, as the electoral politics no longer perform their role as the only dependable channel of democratic transactions for the people due to number of its operative deformities! And one thing is very clear that these posers are growing in importance day by day, due to the legitimacy deficit of the elected representatives and each time they are put forth by a discontented civil society, they only cast a longer shadow on the fate of representative democracy, which often waxes eloquent about the procedural legitimacy, institutional efficacy and neutrality of its political space. One of the members of Team Anna, Prashant Bhushan, observes that 'the representative democracy was developed at a time and in the circumstances when there was no mechanism available to know the views of the people on various issues on a continuous basis. However, with the technological advances attained over the years, we can now move in direction of more meaningful involvement of the civil society in the governance through dialogue and deliberations'. By saying so, he rakes up a crucial issue—the issue of accountability and responsiveness of the representatives towards their constituents in democracy. One of the authorities on the political representation, Hanna Pitkin, has said that responsiveness need not to be a constant, continuous activity in the representative democratic system. However, there has to be a constant condition of responsiveness in the sense that a potential readiness of the representatives to respond should be ever present. The question which stares us in our face today is that whether such conditions obtain in India? Instead of bemoaning the erosion of the authority of parliament and castigating the civil society for poaching on parliamentary prerogatives, both Manmohan Singh and Kapil Sibal should mull over it!

Although recently a lot of people have expressed their unease with the method adopted and the demands presented by civil society, particularly the one which pertained to a demand to participate in the drafting of the Lokpal Bill and the pressure brought on the government to present its version of the bill before the parliament. It has been observed that such an act on the part of the civil society amounts to political blackmail and is an encroachment on the job of the elected members. It has been further stated that in the absence of a formal and mutually agreed method of formulation of demands in civil society, how would one find out what the 'general will' in the society desires? Hence, if such acts, we are warned, are repeated again and again, it might lead to chaos and confusion, which a country like India cannot afford. In short, what is being stressed is that the procedural value of democracy has to be privileged and should override the amorphous structure of civil society, which is masquerading as the 'popular will', if the democratic goods are to be delivered to the people.

It has been further argued that since civil society is not a homogenous category, there are multiple interests and ideologies which work at cross purposes. There is no procedure in place to ascertain and quantify umpteen numbers of choices and opinions within it, the way the periodic election does in a representative democracy. Hence, it is difficult to involve the agents and the agencies of civil society in the legislative and executive acts of the government. Moreover, it is also said that since civil society often speaks in multiple idioms, how can one expect from the state that it would rank one among them to be the true representative voice coming from it? Even the counter argument that in spite of the absence of a formal procedure in place in civil society, the state does not bow down before all the demands emanating from it and engages only with a group which it generates some following for itself, does not cut much ice with the skeptics. The contention that the state only negotiates when it fathoms mass support behind a cause, as was demonstrated in the case of the Anna Movement when the government took many somersaults within a short span of time with the rising tide of support in favor of the agitation against corruption, does not convince these purists.

Undoubtedly, there are many holes in civil society's argument, so far as the representation of the popular will through the non-electoral channel is concerned. Why does the state adopt an ostrich-like approach towards the decade-old fast of Mrs Sharmila in Manipur, who is protesting against the draconian laws? Is it because she has no mass support for the cause that she is espousing? Or, does her demand harm the political class more than the creation of the office of a Lokpal? Or is she being ignored because the middle class of India has not lapped up her movement, the way they have done with Anna? These are some hard questions to be answered by the protagonists of the civil society.

Moreover, the criterion of mass support certified by the state to judge the 'popular will' outside the electoral arena is equally fraught with danger. Who ultimately should be the adjudicator of the popular will? Does it also reside outside the electoral arena? Should the states' inclination to negotiate and engage with a civil society group be the only proof of the legitimacy of the issues in question? Such questions are more relevant today than the conflict between the parliament and the civil society and depiction of the parliament as the only repository of popular will, as is being made out in certain quarters. The age-old conundrum of democratic accountability is as relevant today as it was when direct participatory democracy transited towards representative system. Now it is being proved again and again that accountability and responsiveness issues are valid in themselves and have to be settled on their own terms. They can neither be taken care of within the emotive politics of group rights, as the failure of the social justice politics and their champions in some of the Indian states to stand accountable to their own social constituency, which had reposed so much faith in them, would bear it out. Nor, can they be mortgaged to the abstract liberal democratic discourse of institutional neutrality, constitutional oath and secular fidelity, as their omissions and commissions have now become political folklore. Hence, if such meanings are derived from the Anna phenomenon, it would be a better service to the cause of Indian democracy than hiding behind the political rhetoric of parliamentary sovereignty and the civil society's deformities in India. It hardly needs any mention that India has neither gone for parliamentary sovereignty of the British type, nor has it adopted the judicial supremacy of the American variety. It has, instead, settled for a doctrine of 'constitutional supremacy', which proclaims sovereignty of the people. Can anyone overlook the fact that the Constitution of India swears in the name, 'We the people', at the very outset and this precedes everything else including the institution of Parliament?

6

Anna Hazare's Soap Opera

Ajay Gudavarthy

Anna Hazare's anti-graft movement is now part of the growing epic predicament that Indian democracy seems to be increasingly drifting towards. An epic predicament, like any major epic of India such as the *Ramayan* or *Mahabharath*, is a moment where we know the end result but, or precisely because of that, our interest in the phenomenon sustains. We all knew, watching, the *Ramayan,* who would win and why, yet the story kept us spellbound and of course glued to the television when it was telecast. *Not the suspense, but its predictability is what endears it, and makes it so familiar.* In a democracy marked by everyday uncertainty, here is movement that promises radical change without any risk, pain or unpredictable overtures, which is what only an epic can do. It promises drastic change without shocking us, and in fact, adhering and confirming to the dominant values in the society. We all know for sure that the Lokpal Bill, even if passed, cannot in any significant measure contain corruption in our country, since corruption is a lot more structural and has its roots in the nature of the political economy; yet, we are in no position to brush it aside as a wave but *hope against hope, expecting it to deliver what it is actually promising to do.*

The proportion and the scope of corruption have grown manifold post-economic reforms and the opening-up of the economy. It is due to the manner in which reforms have been both introduced and initiated in India, best described by Jenkins as 'reforms by stealth', and also the changes it brought to our economy from being an agrarian economy to the sudden rise of the rent-seeking class that dominates the state. Today, the economy and its high growth owes a lot to these newly emergent middle-men like classes that are neither an industrial class nor make profits out of manufacturing basic or any other goods. Instead they make big money out of contracts of various kinds. The state is therefore dominated by the rising 'contractor class', including civil, liquor, real estate, and more recently, the mining contractors best typified by the infamous Reddy Brothers of Karnataka. In fact, a bulk of state revenues is today generated from and by this contractor class. The state needs them as much as they need the state. What we identify as corruption is the only way these classes and state can mutually mediate and survive. The old distinction between the economic and political class is collapsing, with these classes themselves entering and controlling the state, as part of its executive organ. In fact, it wouldn't perhaps be an exaggeration if one were to mark the shift of the Indian state from being *a contractual state to a contractor state. The nature of the capital is speculative, and that makes this class indifferent to long-term planning and democratic procedures; it instead relies more on quick and speculative modes for making profits. It is these changes in the nature of the political economy that are inextricably linked to the growing phenomenon of both corporate corruption and that by public officials. There is very little that the Anna's Lokpal Bill can do about setting right this structural limitation;* yet it sustains our interest and looks indispensable for a democracy to deliver whatever it can afford to. More importantly, those sections of the society including the democratic, progressive, and in some cases, radical organisations, are in no position to oppose the movement, knowing very well what it promises is way too exaggerated. This is what frames the response of these sections, as a tempered and essentially a simulated exercise. Simulation or epic predicament, I guess, is part of the very nature of popular democracy, and those who understand this, make good use of it, as L.K. Advani did with his initial Rath Yatra to Ayodhya, meticulously organised with the tele-serial, *Ramayan* as the backdrop, and his recent Jan Chetna Yatra, with Anna's soap opera in the background. Popular democracy appeals at the level of intention and not merely evidence, and this is so with any epic that cannot be questioned with any amount of archaeological or textual evidence, as witnessed with not just the Ayodhya temple but the more recent controversy around *Many Ramayanas* in Delhi University. There was nothing particularly communal about the tele-serial *Ramayan* but the context resignified it into a footage for Hindutva. *Anna's Movement is a worthy cause in itself but the current context entails more than what meets the eye, and is way too complex to either reject or wholeheartedly accept it.* Each entails its own consequence, and also partly explains the massive confusion amongst individuals and political organisations of various ideological hues in terms of its implications for democracy, and for the ruling elite of the nation.

The Left-of-Centre and progressive and radical forces are caught in the dilemma that they have been part of since the days of the death of the 'developmental state'. In the hey days of the developmental state, the Left in India had a safe and a promising posture of critiquing the state itself, and took upon themselves the responsibility of indiscriminately delegitimising it, but once the period of neoliberal reforms began, they were caught unawares as their job had been taken up more robustly and vigorously by the corporates and their associates including the media. They are aware that any excessive critique of the state and public officials only further legitimises and entrenches the global corporate model of development. They are caught with the unenviable position of critiquing the state without delegitimising it to the extent that we lay a red-carpet welcome to the global corporate. *They cannot wholeheartedly side with Anna since they do not raise the issue of corruption by the corporate, nor can they oppose it since they share his angst and concern for the decaying democracy and the moribund state that is best reflected in the mammoth corruption it's ruling elite is structurally dependent on and willy-nilly encourages for its own survival.* Corporations encourage growth and efficiency, while the State is all about corruption is an argument not agreeable to them, and they had the same dilemma while supporting the RTI. The choice they seem to have is to extend measured support while cautioning against exaggerated expectations, which is not an attractive position to take when the mood of the nation is swept with emotional appeal of the movement marked by a sense of hope in times that look increasingly desperate and stagnant. The only other choice is to offer a critique, the way Arundhati Roy did, that only looks absolutist and unrealistic, if not irrelevant. The problem with absolutist critique, however relevant an analysis it might offer, is it gives no terms to negotiate but only outrightly rejects the struggle, since it believes it does not say much about poverty, Greenhunt, and state repression. These are of course terms that are outside the scope of this struggle, and how does one evaluate a critique that does not engage with a movement for what it is, and a critique that can be extended to anything and everything?

The liberal democrats, on the other hand, are worried that Anna's movement undermines democratic procedures and representative institutions, including and above all the parliament. Nobody, according to them, is above public representatives, and undercutting procedures and deliberation in a democracy can be dangerous. Thus, civil society can play a complimentary role and cannot supplant democratic institutions, which amounts to undermining democracy itself. They were therefore unhappy with the so-called 'blackmail' tactics by Team Anna and raised the pertinent question as to who are Team Anna accountable to? And what if those appointed to the Lokpal are themselves corrupt? However, here again, the story is not so simple. We are today witnessing a strange irony where procedures and the endless delay they entail are used by the ruling elite as a shield against being prosecuted. They escape hiding in the interstices of the time-lag that the procedure of checks and balances offers in a representative democracy. However, this does not mean democracy can work without elaborate procedures and checks, since even with all of this we routinely are witness to the brazen abuse of organisations that need to maintain their autonomy and anonymity, including the way CBI is used (which prompted some in the BJP to refer to it as Congress Bureau of India!). *It is a case of democracy turning against itself. Here, again, they seem to have no easy choice; the liberal voices struggle to distance themselves from those in the ruling party,* especially the likes of Digvijay Singh.

Perhaps, it's the Right-wing that managed to put up the best show, not in the least because they are any serious about rooting out corruption in the system. The Right headed by the BJP to begin with had an easy run since they are in the opposition, and it helps them to corner, by whatever means, *the dispensation of the day.* It also could afford a more wholehearted support to the movement since they could sense that the *spectacle of Anna had all the elements that are usually part of the repertoire of the Right-wing's modes of mobilisation in India.* The performative aspect of Anna's spectacle included *his ascetic living, bachelorhood, use of slogans like 'Vande Mataram', and 'Bharat Mata ki jai', which, whether intended or not, come a tad too close to the persona of any RSS*-pracharak, *in spite of his Gandhian believes.* This again is what is strange of Indian democracy. The symbolic can easily subvert the content, because content without the symbolic can be reduced to the synthetic. It is this gloss alongside the commonsensical propositions and the naivety of Anna that is often confused for simplicity in Indian public discourse, well suited to the mobilisational modes of the Right. Anna's soap opera was a Bollywood style hero versus anti-hero narrative that goes well with Hindu-versus-Muslim, or Ram-versus-Ravan type popular narrative style that has distinct and identifiable symbols of good and bad. This indeed is a rich resource, again in the neoliberal times where the targets have become transnational and therefore invisible. To bring alive something that is silent, invisible or dead can be very empowering in the populist mode that democracy works within.

Now, finally we can raise the more difficult question as to why did Congress as the ruling dispensation respond with such alacrity? *The arguments offered—because of the mass mobilisation and the pressure it could build, or the moral pressure that fasting can bring—are, to my mind, insufficient to explain the way they buckled under pressure.* If these were the reasons then how could Congress so blatantly ignore the struggle for a separate state of Telangana that witnessed unprecedented mobilisation in every nook and cranny of its districts; if 'hunger strike is effective because it's the land of Gandhi' holds any truth, then how do we explain the sheer negligence of the suffering by Irom Sharmila for well over a decade now? Congress is not even open to a debate and the blockade in Manipur amounted to nothing more than another day's news, not to mention the way Omar Abdullah has been bargaining for piecemeal withdrawal of the AFSPA. The answer could well lie in the social base that got attracted to the anti-graft movement. While there is some truth in the fact that people from all walks of life, and all classes, including people from the rural hinterlands in the north supported the movement, it was primarily a movement that gained support from the professionals and urban-rich with keen interest avowed by the NRIs. Their interest overlapped with the belief not only that a corruption-free India would directly benefit them but also that India would become a more attractive destination for global investments. Better infrastructure, work culture, and violence-free India with a strong 'law and order', at any cost, it is believed, would enrich the global image of India and would move a step closer to being a super power in a foreseeable future. In this frame, a corruption-free India is a cause worth fighting, notwithstanding how much of the growth and prosperity of these classes is due to prevalent corrupt practices in the system. This anomaly could not hold these classes back and instead, it is their firm belief of serving national (read global) interests that motivated these privileged sections of urban India and propelled them to occupy the streets that have been, for some time now, vacated by the poor who with growing distress levels, it seems, have little time for protest politics at their disposal. Again, ironically this dream of India going global was initiated by the Congress itself, and by, more than anyone else, Prime Minister Manmohan Singh. Nevertheless, this is precisely the reason for the protest. Democracy has again this strange dimension where, within a fractured polity, parties and governments are identified with a constructed social base, and are expected to be loyal to that base. Today, while there is enough pressure that governments are supposed to represent all sections of the society, we seem to be reconciled to fact that they rule in the name of certain sections and which in turn, it is expected, will benefit everyone. It seems, in contemporary Indian democracy, it is not so much of an issue if governments fail to keep the promise of representing everyone's interests—as conflict of interest looks like an irreducible fact of modern democracies—but it does assume eruptive proportions when governments fail to serve the agenda of the class and sections of the society they actually work on behalf of in reality. Congress, under Manmohan Singh, notwithstanding its elaborate welfare regime, always projected itself as a government in favour of the private, and global corporate capital, and professionals working for it. When corruption, as they perceive, hurts their interests, and Congress looks reluctant to act, then it is construed as not only an inefficient government in power but also a party that is betraying and disloyal to its own stated ideals and social base. It is now a more important criterion for efficiency and democracy to stand to one's stated ideals and represent its distinct social base, however partisan it might be, than to be actually democratic in terms of representing all conflicting interests. We might be actually, as a society, getting reconciled to this partisan nature of democracy rather than expecting it to be close to its ideal-type functioning. It therefore makes for dramatic change in the democratic current whenever parties or individuals representing them overstep the brief they have offered the polity. There is therefore more uproar when Advani makes what were considered pro-Jinnah comments, without much interest shown in the veracity of the historical truth or accuracy of these observations. Even if what Advani observed about Jinnah were to be historically true, coming from him makes them false. He could never perhaps recover the stature he enjoyed before those comments, however well meaning they might be or however desperate he might be to switch to a more moderate image in the interest of the future prospects of his party. Similarly, the CPM could never recover from the damage it inflicted upon itself after they ostensibly betrayed the very peasants they had once mobilised. This betrayal, even if it involves a move in the positive direction, is seen in popular democracy as graft. Chandrababu Naidu in Andhra Pradesh, after he began to raise the issues of the farmers, came to be looked upon as a more cunning and opportunistic politician, than when he proudly projected himself as a CEO of the state and pronounced the irrelevance of agriculture and history. What Congress therefore faced was a crisis from 'within' its own social base, and it is this anxiety of loss of an image it constructed and stood by that propelled it to take the Anna's movement so seriously and begin to work towards a possible resolution. The same Prime Minister, who has worked overtime not to respond to a popular movement like Telangana, went to the extent of dissolving his government over the nuclear deal. This is not the pressure of democratic mobilisation, even if it is a part of the logic, but more an implosion from within that politics seems to be succumbing to. Anna's movement appealed to the 'dominant' social, as against mass, base of the ruling party and it could ill afford to ignore it lest it looked inefficient and 'corrupt'.

It is this drama marked by compounded confusion that gave Anna's movement a larger than life image, and an aura of a epic, where merely knowing and harping on the outcome is not only insufficient but actually contributes in making it the epic soap opera it has become. The saga might now be running its last few episodes, but will nevertheless continue to engage us till it comes to be replaced by a more enthralling soap opera, where not merely the subject but even the actors might nave to be new and fresh but predictable.

7

The Neoliberal Revolution

Anand Teltumbde

Expectedly, the high-pitched media-supported Anna *anshan* at the Ramlila Ground has come to an end with Parliament passing a unanimous resolution as dictated by Team Anna. The three conditions—that the lower bureaucracy should be within the Lokpal's ambit, Lokayuktas in the states should be brought in through a central legislation like the Lokpal's, and a citizen's charter detailing the responsibilities of government functionaries and the penalty for non-fulfilment should be instituted—were favourably discussed by Parliament but the government initially avoided passing the resolution, retracting its commitment to Team Anna and thus adding one more point to its score of foolishness. Soon thereafter, it retracted again and managed a unanimous resolution in Parliament, which would satisfy Anna Hazare to give up his fast on the 12th day. The media screamed 'Anna wins full victory' while Hazare himself cautioned the ecstatic crowds that it was just a half-victory. He announced that he had suspended his fast; his agitation would continue until the Lokpal Bill was passed.

Although the media is still fraught with the Anna euphoria in the absence of some other 'breaking news', it is cooling off on the episode and coming to terms with the fact that it is a long circuitous way to go for getting the Bill passed. In the process ahead, whether the Lokpal Bill would really conform to the Jan Lokpal draft, is anybody's guess. While Parliament's commitment to the three conditions is of a 'moral' nature, in the situational context, it may be reasonably relied upon. However, since it is linked to the architecture suggested by the Jan Lokpal Bill, it is necessary that the final Bill conforms to the latter. As of now, there are already nine alternate drafts of the Lokpal Bill, and by the time the Standing Committee considers them, there shall be many more. They will all be considered by the Standing Committee. In all probability, the final Bill that will be put before the House would significantly differ from the Jan Lokpal Bill, architecturally as well as in content. Will the entire episode then be repeated once more, after months? Going by Hazare's resolve, the answer is yes; but will that not be dangerous?

Emboldened by the nationwide support he received, he has already announced his next step to take up electoral reforms in demanding inclusion of an option of 'none-of-the-candidates' to exert pressure on the system to have 'good' people in governance. There is no doubt that he would be hugely supported by the burgeoning middle classes in all his moves, now that they have seen in him a second Gandhi. *However, the point to ponder is whether all these legislative reforms will really arrest the craving for accumulation in the dominant classes, legitimised by the neoliberal ethos; which class interests are driving them; and in what way they will serve those interests.*

Government's Game Plan

The government's flip-flops, nay, the series of blunders, has surely facilitated the movement. After tasting success in its high-handed demolition of the Baba Ramdev show at the Ramlila Ground, the government could use force against the crowds that showed up in support of Anna Hazare and possibly demolish it. However, it did not do so. If one takes a cursory look at its behaviour right from the beginning of this movement, one could sense an astounding ineptitude of the government in handling it. To start with, it should not have driven Hazare to go on a fast. Within hours of sitting on fast, the government began discussing with his team and made a volte-face on its foolish plea that drafting the Bill was the government's prerogative, in making it a part of the joint drafting committee. If it was to be the joint drafting committee, it could have involved representatives of all political parties and pre-empted future hurdles in the process. Not only did it not do it, it also made another somersault by rudely abandoning the exercise, discarding the Jan Lokpal draft under discussion and forwarded its absurdly drafted Bill to the Standing Committee.

When Hazare declared his second spell of fast, the government could easily guess what was in store for it and plan its move in advance. However surprisingly, it became further ludicrous: the Delhi Police, which is controlled by the Central Government, put unreasonable conditions for the agitators; they arrested Hazare and then released him, both without any plausible reason; the Ramlila ground was prepared as the venue for his fast; and the people's frenzy all over the country was allowed to reach its zenith over 10 long days, is certainly unbecoming of the government of such a large country. It was too foolish for the government to do so. However, was it just foolish for having been seen by most people? It was not an isolated act or acts but a long series of foolish actions, which should prompt suspicion of some game plan of the government. *After all, could experienced politicians like Pranab Mukherjee, Salman Khurshid, or even Kapil Sibal and Chidambaram, who may appear brash but are certainly not brainless, be so foolish collectively to let it happen? And that, too, under the leadership of our Oxford-Cambridge educated Prime Minister? It appears unlikely.*

With hindsight though, one can see this series of apparently foolish actions of the government has only served one purpose: allowing long enough time to build up hysteria all over the country against the political class and government. How could the political class or government scheme against themselves? What could be its possible utility to them? What possible purpose could it serve? *One may guess, it serves a definite purpose of the government in building a strong public opinion in the country against the government and the political class dabbling in matters of economy, and therefore, in corollary, in favour of free-market reforms. The uncongenial context of the series of scams, untamed inflation, rising people's movements against various kinds of land grabs, growing unemployment, and so on were exposing the anti-people character of the pro-elite neoliberal policies of the government. The government badly needed a strong voice from among the people that could overcome this anger of the masses and pave the way for further reforms for which the neoliberal Team Manmohan has been craving.*

The Anna movement actually has come as a blessing in disguise for the government to accomplish this. Do not make any mistake, the Lokpal is nothing but essentially a regulator which is prescribed by the neoliberal framework to ensure that the free market operates by certain guidelines. This regulator could be conceived to regulate the political and bureaucrat market so as to keep it attuned to the process of deepening neoliberal reforms. As such, Manmohan Singh is not averse to the idea of a Lokpal; he would genuinely want it. It is not because he is concerned about corruption; rather, he is not at all. People were bewildered at his silence when scam after scam unfolded and stunned the country. They do not know that for a hardcore neoliberal, corruption is not an issue at all. It is the grease that lubricates the economic growth machine. After all, it is a part of the market mechanism. If people paid some bribe to get 2G licences and caused the 'notional' loss to the exchequer of Rs 1,76, 000 crores, it was the perceived price the licensees were prepared to pay for the 2G spectrum in the existing market.

The monumental ineptitude exhibited by the government may only be understood by this possible game plan. *The longer the frenzy over the Lokpal lasts, the better it is to create and deepen the resentment against the politically driven staus quo and pave the way for the market driven reforms. The government is only worried about creating any structure that would impede these reforms and would surely ensure its will prevails even in the face of euphoric demands.* It is not really worried or scared of the Lokpal, because it very well knows that that will just be another wheel for its applecart, which will not change its direction. It is only worried that it should not slow it down.

BJP, the Net Gainer

The beauty of India's parliamentary system is that there is essential similarity between all ruling class parties on most core policy matters and behaviours, whether it is economic reforms or foreign policy or secularism and communalism. They differ at the most in shade. In class terms it may thus be called political oligopoly. They would, however, fight against each other to the hilt to capture power. *In the current contention between the 'civil society' and the government, the BJP sensed a great opportunity to embarrass the Congress-led UPA and score political points.* The pathetic performance of the UPA-II has enlivened its hopes of winning the next elections. On corruption, however, it was not in a position to come clear because of the fear of skeletons tumbling out from its own cupboards, notwithstanding its apologetic defences. It was amusing to watch the TV debates in the wake of this Lokpal imbroglio with the Congress and BJP spokesmen hurling accusations at each other. That rather truly reflected the state of the nation, where corruption is no more an absolute evil but a relative measure. Other regional parties, also having tasted meat in some form or other, did not fare any better.

The BJP used every opportunity skilfully in the debate over the Lokpal drafts to embarrass the government, without opening its cards. When Anna Hazare came out on the road, it actively supported him. During his fasts at Jantar Mantar, Raj Ghat and lastly Ramlila, its progenitor, the Sangh Parivar, took an active part in mobilising people. Many people had commented upon its imprint in the picture of Bharat Mata in the form of a Hindu goddess that constituted the backdrop at the Jantar Mantar, strikingly similar to the one used by the Sangh Parivar in their programmes. Although the organisers belonging to 'India against Corruption' might have had Hindutva proclivities (and some people did accuse a few individuals of that) that led them to put up the Bharat Mata there, Team Anna by then had incorporated progressive people like Prashant Bhushan, whose secular credentials could not be suspect. The fact that the comments emerged from outsiders and not from the motley crowd is also significant in understanding the character of the crowd. The slogans of *Vande Mataram, Bharat Mata ki Jai* and many others reflected the influence of the Sangh Parivar on the crowd.

Although they carried on with their apologetic explanation, that the picture of the goddess put up on the stage was actually of Mother India and not that of the Hindu goddess, the organisers were embarrassed enough to change it to the picture of Gandhi at the Ramlila Ground. The government's mishandling came handy for the BJP to embarrass the government. The commentators, sans touch with the ground reality, did not see the Anna movement being actively driven by the Sangh Parivar, but with every BJP person speaking in unison of her/his support to the movement halfway through, it testifies to this truth. At many places, people have noted the Sangh *pracharaks* actively mobilising people to participate in their processions and demonstrations. Ashok Singhal of the VHP proudly claimed that they had provided free food to the people gathered at the Ramlila Ground. Insofar as the BJP aimed at embarrassing the government, it accomplished it in full measure. *Both ways, in terms of preparing the general public opinion in favour of further neoliberal reforms as the government perhaps wanted, and in the process causing embarrassment to the government, the BJP was the gainer.*

Alienation of the Masses

While the crowds surged with every passing day in support of Anna, it was mainly drawn from the middle-class segment of the population, which could be described as urbane, English-educated, upper-caste, upwardly mobile young people. The frontal organisations of the Sangh Parivar also significantly contributed to the swelling crowd. This is the neoliberal generation of India, most of them having grown up during the last two decades, seeing the Indian economy growing at an impressive rate. They do not share the shame and apology for India that their elders had because of her so-called Hindu rate of growth which refused to transcend the 3.5 per cent marker and visible poverty. The times this generation lived through was marked by the 'licence-permit raj', domination of the public sector, rise of the backward castes, and cultural build-up of the lowest strata of dalits. Although the government policy had systematically been driven towards capitalist development without in anyway denting the feudal classes, and in the interests of the bourgeoisie, the Nehruvian rhetoric had succeeded in creating an impression that it was pursuing a socialist path. During the Cold War period, its association with the USSR and consequent annoyance of the US camp also strengthened this impression. *The Nehruvian project did aspire to see India emerge as a modern nation shunning its decadent traditions and customs. People tended to intellectually believe that India needed to change its beliefsystem and culture, and they seemed to carry a sense of apology for the past. Although it did not make much dent to the practice, nobody, except the hardline Hindu, could dare to justify the caste system, communalism, religious rituals, gods and godmen in public.*

The neoliberal era began informally with Indira Gandhi taking the then biggest loan from the IMF of $ 5 billion immediately after her second coming, which was soon identified with Rajiv Gandhi after her assassination, and formally in July 1991 under the Narasimha Rao Government which brought in a systematic reversal in the previous trend. The 'free-market' propaganda of the global capital appeared sensible in rescuing the world economy in crisis, which was associated with the statist blockade. The decline of the socialist regimes also boosted the belief. The Indian economy generally began looking up with visible markers of 'development' like foreign brands being freely available in the Indian market, foreign models of cars appearing on roads. The reversal of the economic trend created reversal of the apologetic thinking of India. India's emergence as a major player in the IT sector, Indian professionals in the US gaining prominence, whether as a cause or consequence, rather enhanced the pride in 'India'. *Young people generally blamed their parents' generation and the ideological baggage of socialism for the recent past and believed in the intrinsic superiority of India, along with all its customs, tradition and beliefsystem. Caste, communalism, religious rituals, culture and tradition, which were being apologetically spoken about, began to be openly justified in public. This reversal overlapped with the Hindutva ideology. This has been one of the major factors behind the BJP's rise from oblivion to political power in the 1990s.*

These policies being inherently elitist, they helped the typical upper-caste, English and technical educated youth of cities and towns in constituting a rising middle class. It imagined India as an emerging superpower, and in its superficial ways, identified political and bureaucratic corruption, the overall system of governance, and perhaps the Constitution that dampened 'meritocracy' as hurdles in its path. The huge support that the Jan Lokpal campaign received from this segment could be understood in this manner. While they would like freeing India from these evils, this segment, true to its class character, cannot stomach the idea of a thorough overhaul of the system, a la revolution that, say, the Maoists want to bring about. The Maoists also speak in the name of the people, the vast majority of the toiling people who are rendered invisible by the neoliberal onslaught. *The social engineering, non-violence, civil society, people's power are the typical wordy armour of this class which tend to exclude those who are not part of them. It is natural that the lower strata, certainly the dalits, adivasis, minorities and artisan castes untied to the dominant castes, do not identify with their show and rather would oppose it even in an aberrant manner.*

It is not that they favour the current governance or like corruption. Being the biggest victims of these evils, they would rather want them to be rooted out. However, they do see the campaign being driven with class interests inimical to theirs and not particularly aimed at eradication of these evils. The legislation of acts has been a veritable means to pacify them at various times. Take, for instance, the enactment of the Atrocity Act, which aimed at curbing the incidence of caste atrocities against SCs and STs. What is the reality? Since its enactment, the caste atrocities have rather consistently risen. Take another case of the much acclaimed Right to Education Act. This act in reality has taken away the inherent constitutional right of the poor children to get education in common schools and rather legitimised the multi-layered education system that was introduced under the neoliberal ethos. The result of it will be soon seen in the huge disempowerment of the entire rural people in general and the SCs and STs in particular. The crowds at Ramlila thought (indeed it is reported as such in a section of the press) that these 'undeserving' people do not have brains. They shouted provocative slogans and held placards that reservations were the root cause of all corruption. Some of their key leaders were reported to have been associated with the anti-reservation campaigns. An editor of one Hindi periodical, *Diamond India*, Bhanwar Meghawanshi has listed many such provocations in his article 'Why Are Dalits Not Enthusiastic About Anna's Movement?' Provocation apart, *there has not been any remote reference to the caste culture which could be easily discerned as the mother of moral corruption or the neoliberal policies of the government which can be directly linked to the kind of corruption that provoked the campaign.* The complete tone and tenor of the campaign was slanted against the lower strata of the society which, though invisible on TV channels, constitute the vast majority of this country. Team Anna wanted to dispel this impression in a symbolical manner, again ironically borrowed from the Sangh Parivar's repertoire, by being offered coconut water to break his fast through two girls, one a dalit and the other a Muslim. It needed to know that alienation of these communities has gone a little deeper to be dispelled by such a stereotypical symbolism.

Lokpal as a Saviour

Nobody can oppose the need to strengthen the mechanism to curb corruption in the country. However, to believe that something like the new oligarchic set-up of Lokpal will do the magic, just because it worked in Scandinavia and other such countries, is unjustified. Most acts in most countries are essentially similar but the result they produce is drastically different. It has to do with the cultural paradigm in which they work. There is a case to take cognisance of these issues at this stage. Corruption can be seen as the outcome of the power asymmetry in society; unlike other societies it appears qualitatively endemic to our caste culture with its rigid hierarchies. *This culture has produced the doublespeak of the elite, expressing altruistic concern for the people but at the same time continuing with their exploitation.* It is an integral part of our culture that distinguishes us as arguably the most corrupt people in the world. India's corruption ranking by *Transparency International* also does not catch this reality. The African countries that appear more corrupt than us by those ranks were also basically taught corruption by the Indian migrants. The Swiss Banking Association report of 2008 had indicated (mysteriously it is not being mentioned anymore these days) a whooping $ 1891 billion of Indian black money deposits in the Swiss banks, more than all the black money deposits of all countries in the world. This perhaps best portrays our character. *The remedy, therefore, becomes eradicating socio-economic inequality from the society. The Lokpal prescription does not reflect this diagnosis of the disease and instead focuses on the mere symptom.*

Anna and his team believe that 50–60 per cent of corruption can be eliminated if their Lokpal is installed. The entire premise of the campaign is on creating an independent and incorruptible agency, which will curb corruption from the entire political class and bureaucracy. Theoretically speaking, the constitution of such an agency itself is next to impossible because in our culture, those in public prominence, from amongst whom such a selection would be made, cannot be conceived to be beyond corruption, the honest and sincere people having been thrown out of the arena. Paradoxically, they may be found in Indian jails charged under the Sedition Act. Many people have raised genuine issues in regard to its practicability and efficacy and they cannot be just ignored. *The Lokpal or Jan Lokpal will be one more oligarchic institution to be borne by the toiling masses of this country.* Take, for example, any of the recent scams and ask a simple question: *would the Lokpal have really deterred these scamsters? Would this Bill have prevented the CWG scam, the NTRO scam, the CVC appointment or any of the recent embarrassments? Only the incorrigible optimist might answer the question in the affirmative.*

The kind of corruption Team Anna speaks about also has its identifiable source but it scrupulously avoided speaking about it. The Global Financial Integrity (GFI) study titled *The Drivers and Dynamics of Illicit Financial Flows from India: 1948-2008* by economist Dev Kar estimates that out of $ 462 billion siphoned out of India during the last 61-year period, 68 per cent is attributable to the post-reform period of just 18 years. There are many such country studies and acknowledgement from the protagonists of neoliberalism itself that confirm that neoliberal policies have caused the new genre of corruption. *Instead of pointing at this source, the Lokpal campaign rather effectively diverted the people's attention from it.* Let Anna undertake fast-unto-death for stopping the economic reforms of the government in order to curb corruption and then see how many people come to Ramlila and in *what way the state reacts! Instead of identifying the prevailing structure and system as the source of corruption, the campaign is focusing on individuals, forgetting the fundamental dictum that individual behaviour is largely of the situation and less of the self. This country has been after saviours for far too long. We had many saviours; every caste and community has its own. The middle classes found their saviour in Anna Hazare to cleanse this country of evils. They propose the saviour in the Lokpal. Saviours have come and gone; the only thing that they did was to damage the consciousness of the people by presenting themselves as the harbingers of change.*

Conclusion

Anna Hazare, a simple old man, that benevolent chieftain of sorts from a remote village, who has earned a certain reputation by pursuing causes that he believed in steadfastly, has come up at the national level as a miracle man throughout this movement. However, the credit for the miracle halfway through must go to the media that worked relentlessly to build up and project his image. The media, which easily adopts a holier-than-thou kind of attitude, can itself be marked for corruption in its omissions and commissions. That it is a business, pure and simple, conducted with certain business strategy is a settled question. Even in earlier times, notwithstanding its pretentions to responsibility and ethics, it was a business. However, then the business strategy had a dimension called the *'long term'* which impelled the media to establish its credibility and ethical image, ignoring the lures of the short term. Now, the product life cycles have become so small that this long term has almost disappeared from the strategy consideration and the short term has overtaken everything. The media, therefore, *unabashedly seeks revenue maximisation through TRP and for that goes to any extent manufacturing news.* Taking its social consequences, this very process itself can be condemned as corruption. However, who will say this to whom when the media controls the entire communication in our age? The enormous power the media wields can easily create miracles of the kind out of practically anything, if it finds the potential to serve its own interests.

As discussed above, this movement has steered clear of the root causes of the disease of corruption and pitched its prescriptions around corruption as a symptom. It is also indicated that if it had done the former, it would have never got the kind of support it received. *Such simplistic and superficial diagnosis of social matters is characteristic of the neoliberal ideology and fits well with the class character of the middle classes who like just a patchwork solution that can bring them incremental benefits while preserving what they already have. Instinctively they are scared of going to the roots of the problem because that would demand a radical overhaul of the system which could threaten their own possession.* Taking the aspirations and frustrations of this class, this movement had just the right mix to attract it. *Their perception of corruption is constricted; it is limited to the politicians and bureaucracy. They would not, even by mistake, touch the corporations and businessmen who are the main feeders, the fountainhead of this corruption. They would not similarly touch NGOs of various hues that are conduits of the neoliberal ideology and yes, the media.*

The greatest success of the movement lies in galvanising the neoliberal middle class, which generally remained apathetic to politics, to make a statement on the road. They have effectively created an illusion that the system could be 'revolutionised' by introducing legislative reforms like the Lokpal and other changes in the election system or by bringing in 'good' people in place of bad ones. They attempt to *thwart the possibility of revolt towards which the situation is fast driving the people. The campaign has already prevented people from seeing the real rot in the system, the nature of the disease and has diverted their attention to the symptom. Many people called it a revolution, not knowing what stuff revolutions are made of. Well, if it qualifies to be a revolution, we may as well have to call it a neoliberal revolution!*

8

The Old Man and the Sea of Troubles

Shailaja Menon and N. Sukumar

> Constitution is not to be construed as a mere law, but as the machinery by which laws are made. A Constitution is a living and organic thing which, of all instrument has the greatest claims to be construed broadly and liberally.[1]

A hearty welcome to the new poster boy of 'India Shining'. Surely, he will share space on T-shirts of Gen X along with Che Guevara and Bhagat Singh. Yes, it is none other than Anna Hazare. For many Indians, he is a worthy claimant for the Bharat Ratna. After Tahrir Square, it seemed that the social network was alive and kicking at Jantar Mantar or so the English press would have us believe. A friend called up to enquire, 'Were you not part of the carnival at Jantar Mantar?' A plethora of SMSes and Emails testified to the ordinary Indian's repugnance to corruption. It seemed as if Bharat and India finally met and luxury sedans rubbed shoulders with the *jholawalas*, from *galli* to *Delhi*.

However, the feel good factor raises some disturbing questions about the hydra-headed Indian State. All of a sudden, the ruling elite sided with the '*aam aadmi*'. Did the state and civil society suddenly wake up to the canker of corruption? Surely not! The present generation might not recollect the Bofors scandal which cost the Congress a general election in the late eighties. Even after numerous commissions of enquiry, no culpability has been fixed. India's rogue gallery is filled with such interesting innumerable characters, from the Big Bull to the 3G. Every Indian should feel happy that we hold the patent of discovering 'zero' since the numerical value of zero has grown exponentially with every scandal. As a nation, we should be ashamed as even the coffins of the bravehearts who rendered the supreme sacrifice during the Kargil war was not spared from the virus of corruption. Hence, unsurprisingly, Anna Hazare emerged as a phenomenon to rescue the Indian people from the nadir to which we have sunk.

With due respect, Anna Hazare is not the only conscience-keeper this nation has witnessed in recent times. Why do we forget Manjunath, Satyendra Dubey, Amit Jethwa in Gujarat, Satish Shetty in Pune, Datta Patil in Kolhapur and more recently, Yehwant Soanwane, all of whom who paid with their lives while struggling to uphold honesty in public life? A few candlelight marches, some sloganeering and tokenism from middle-class India including *baba*s and *babu*s and the entire issue was forgotten. However, even the response of the ruling elite to any form of protest is highly skewed and selective. The irony is that people accused of corruption roam free while a barefoot doctor had to spend time behind bars for providing succor to the needy. The mighty state feared a healer, Binayak Sen, more than the corrupt political class who has forfeited any loyalty towards the people. How can one make sense of the farcical nature of the entire episode of sedition that has been imposed on Binayak Sen by the state? The only crime that he committed was that he held up a mirror to the dysfunctional state, far away from the prying eyes of the media. Anna Hazare chose to protest with the entire media circus glamorising his every gesture.

Jantar Mantar is the hallowed ground to register any disenchantment with the '*system*'. Anna Hazare and his followers became instant heroes, supported by the 24x7 live telecasts. Does anyone, including the cheerleaders at India Gate and Jantar Mantar spare a thought for Irom Charu Sharmila who has been on a fast for more than a decade protesting against the draconian laws? The state has ensured its survival by forcibly keeping her alive. The stone pelters in Jammu and Kashmir were met with bullets. The cold-blooded murder of Azad and Kishanji when they sought to negotiate with the state to uphold the constitutional values is incomprehensible. For the average Indian, fighting the corporate takeover of his/her livelihood in Orissa, Andhra Pradesh or Chattisgarh, the state responds with a ready-made package-Rapid Action Force, CRPF, increased surveillance and arms and ammunition. Will all the fasts at Jantar Mantar succeed in restoring real power to ordinary Indians in deciding their lives?

How does one make sense of this hierarchy of protests? What makes a protest newsworthy? Does the success of a protest revolve around a particular personality dressed in the theatre of Gandhi? Why the thundering silence by the same group of media-savvy protestors when confronted by systemic deprivations? The consumer-citizen, being pampered by the ruling elite cutting across political affiliations will be satisfied with a few crumbs of face-saving legislative measures like the Lokpal Bill, which has been under scrutiny for the past several decades. What is of concern is why the systemic checks and balances failed to work to stem the rot in the system. We have witnessed in innumerable cases when a collusion of interests between the ruling elites and the civil society resulted in maintaining the statusquo. One should bear in mind that the civil society also reflects social hierarchy and is highly selective in the causes it champions. Anna Hazare sat on a fast earlier also to cleanse the politics in Maharashtra which witnessed the Telgi scam, and Adarsh scandal to name a few, and ultimately resulted in the unfortunate death of Yeshwant Soanwane. Scores of farmers committed and continue to commit suicide in Maharashtra and not a word from a 'messiah' who worked for rural regeneration. The caste massacre at Khairlanji has been erased from public memory and the survivor of this heinous atrocity languishes in misery. The media and civil society groups are yet to effectively audit Anna's earlier fasts and its repercussions.

No wonder, the malnourished and deprived millions of ordinary Indians are still awaiting the fulfillment of the moral consensus arrived at on 26th January 1950. The Directive Principles of State Policy, are clearly enunciated in Article 38 and 39 that the state will minimise the inequalities in income and endeavour to eliminate inequalities in status, facilities and opportunities, not only amongst individuals but also amongst groups of people residing in different areas or engaged in different vocations. Further, it also states that the ownership and the control of the material resources of the community are so distributed as best to subserve the common good. Unfortunately, Team Anna has failed to provide a coherent strategy to negotiate the values enshrined in the constitution.

The Theatre of the Absurd

Once the initial euphoria subsided, the fissures in the movement became too apparent. It occupied a highly dictatorial space in the political imagination. What was sought to be established was a patron-client relationship. Team Anna knows best what is required for India to root out its social evils and woebetide anyone who thinks differently. This was amply reflected in some of the posters, '*Anna nahi aandhi hai: doosra mahatma Gandhi hai*' (It is not Anna but a storm and the second Mahatma Gandhi). Many people wore with pride the caps emblazoned '*Mein Anna hoon*' (I am Anna). In all the sloganeering, sane voices arguing for alternative paradigms were sidelined and also condemned as anti-national. It seemed as though Anna was the only guardian of democracy.

Historically, every movement lays claim to great leadership which can be rationally justified and morally legitimised. Such movements are 'owned' by the people and continue to inspire generations. What transpired at Jantar Mantar was orchestrated by urban-based specific groups interested in continuing their unchallenged grip over power. The media was a willing accomplice to the entire melodrama. It is very pertinent to recall the alarm bells sounded by Dr Ambedkar who rightly realised and condemned the hero-worshiping tendencies embedded in Indian culture. He was immensely concerned over the political culture of 'laying down the liberties at the feet of great men or to trust them with powers which enable them to subvert their institutions.' He believed that there is nothing wrong in being grateful to great men who have rendered life-long services to the country. However, there are limits to gratefulness. No man can be grateful at the cost of his honour, and no nation can be grateful at the cost of its liberty. This caution is far more necessary in the case of the people of India than in the case of any other country, for in India, *bhakti*, or what may be called the path of devotion or hero-worship, plays a part in politics, unequalled in magnitude to the part it plays in the politics of any other country in the world, argued Dr Ambedkar. He went on to add that *bhakti* or hero-worship in religion may be a road to the salvation of the soul, but in politics, *bhakti* or hero-worship is a sure road to degradation and to eventual dictatorship.[2] Once, people mortgage their intelligence and free will to the 'hero' it is a sure road to moral degradation. 'Hero worship is a source of positive danger to the state'.[3]

On the day Anna broke his fast, symbolically, a dalit and Muslim child shared the dais. These communities were conspicuous by their absence in the arena of stage-managed protest. It seems that Team Anna's advisors sought to make the occasion more 'inclusive'. Certain sections of the intelligentsia argued that the movement was urban-centric, the aspiring middle-class and upper-caste dominated. It was insinuated that many Right-wing and anti-reservation groups actively mobilised support for Anna. The subsequent events proved Dr Ambedkar's prescience. Gradually, Anna assumed a larger than life presence, thereby undermining the political legitimacy of the state. He challenged the constitutional authority of the parliament and its elected representatives, in short the collective consensus of the citizens of India. Team Anna dictated to the Indian state to accept their version of the Lokpal Bill, unconditionally.

This begs the question as to what is the fundamental difference between a *khap* panchayat and Anna. Both seek to undermine constitutionally created structures and instead emphasise personal dikbats. This was made amply clear when Sharad Powar was slapped by a disgruntled citizen. Initially, Anna queried as to why Sharad Powar was slapped only once only to apologise under duress. The same dictatorial attitude made Team Anna to campaign against particular political parties during a bye poll in Haryana. Such narcissistic behaviour reflects the feudal tendencies of the movement and dilutes the issue which primarily catapulted them into the public imagination.

This is not to undermine the pernicious issue of corruption which has chipped away the development process. However, to create a vast independent super bureaucracy to keep surveillance over government officials as envisaged by Team Anna under the Lokpal would usher in more problems for the vulnerable sections. Such an agency would be outside the checks and balances of India's constitutional system. Despite numerous constitutional safeguards, the ordinary citizen finds it extremely difficult to enforce his/her rights. How far can they negotiate with yet other behemoth created to root out corruption? Additionally, how does one ensure that such a structure will not be utilised to settle personal scores (by filing false cases)? As it is, India is riddled with structural problems of caste, class, gender, ethnicity, minority issues etc. An overarching umbrella in the name of eradicating corruption will again shackle the oppressed. Another issue is the nature of the bureaucracy. Post-Independence, the state continued with the British bureaucratic legacy which was created to safeguard the interests of the colonial state. The manner of selecting, training or even the life choices of the upper echelons of the bureaucracy reflect the elite colonial character. The present educational apparatus only permits a 'meritorious' few to be part of this upper crest. It does not require a deep political or social analysis to ponder as to who actually is ruling and administering India. The brahaminical mentality inscribed in the body-politic of India has not been cleansed. Will Lokpal ameliorate the situation or further muddy the waters of society by excluding the already underprivileged?

No wonder then that the inherent contradictions of the movement have ridiculed the symbolism of a Gandhi-lookalike who has been reduced to giving sound bytes and *maun-vrats* to remain relevant. The state found it extremely easy to target the Team Anna members individually on various charges of omission and commission. The movement began with a single agenda of cleaning up the corrupt public life and ironically some of the members are fighting corruption charges. Till date, the average citizen is not aware of the financial resources of the movement. The association of sundry religious figures reflects the ideological paucity and future political motivations. As long as Anna's experiments were confined to Ralegaon Siddhi, his halo remained intact. When he chose a bigger stage, he invited bouquets and brickbats in equal measure. What worked in a village of few thousand people need not be successfully replicated at the national stage. Undoubtedly, corruption is an emotive issue. A movement designed to tackle it has to be more organically structured in terms of ideology, strategy and leadership. A one-man army and a single point agenda failed to convince the larger masses beyond the national capital and certain urban areas. The stage was prepared, the media was ready, the network was effective and the finances were mobilised. Unfortunately, it collapsed with the weight of its own contradictions. For 'India Shining', corruption is the only issue, but for 'Bharat', there are multiple deprivations.

Conclusion

What we witnessed and will again witness at Jantar Mantar/Ramlila Maidan was only a trailer of the gradually unfolding script. Once, the moral consensus was unilaterally breached by the ruling elite, the faceless mass is straining at the leash to break free from the systemic bondage and claim their place in the sun. An uneasy calm prevails across the country as a million mutinies ebb and flow to strive to fulfill Articles 38 and 39 of the Constitution that upholds the vision of an inclusive, egalitarian and just society. Nehru's tryst with destiny and Ambedkar's dream of social democracy have been deliberately sidelined in the mindless pursuit of crony capitalism. In passing, we can only echo Tagore's fervent plea, 'Into that heaven of freedom, let my country awake'. A million mutinies characterise Indian democracy and any movement will have to make sense of them to remain relevant. What Dr Ambedkar commented on the reality of untouchables despite the efforts of several mahatmas can be contextualised in the case of the oppressed citizens. As long as the undemocratic order prevails, the value of the franchise will remain a distant chimera.

REFERENCES

1. Goodyear India v. State of Haryana, AIR 1990 SC 781: (1990) 2 SCC 712, Paragraph 17
2. S. Thorat, 'Ambedkar's Way and Anna Hazare's Methods', *The HIndu*, 23 August 2011.
3. http://bahujannews.blogspot.com, 6/12/2011, 11.15.pm

9

Media as an Echo Chamber: Cluttering the Public Discourse on Corruption

Sukumar Muralidharan

In its approach to Anna Hazare's 13-day long protest fast, the media again made itself part of the story. Missing in the frenzy was any effort to arrive at an understanding of what 'corruption' meant to the people joining the protest. Also lacking was a sense of tolerance for alternative views on a complex social phenomenon. Far from reflecting the complex and multilayered anxieties that underpin the growing popular restiveness with governance processes, the media chose to present a singular authoritarian point of view as the true and authentic voice of all Indians. The implications for the quality of the public discourse on the future of democracy are grim.

Facts have a certain pliability about them. They can always be moulded into a shape that suits prior conceptions. At a discussion in Delhi on the 'Media and the Politics of Corruption' on 31 August – just a few days after a hunger fast by Kisan Baburao Hazare, alias Anna, in the cause of a high-powered anti-corruption body had been called off—two television news anchors, aware that their conduct through the 13-day long event was under scrutiny, chose aggression as the best strategy of self-defence.

The coverage of Anna's indefinite hunger fast at the Ramlila Maidan in Delhi, they said, was perfectly in tune with the magnitude of the event and its importance to all Indian citizens. The crowds that gathered at the venue of Anna's fast were deeply stirred by the personal example set by the 74-year-old social campaigner in the struggle against corruption. To call their fervour a contrivance of the media was an illusion of an out-of-touch intellectual elite, and an insult to basic human integrity and intelligence. The media's only sin was that it had refused to be 'embedded' with the government and uncritically parrot the official line.

Unsurprisingly, TV news anchors have consistently been in the forefront of the public debate about the media's role—to adapt Noam Chomsky's adaptation of the famous Walter Lippmann term—in the 'manufacture of dissent'. Another well-known TV personality sought to tackle this matter frontally in a newspaper column and arrived at the self-extenuating conclusion that the fault, if any, lay at the government's doorstep, since it had consistently failed in putting across its point of view cogently and comprehensibly, allowing the forces of dissent to carry the day by default.[1]

Coverage Time

Available for public scrutiny by this time, were the results of an exhaustive media monitoring exercise—involving two news channels each in English and Hindi—by the Centre for Media Studies (CMS), a research organisation with long years of experience in the field. Between 16 and 28 August, the exercise found that the two Hindi channels, Aaj Tak and Star News, devoted 97 per cent of total news time during prime viewing hours (7 to 11 pm) to the Anna fast. For the two English channels monitored—CNN-IBN and NDTV 24x7 — the corresponding figure was 87 per cent. Left out of this exercise was Times NOW, which was widely seen to be the most brash, bumptious— indeed, noisy and intolerant—news channel in respect of the Anna Hazare fast.

Taking the pattern of total time utilisation on the English channels, the figures were roughly about 65 per cent of broadcast time for the Ramlila event, 23 per cent for advertisements and the rest for other news. The Hindi channels were not very different in terms of the total time dedicated to the Anna fast, but with advertisements occupying about 30 per cent, they had virtually no time for other news.[2] It is also estimated that through Anna's 13-day fast, the viewership of English news channels increased by over 70 per cent and of Hindi news channels by over 85 per cent.

Revenue from the Coverage

From another source, we find that in the earlier phase of Anna's protest fast in April, news channels raked in Rs 175.86 crore in advertisement revenue over a nine-day period. Coverage totalled 5, 576 news clips, of which prime time news coverage numbered 1, 224 clips across 152 hours, with an ad value of Rs 52.47 crore. Classifying the news clips by their tone, 5, 592 were positive towards Anna and his cause, while 92 were characterised as negative.[3]

Viewership and audience demographics are the principal criteria in determining ad placement decisions. Yet, the pattern of coverage of the Anna fast was so distinctive across all news channels, that it suggests a strong linkage between quantum and tone of coverage and revenue implications. The matter needs to be carefully dissected and thought through. Media companies, for the most part, are private limited companies, not legally obliged to publish annual statements of accounts. Even less are they under compulsion to disgorge the finer details of commercial strategies to maximise ad revenue.

However, an indication that Anna's fast was a lucrative source of revenue for the media is available from the conduct of Bennett Coleman and Company (BCCL), publishers of the *Times of India* (TOI) and owners of the TimesNOW channel, which has shown itself over the years to have the best sense of the 'editorial context' that advertisers most appreciate.

Concept of 'News-Hole'

Derived from print media practice, the 'news-hole' is a concept that media analysts frequently work with. It is a term that originates in the practice of making up a page, where space is already committed for advertisements and news content can only fill in the 'holes' in between. That concept of the 'news-hole' has now been adapted to the visual electronic media, though its measure is not in units of space, but time. Its essential connotation is that news has only the second claim to media space and time, after ads. It does not yet reveal the subtext that news content is itself influenced by the ads that surround it—or that news content can be manipulated to provide the best 'editorial context' for ads placements. As with much else in the Indian media over the last two decades, the new paradigm was forged by BCCL, which proudly invented a mutually supportive relationship between the news-hole and the surrounding ads. Since the money came from the ads, the burden of adjustment had to be on news content.

Within all the limitations of the print medium, BCCL's flagship newspaper, the TOI, was a stellar performer in mobilising crowds for the Anna fast. A perceptive analyst has provided all the basic data here. The TOI's Delhi edition covered the 13-day event over 123 broadsheet pages branded 'August Kranti', hijacking a talismanic moment from India's struggle against colonialism. Overall coverage included 401 news stories, 34 opinion pieces, 556 photographs and 29 cartoons and 'strips'. On seven of these days, the front page of the ToI had eight-column banner headlines. Negative stories, if any, were run with attributions to public figures—such as the Islamic cleric who heads Delhi's Jama Masjid and the leader of a nationwide confederation of government employees from the scheduled castes—who are known to evoke a reaction of some scepticism, if not disdain, among the main readership demographic of the TOI. And the newspaper launched a toll-free number for readers to give a 'missed call' if they endorsed the demand for a 'strong Lokpal Bill'.[4]

By way of a sampling of the banner headlines in the TOI, on 25 August, the ruling United Progressive Alliance (UPA) was deemed to have hardened its stand after an all-party political meeting the previous day endorsed the sovereign right of Parliament to determine the appropriate law to deal with corruption.

The popular expectation that Anna's agony would end was belied and despite the official spokespersons' deliberate effort to put a different construction on events, the TOI headline read 'From Breakthrough to Breakdown'. Subsequently, a collective appeal by the prime minister, leader of the Opposition in the Lok Sabha and indeed, both houses of Parliament, failed to deflect Anna from his resolve to go for his maximal agenda. On 26 August, TOI determined that the moral advantage from these

exchanges had accrued to Anna with the loud banner that read: 'PM Walks the Extra Mile, Anna Unmoved'. Two days later, the TOI reported the culmination of Anna's fast, which came about in ambiguous circumstances that fell conspicuously short of his maximal demands, under the headline: 'Anna wins it for the people'.

Missing Discussion

Missing through this entire 13-day long frenzy was any informed public discussion of what was at stake. Daily experiences with corruption were narrated with a pronounced bias towards the common irritants that the middle and upper strata face. Typically, delays in obtaining passports and business clearances were talked about, not the difficulties with getting names registered on daily muster rolls for the rural employment guarantee programme. The Anna Hazare group's insistence that its conception of a vertically structured, rigidly hierarchical body was the only way to deal with corruption, generally escaped without serious scrutiny. The few who sought to raise questions about the appropriateness of a body conceived with conspicuous disdain for participatory democracy were typically characterised as divisive elements, disrupting a moment of rare unity within civil society, effectively giving the government a free pass.[5]

There was, in short, much discussion of the need for a 'strong Lokpal Bill', but no clarity about how this end could be achieved. Characteristically, during an hour-long programme of studio-based debate and discussion titled *The Big Fight* on 20 August on the news channel NDTV 24×7, the entire audience declared itself to be in favour of Team Anna's Lokpal Bill. Yet, no hands went up when the next question was asked: about how many among the audience had actually read the draft bill.

Yet, there are obvious difficulties, both logical and ethical, in putting down the widening public ferment to media manipulation. People today are stirred up like never before over the quality of governance and willing to express themselves forcefully. And the 24-hour news channels that have multiplied over the last half-decade provide them with a platform.

Consequence of Disquiet

It is a plausible conjecture that the restive spirit about is a consequence of the threats seen today to India's growth story. Though indifferent for the first decade-and-a-half of India's liberalisation process, economic growth began picking up momentum from about 2004 and showed enough dynamism for a sufficient number of years to earn worldwide recognition as a force that would influence global balances into the near and distant future. This period also saw the coming of age of the great Indian middle class which had ostensibly earned its belated freedom after spending decades under an oppressive state-controlled economy. Media growth is a sub-plot within this broader story, propelled by advertising expenditure which, as is invariably the case, outgrew increases in corporate profitability, but tended to mirror the underlying patterns of consumption of the middle and upper strata.

The global economic downturn since late-2008 is only beginning to show up in India's official economic statistics, but it is a part of peoples' lives. Inflation has become a more perceptible threat than ever before in two decades. The vaulting ambitions of India's bulging 'youth demographic strata' are under stress, making nonsense of the beguiling prospects held out by the media just over two years ago. And as the global economy itself lurches into a possible double-dip recession, the prospects of India's emergence on the world stage as a superpower seem rapidly to be diminishing.

These factors have engendered anxieties across all strata, expressed in diverse ways. On 23 February this year, India's principal trade union confederations jointly organised a mass rally in the national capital. Despite acute concerns among the working class over the direction that policy was taking in a context of growing livelihood stresses, official thinking showed little inclination to go beyond the standard story-line that the labour market needed to be 'reformed'—that enterprises in other words, needed the power to hire and fire at will.

Coverage of February Rally

The trade union rally was a way of showing the world that there was another way of looking at things. It was an alternative discourse that the many news channels based in Delhi and elsewhere proved fairly indifferent to. The following day newspaper coverage mostly focused on the massive traffic snarls the rally had caused. The TOI's Delhi edition ran a full page of coverage under the banner headline: 'Red Wave Sweeps City, Halts Traffic in Central Delhi'. In three chosen samples of public reaction, representing presumably the whole range of opinions heard that day, one of the sufferers of the day's traffic chaos was quoted saying: 'If I find out which party is behind the rally, I will never vote for it'. Others complained of vital appointments missed and tasks left unfinished.

The first day of mass gathering on Delhi's streets in support of Anna in his most recent phase of agitation was 16 August. Within moments of the preventive arrest effected to stop Anna from beginning his protest, Delhi's news channels had fanned out across the city to provide saturation coverage for the ensuing demonstrations. Traffic was thrown out of gear in several parts of the city when the crowds came out, but the media cared little. As the TOI's Delhi edition put it in its main local news page on 17 August: 'City Centre Comes Alive With Marching Throngs'. And elsewhere, under the headline "Massive Jams in City But Few Were Complaining', the newspaper made a special effort to record that city commuters with nerves frazzled by the chaos, were 'pacified' by others who explained the issue at stake.

Framing of Issues

Yet, doubts persist about how clearly the media has framed the issues. 'Corruption' is in the discourse of most of those who have joined the Hazare campaign, a convenient target onto which a whole complex of anxieties can be shifted. And the seeming urgency of creating an authority superior to all others, meshes neatly with elite convictions that representative democracy has been a colossal failure. However, since the Jan Lokpal, a body conceived as the magic bullet to end all corruption, has failure—and endless conflict with all other institutions—virtually encoded in the circumstances of its genesis, it should be asked what the consequences of manifest failure would be. Would the target then shift from 'corruption' to 'politics' itself? Would representative democracy itself fall victim to awakening Indian middle-class rage?

When completely stymied by phenomena that seem unique and mystifying, it often helps to borrow analogies from the physical sciences. An amplifier is an appropriate analogy here: taking in a signal as input and processing it through its circuitry to generate an output signal. The quality of the output can never quite match what is received by way of a primary signal, though technology has been seeking to achieve the most faithful reproduction. Among the first significant discoveries in this respect was that of feedback: channelling a part of the energy output back into the input stream influences the performance of the device in various ways.

Feedback

Negative feedback, that is, a loop that feeds back a part of the energy output in a manner that is not congruent with the input signal, enhances performance and provides for faithful signal amplification and stable system performance. Positive feedback, which channels an identical signal back into the input stream, leads to a distorting spiral of noise, system instability, a cacophonous listening experience for the audience, and finally, a potential breakdown. Clearly, this seems the pathway that the media is embarked upon, by its resolve to function as an echo chamber for elite perceptions, amplifying and reinforcing them in every manner possible.

REFERENCES

1. Barkha Dutt, 'Digging Its Own Grave', *The Hindustan Times* (Delhi), 19 August, editorial page, available at: http://www.hindustan times.com/Digging-its-own-grave/H1-Article1-735205.aspx.
2. The basic data on time devoted to news is available at: 'Anna Obsession Boosts TV News Channels', http://www.indiantelevision.com/ headlines/y2k11/aug/aug212.php. The time that went into ads is not available from this source and was obtained directly from CMS.
3. Full details of this study are not availabe, undoubtedly because this manner of information normally comes with a price tag. The bare details presented here are taken from the media watch website, *The Hoot*. The obvious gaps make it essential that the information be used with discretion. For instance, the number of news channels surveyed remains unknown. See here for all the information currently available: http://www.thehoot.org/web/home/story.php?storyid=5448&mod=1 &pg=1§ionId=4&valid=true.
4. Pritam Sengupta, 'How the *Times of India* Pumped Up Team Anna', available as on 1 September at: http://churumuri.wordpress.com/2011 / 08/31/how-the-times-of-india-pumped-up-team- anna/.
5. Embodying this attitude with extreme aggression and inattention to minor inconvenience of fact, was the TimesNOW channel's main news anchor, on which see: Mihir S Sharma, 'Revolutions Eat Their Own', *Indian Express* (Delhi), editorial page, 27 August, available at: http:// www.indianexpress.com/news/revolutions-eat-their-own/ 837710/0.

10

Understanding the Dalits' Critique of Anna Hazare's Movement

Harish S. Wankhede

In the recent past, corruption has become the biggest matter for the media. A mosaic of *urban middle classes* (non-political social groups, Non Governmental Organisations (NGOs), Residential Welfare Associations (RWAs), business corporate houses and certain Right-wing *cultural* groups, et cetra) in association with the media have constructed an illusion of a 'national movement' and have taken the political class to ransom. Most of the political parties (including the Communist Party of India and the Communist Party of India-Marxist) have also extended their support behind the anti-corruption movement led by the Gandhian, Anna Hazare, and rallied behind the 'Jan Lokpal Bill' without critically engaging with the constructed hype. The popular upsurge of the middle class (mainly at New Delhi) was one of the most debated and viewed events of the recent times. It was argued by many as the 'second independence struggle', by comparing it with the 'Tahrir Square upsurge' and was also seen as the emergence of new conscious and responsible middle class. Along with such heightened appreciation and support, the movement has also witnessed some rounds of criticism mainly from the Left-intellectual circles and also by certain political leaders (Lalu Prasad Yadav and Sharad Yadav in specific)[1]. *Most of the criticisms were concentrated mainly over the technicalities of the Bill, its constitutional validity and also the legitimacy of civil society to dictate terms to Parliament. Within such discourse, there were very few who categorically objected the political objectives of the movement and its relationship with other democratic churnings. Amongst the critics of this movement, the dalit perspective has emerged as one of the most vocal and visible forces.*[2]

The anti-corruption movement has brought many contentious issues into the mainstream debates. It has questioned the political will and institutional incapacity of the state to tackle this menace. The Left parties demand the inclusion of business corporate houses in the purview of the Lokpal and try to broaden the purview of the proposed Bill (Karat 2011). However, most of the debates have peculiar middle-class sensitivities and operate within the typical urban vocabularies, far distant from the issues of socio-economic hazards that the deprived and depressed classes witness in their everyday life. *The anti-corruption campaign does provide a sensible anti-thesis against the current economic and political maladies but fails to impress those sections that are living on the margin and has most vulnerable conditions. The dalit socio-political movement in general locates itself as the voice of these deprived and marginalised communities and on their behalf they have criticized the current movement for the Jan Lokpal Bill.* It was first to take an open public position and mobilised people's opinions against the Hazare movement.

Democracy has dual role to play in the liberal political churnings. On the one hand, it has to justify its utilitarian merit by engaging with the concerns and interests of the majority of the people and on the other hand it has to provide equal and legitimate space to all the group/individual voices against the difference blind hegemonic ideas. A complex balance between these two ideals provides democracy its real meaning. The emergence of the dalit perspective in Indian democracy is the product of the later argument which quintessentially democratizes the whole socio-political milieu in favor of the most deprived and depressed social classes and provides them a meaningful presence in the discourse of nation building. The current criticism of the dalits against the Hazare movement should be understood through the ideological merits and political commitments that the widespread dalit socio-political movement has demonstrated in the recent past.

Dalits have three important arguments against the current movement for the passage of Jan Lokpal Bill. First, there is a visible absence of the issues, concerns and representation of the socially marginalised sections during the movement and in the broader conceptual framework of the proposed Bill. Second, the symbolic and ideological gamut of the movement is mostly borrowed from the brahmanical socio-cultural domain and third, it discredits the constitutional authorities (mainly Parliament) in favor of a new institution having centralized supreme power.

The Question of Social Justice and Representation

The anti-colonial movement dominated by the upper caste nationalists met many challenges from the internal class-caste contradictions. On the behalf of the dalits, Ambedkar formulated an independent rational-radical opposition to the Congress claiming that the party privileges mainly the interests of the upper caste Hindu elites. He legitimised the need of a 'special representation' of the marginalised communities as the essential norm of the modern democratic principles. (Ambedkar 2002: 91) The hypothesis that somebody else can represent my concerns in the general assembly was critically evaluated to demonstrate the possibility that the dalits have its own capacity and capability to articulate their issues more authentically. *The Ambedkarite politics thus proposed two canonical elements for the dalit political Movement, first, independent analysis and articulation of the concrete socio-political realities in favor of the most deprived sections and second, adequate representation of the socially marginalised communities to make democracy more inclusive.*

Most of the 'national-people's' struggles are led by the educated upper-caste urban elites in India. These elites act as the responsible enlightened agency acting in the interest of marginalised and deprived groups. More than the ideas of community representation, these movements champion the qualitative abstract cause of the poor and backward communities. Their constructed moralistic agenda provides them the legitimate right to become the leader of such movements. For a long time, the dalits and tribals have followed the 'secular-sensitive' appeals of such leadership without interrogating the exact need of the upper caste leadership in such forums. They have hardly questioned their social credentials to become the part of such grass root movements. *For many (including sections amongst the dalits), the shared characteristics and objectives of the movement become more important than the quality of the leadership. The Left political parties dominated by the upper caste elite gather impressive support from the dalits and tribals because of their ideological commitments and pro-poor moralistic objectives.* However, *in most of the abstract 'people' based movements (Congress in general and many grass root mobilisations in particular) the Dalits have witnessed a categorical exclusion (or token representation) of their concerns and issues.* These movements do not sufficiently engage with a widely felt sense of caste discrimination, social exclusion and economic marginalisation experienced by the dalits and the tribals.

Providing adequate representation to the ascriptive communities in the decision making was one of the focal point discussed during the Constituent Assembly Debates (CAD). However, outside the parliamentary functioning, the representation of the marginalised communities (including the religious minorities) has not only been inadequate but almost absent. The political parties occasionally celebrate the 'symbolic leadership from these sections as a patch work exercise and keep the upper caste leadership intact and consolidated. The majority of the public forums (NGOs, socio-cultural groups, activists' clubs, et cetra) usually show their die-hard *commitments to the cause of caste annihilation and social equality but hardly provide necessary support and infrastructure, so that an organic leadership of the dalits can independently emerge and can take a lead.*

The idea of social justice (for example, reservations) is viewed as 'debatable' question, mainly related to a small minority and has never became the mainstream agenda for most of the social movements. These movements celebrate their struggles for 'basic human rights' and sustainable economic development without categorically building a roadmap through which the dalits and tribals can become the equal participants in the socio-economic affairs. The shaky opinions of the non-dalit leadership on the fundamental questions of social justice and atrocities against the dalits have alienated most of the dalits from such movements. The failure of the popular movements to provide a legitimate space to the deprived sections has resulted into a growing resentment against the elite upper-caste leadership. As a consequence, the demand for authentic representation has increased, building an alternative caste-based socio-political movement against the domination of 'insensitive' elite leadership. Identity politics is the product of non-recognition and non-representation of the marginalised social groups in the mainstream socio-political movements led by the upper caste elites.

In this respect, the Hazare movement is also not exceptional. The responsible leadership of the movement has categorically possessed the urban middle-class credentials, an upper-caste social identity and has never aligned with the agenda of social justice in their entire carrier. In contrast, one of the most prominent voices of the movement, Arvind Kejriwal, has been alleged to have openly supported the anti-reservation stir of 'Youth for Equality' brigade and has argued against the reservation for the Other Backward Classes (OBCs) in higher education. Further, the leadership has failed to categorically mobilize the poor (majority of them are the dalits), peasants (backward classes) and the labor class in favor of this movement. The leadership also has not tried to demonstrate how corruption is a real 'social problem' for the socially marginalised groups and how does their socio-economic hazards will be removed because of the Jan Lokpal Bill? The visible absence of leadership from the marginalised communities (including the Muslim) who could have mobilised their counterparts to join the movement, led the movement to become a non-political assemblage of a passive middle class populace. The hyped 'national movement' has not seriously studied the disturbed social realities of India and has tried to mobilise people on a narrow and shallow battle against corruption. The populist 'Indian' identity created by the media was a collective jingoism of the passionate urban classes who hardly associate with the persisting problems of rampant poverty, caste discrimination and gender violence.

The Brahmanical Language of the Movement

The brahmanical Hindu identity and its cultural connotations are seen as antithetical to the political projects of the dalits. The overarching cultural identity based on the logic of Brahmanical idioms, like *Bharat Mata* has been crucial in promoting the Hindu religious symbols as universally applicable values. During the first phase of the Hazare Movement (the Jantar-Mantar episode), the portrayal of *Bharat Mata* has occupied the central space on the stage supplemented by passionate sloganeering of controversial *Bharat Mata ki Jai* and *Vande Mataram*[3]. Whoever has any little sense of the political history of India will understand that both the elements in the past have been categorically used by the *Hindutva* forces mainly to distance the Muslims from the nationalist struggle and to disturb their religious sentiments. Its usage will not only limit the participation of the Muslims, but will also have the potential to disturb the *dalit-bahujan* social consciousness who regard the renewed Hindu cultural symbols as yet another attempt to promote elite brahmanical cultural values. (Ilaiah, 2003:184–5) The political appropriation of hegemonic Hindu religious symbols categorically deny differences based on ascriptive social identities and try to assimilate every one under one hegemonic 'spiritual domain' of 'Hindu India'. The dalit movements criticise such integrationist goals and argue that under the veil of metaphysical abstract spiritual notions, the social elite is cheating them along with the other socially deprived groups. The dalit assertion rejects such political gimmicks of the social elite which celebrates and establishes the cultural and religious notions of Brahmanical Hindu traditions.

In the later phase (Ramlila ground), Hazare has convincingly tried to mimic the Gandhian mode of protest and re-fetched the position of Gandhi as an ideal personality to be followed. However, he has categorically forgotten the historicity of Gandhian ideas and its relationship with the subaltern masses, mainly with the dalits. For example, during Gandhi's lifetime, most of the communities/groups developed their own independent leadership against the hegemonic appropriation of Congress as the leader of the entire nation. Most of the community leaders like Jinnah (Muslim League), P.V.R. Ramaswamy (leader of the Dravidian Movement) and Ambedkar (tallest leader among the Dalits) have not only opposed Gandhi for his bias towards Hindu upper castes but have also rejected all his political methods. Gandhi was opposed to and ridiculed not only by the 'community and group leaders' but even the other leaders of 'nationalist' attire had no strong camaraderie with him (Subhash Chandra Bose, Bhagat Singh and even Nehru can be counted on this list). He retained his leadership over an abstract mass, but most of the constituents of that 'masses' already developed their independent movements for complete liberation, empowerment and social justice. His rhetoric of 'religious reforms and unity' was understood by them as an open ploy to keep socially deprived communities attached with the political ambitions of the upper-caste Congress leadership. (Omvedt 2011: 49-50) The dalits therefore regarded the Gandhian ideals as conservative, orthodox and antithetical to their modernist-secular aspirations.

Gandhi and his 'isms' on many accounts have not only defended conservative and regressive ideas (caste system and *varnashrma dharma*) but also had backward-looking non-scientific values (in his classic *Hind Swaraj* he rejected machinery as the root of all ills and described the western world as 'Satan civilization') (Gandhi 1938). Importantly, he had no faith in parliamentary democracy and he compared it with 'prostitute' or 'sterile women'. (ibid: 8) Hazare also have identical opinions which can be termed as regressive and backward through a modernist dalit perspective. For the dalits, Gandhi can become ideal for those who believe in middle class political values and are ready to negotiate with the state without really making any radical change in the degrading socio-economic conditions of the people. Gandhi and Hazare thus have competent similarities because in both the movements, one can notice the seer presence of patronising moralistic ideals but a visible absence of the ideas and concerns raised by the dalits, Muslims and OBCs as equal partners.

Democracy has become more vibrant and socially rooted as the political mobilisations and participation of socially deprived groups become more independent and participative. The dalits have understood that the Gandhian ethics of Hindu social order and its political articulation (Hindutva) is antithetical to the ideological merits of the dalit movement and its emancipatory politics. Any submission to such quasi-moral socio-political construction of the Brahmanical elites will again relegate the dalits into the margins. The specific socio-cultural experiences provide the dalits a critical perspective to judge the legitimacy of political movements that claim to represent the voice of the nation. It upholds the voices of the oppressed sections against the historically privileged communities and their political notions. The political usage of brahmanical symbols and non-critical presence of Gandhi as the mascot at the Hazare movement, thus have a defining potential to alienate the dalits and the Muslims from its platform.

Defend the Supremacy of Constitutional Democracy

Harsh criticisms against the political elite is one of the most important characteristics of liberal democracy. Various democratic forums formulate their own critical understanding about the governing authorities and propose their own alternatives to correct the executive functioning into a fair and responsible agency. The heightened debate over the Lokpal Bill similarly addresses the same issue of political nepotism and growing practices of corruption in the high offices. Here, the Hazare movement is unapologetically vocal against the parliamentary democracy in India, while debating the importance of this Bill. It has criticised the political class not only as corrupt and unethical but also demeans them as uneducated and irresponsible. It was argued that such critical observation was based on certain factual and visible truths related to many infamous events of corruption in recent times. It is portrayed (mainly by the corporate-controlled media) that there is a widespread discontent among the public against the political class and the whole nation wants to get rid of this malaise on an immediate basis.

The Hazare movement is described by the influential sections as the resurgence of the civil society for a better change in governance against corruption. The movement has certain moralistic episodes; however in its methods and objectives, it degrades the logic of constitutional democracy and promotes unprecedented procedures of law-making. Firstly, it undermines the fundamental rights of the legislative houses to discuss and formulate a law. It pressurises the government with its quasi-ethical sensationalism and celebrates the non-compromising model of protest 'satyagraha' as the principle mode of demand articulation. The coercive tactics of 'fast-unto-death' have been instrumental in advancing just one version of the Jan Lokpal Bill as ideal and suitable without giving any space to other counterparts to flag their independent opinions and suggestions. As a result, the contentious issues within the Jan Lokpal Bill have been adopted by the parliament under the stressed and non-compromising attitude shown by the Team Anna. The supremacy of the parliament to formulate a bill and make a law has been thus mortgaged to satisfy the demands of the newly empowered people's representatives namely, the 'civil society'.

Secondly, the blanket raw criticism against all the political representatives during the movement has a subtle accusation against the changed demography of the legislative bodies. In the last two decades, the social composition of the parliament has remarkably shifted towards the OBC legislators and there is a significant decline in the upper caste representation, mainly of the brahmins.[4] This phenomenon, in general social science discourse, is understood as 'silent revolution' and greater democratisation of the political system. (Jafferlot 2003) However, for Team Anna there is no appreciation for such a revolutionary phenomenon, which otherwise showcases the growing consciousness of the marginalised and deprived communities to independently articulate their own political positions. The members elected from marginalised communities represent a platform which in times pressurized the government to carry forward the agenda of social justice. This group is further instrumental in many ways to suggest pro-poor policy mechanisms and keep a check on the aggressive neoliberal economic agenda of various regimes. The changed nature of the parliament and its interventionist attitude thus challenges the pro-market corporate houses which seek just a minimalist regulatory intervention of the state in the economic affairs.

Thirdly, the categorical silence over the issue of corruption in the private business houses, NGOs and religious institutions in the Jan Lokpal Bill has raised many questions. Many of these institutions, in nexus with the political elite, have not only possessed undeclared property and unaudited financial assets but also utilise unethical practices and threatening tactics in corrupting the civil servants and political leaderships. The private corporate houses (controlled mostly by of the upper-caste elites) have shown open disrespect to the policies of 'Affirmative Action' in their enterprises and most of the job appointments are done through unfair internal consultations (nepotism).[5] The influential NGOs have tactical alliances with the international funding agencies (Ford Foundation, in general) and in their various projects, they categorically follow the dictates of their international masters. Finally, many religious institutions have amassed uncalculated wealth and there is no account of how the property of the temples and other related institutions has been utilised apart from the religious services. These unregulated institutions in many respects are far more corrupt and unaccountable than the political class of the country.

The dalit perspective locates a hidden agenda in the exclusive targeting of political leadership by the Team Anna. They want that the 'discredited' parliament and its executives should be under the constant vigilance of a supreme and centralised extra-constitutional body (Lokpal). The dalits have expressed their fear that the institution of Lokpal will have the capacity to put the legislative and executive class on ransom and can coerce them to follow a particular kind of dictates. They assume that the upper-caste elite are planning such institution mainly because the political control of the parliament is periodically going out of the hands of the social elite. To retain their exclusive control over the democratic institutions, this movement is seen as a latest upper-caste ploy.

Conclusion: Understanding the Normative Aim of the Movement

Contemporary Indian democracy has offered a critical space to the dalit voice. As a political tool, the dalits have utilised democracy to understand the limitations of the hegemonic identities/ideas that the upper-caste elite has celebrated till date (secularism, citizenship, *Hindutva*, proletariat, et cetra). Dalits utilise their own independent ideological scale to judge the merits of any idea or movement. The anti-corruption stir of Anna Hazare may have influenced significant sections of the urban middle class; however it has not mobilised the dalits to become its integral part. As conscious political participants, the dalits judge the legitimacy of any movement by visualising how it makes the public institutions more inclusive and responsible towards the welfare of the downtrodden masses. Any movement under such scrutiny can be called ineffective if it does not endorse such responsible pro-poor socio-economic ethics. In this respect, the normative objectives of the Hazare movement may appear national but it does not supplement the ethical posturing of the dalit socio-political movement.

The anti-corruption movement in its final objective offers three new political possibilities. Firstly, it proposes a non-political association of a middle-class elite (popularly known as 'civil society') to replace the party politics and political opposition. Civil society is a platform of unaccountable voluntary groups (they don't contest elections), mobilised on certain temporary issues to build pressure on the government. It acts as non-political actors, but in a subtle way, subscribes to a certain brand of political ideology. It limits the engagement of the participants on a specific and limited issue (mostly policy related) without dwelling with the deep rooted reasons for the growing socio-economic maladies. More importantly, it disrespects the democratic process of elections and condemns all the political parties and leaders as 'corrupt' without distinction. However, in the democratic processes it has little authenticity whereas the political parties are the legitimate agencies to represent the voices of the people. The middle-class elite belittle the electorates as illiterate and not conscious enough to understand the 'dirty politics'. There is an acceptable understanding amongst these professionals that the elections are farce and political leadership is immoral. Therefore, it becomes the responsibility for these 'concerned citizens' to take the final call and clean the system.

Secondly, the Hazare Movement and the assertive civil society *avatar* appear democratic and peaceful, but the growing importance of this brigade is dangerous for a functional democracy. This platform of independent assertions (Gandhians, NGOs and religious-spiritual leaders) has little interest in strengthening the democratic process in a substantive way. It has the capacity to undermine the revolutionary process of periodical elections and can legitimise the non-constitutional modes (civil disobedience, Fast-unto-death agitations and mass pressure) to make policies and laws. A peaceful democracy will be in trouble, when more such independent actors (without any comprehensive political agenda of democratic participation) of civil society will rise and confront the constitutional system. The idea of civil society is not to turn democracy into anarchic mob-o-cracy but to substantiate it with qualitative democratic participation.

Finally, the heightened discursive privilege given to the unified idea of 'people', without dissecting its pluralist social composition, will only serve the interests of the dominant elite upper-caste sections. Democracy in India has been heralded by the socially marginalised communities because it has provided them a meaningful space to articulate their socio-economic and political objectives. Their independent assertions have contributed in making democracy more inclusive and vibrant. The overarching attempts by the civil society to create influential space for superficial identities (Indian/national/people/citizens) without providing due cognizance to the plural identities of the ascriptive groups will harm the political value of the groups who are struggling for fair recognition and representation.

Dalits' critical perspectives against the movement and the Bill mainly highlight its exclusiveness and non-democratic functioning. It is widely accepted that Hazare's anti-corruption stir was instrumental in bringing the anger and frustration of the middle classes in the public sphere. In fact, the movement has a majoritarian appeal as it engages with the legitimate concerns of the population; however it belittles the importance of social identities and its democratic value in contemporary India. Caste and community identities are essential means through which individuals decide their participation in the public spheres. A fair recognition and equal respect to these identities in the movement will not only make it more inclusive and democratic but will also attach the aspirations of the majority of the people to it.

REFERENCES

Ambedkar, B.R. (2002). 'Representation' in Valerian Rodrigues (ed.) *The Essential Writings of Dr B.R. Ambedkar*, Oxford University Press, New Delhi.

Gandhi, M.K. (1938). *Hind Swaraj or Indian Home Rule*, Navjivan Publishing House, Ahmedabad.

Jafferlot, Christopher (2003). *India's Silent Revolution: The Rise of Low Castes in North Indian Politics*, Permanent Black, New Delhi.

Karat, Prakash (2011). 'For a Strong and Effective Lokpal' *The Hindu*, 25 August.

Ilaiah, Kancha (2003). 'Productive Labour, Consciousness and History: The Dalitbahujan Alternative' in Shahid Amin and Dipesh Chakrabarty (eds.) *Subaltern Studies IX*, Oxford University Press, New Delhi.

Omvedt, Gail (2011). *Understanding Caste: From Buddha to Ambedkar and Beyond*, Orient Blackswan, New Delhi.

Phillips, Anne (2003). *The Politics of Presence: The Political Representation of Gender, Ethnicity, and Race*, Oxford University Press, Clarendon Press, Oxford.

Sarkar, Tanika (2006). 'Imagining Hindu Rashtra: The Hindus and Muslims in Bankim Chandra's Writings' in David Ludden (ed.) *Making India Hindu*, Oxford University Press, New Delhi.

Shanker, B.L. and Rodrigues, Valerian (2011). *The Indian Parliament: A Democracy at Work*, Oxford University Press, New Delhi.

NOTES

1. Both the leaders presented their elaborative critic of the movement during the discussion on the Lokpal Bill in the Parliament. Uttar Pradesh Chief Minister, Mayawati, also raised her reservations against the movement in a press conference. See 'Mayawati Rejects Jan Lokpal' The Hindu, 27 August 2011.
2. The only public protest against the Anna Hazare movement and its proposed Jan Lokpal Bill was witnessed on 23 August 2011 when under the banner of 'Sanvidhan Bachao (Save the Constitution)' a mega rally was organized at India gate by Indian Justice Party led by Udit Raj. See, Dipanjan Roy Chaudhary 'Dalits to Launch own Version of Lokpal Bill', India Today, 24 August 2011.
3. During the colonial period, the Hindu nationalists constructed many ideas bestowed with Hindu religious symbols (cow protection, Hindi as national language, the 'maternal metaphor' of India as Bharat Mata and singing of Vande Mataram) aimed to shape a common spiritual identity for the entire Hindu fraternity and as an aggressive symbol against the Muslim religious ethics. See, Sarkar (2006). Also, as early as in 1930's the Muslim leadership opposed the usage of Vande Mataram in the public spaces, accusing it as idolatry and against the ethos of Islam.
4. From the first general elections (1952) till 2004, the SC/ST representation is stagnant due to the reservation of seats, however the OBCs have doubled their numbers in the last two decades (in 1952 the OBCs has just 59 members as compared to the 128 members in the 2004 Lok Sabha). on the other hand the representation of Brahmin members has significantly lowered down from 119 in 1952 to just 41 in the 2004 elections. (Shanker and Rodrigues 2011: 77–101).
5. The business houses have univocally criticized the social justice agenda of UPA-I to extend the Scheduled Castes/Scheduled Tribes (SC/ST) reservations in the private sector enterprises. Instead they showed their readiness 'to train people in various vocations across the country in service and manufacturing to make people employable'. See. 'No Job Reservation in Private Sector: CII' Times of India, 21 June 2004.

11

Nouveau Claims on Traditional Visions of Indian Democracy

Atul Mishra[1]

One of the features of democracy is that it does not usually conform to the modern experience of time. There is inherent swiftness to temporal modernity; and this means that objectives set up by institutions of modernity must be reached apace. Thus, efficiently bureaucratic and centralised states can, for instance, attain rapid industrialisation or create ordered societies by levelling differences. Such achievements usually rest on institutionalising and perpetuating insensitivity towards constituencies that matter.

The task with a democracy of consequence is different. To deepen the ambit of its transformative potential, it must not only remain sensitive to rightful claims of existing constituencies that matter, but also anticipate the emergence of new constituencies and their claims. Consequential democratic deepening often involves a measure of uncertainty with regards to creation of new constituencies. Though they may be the products of democratic deepening, new constituencies do sometimes generate forms of traction that contest the ethical grammar of that democracy. This is even more likely in societies lacking in even minimal consensus, marked by economic unevenness across regions and strong cultural diversity.

Since a democracy takes its own time, at least relatively, it is likely to be faced with challenges produced by other, swifter sources of modernisation. Thus, in India, while political democracy may move assuredly to ensure inclusiveness, market economy is unlikely to slow down the pace at which it marketises the economic orientation of Indians. This asymmetry in the temporal workings of the two institutions can create instructive instabilities with consequences for Indian democracy.

This chapter examines the context of the Anna Hazare movement and his supporters to explore the following possibility: that the movement itself is born out of that instability which ensues from the asymmetry. If this argument is true, then, it could be argued that the forces underlying the movement indicate important possible shifts in the grammar of Indian democracy. In pursuing these two tasks, its emphasis is on *contextualising* the movement rather than enumerating and analysing its specific features. Similarly, it does not try to speculate on the specific transformations this movement may visit on Indian democracy. Though references to specifics are often necessary to illustrate parts of arguments, they are not the analytical focus of this chapter. Additionally, the claims forwarded here are outlined from (loosely) structural properties. They are not totalising claims about domestic or international politics. Structural outlines are minimalist expressions that can be obtained when we think of a political phenomenon as a whole. Though they can be read as specific political claims in the empirical sense, it serves intellectual discipline if they are primarily seen as relatively abstract knowledge claims from which empirical political conclusions may or may not be extrapolated.

II

Movements usually signify creative frictions in society. As signposts, they can help consolidate the institutional directions of democracy—a prudent necessity to moderate its ideational ambitions. Movements in democracy can also, variously, express dissatisfaction with the workings of democracy—its vision, the institutional articulation of that vision, its pace, the method of its unfolding and so on. Movements generally enrich the substance and process of democracy. In one sense, all of these conditions could be found in the movement lead by India Against Corruption (IAC). However, a persistent and contextual look at the movement provides more helpful leads into its nature and, more importantly, the forces underlying it.

There has been widespread agreement over the primary orientation of the movement. Critics and supporters have equally acknowledged its essentially 'middle-class' character. This is a tricky description because both the term and the constituency are yet to attain conceptual and empirical stability, respectively, in India. The conceptual dimensions of this middle class, some notable attempts notwithstanding (see, Misra 1961 and Varma 1998), are yet to be substantially explored, especially for its political features. A reasonable range of its share of India's population is anywhere between 5 and 15 per cent. Numbers matter here; but more important are the two features of this new Indian middle class: its growing size and its aspirational drive. Both carry the potential to influence the political domain of Indian democracy.

Like all classes, the middle class is fundamentally an economic category. It is constituted through its ability to absorb the ambition of the market. The new Indian middle class is also being constituted in the process of the market's expansion.[2] Two related tendencies of the market are worth noting here. One, the market relentlessly seeks to turn citizens into consumers. It seeks to replace citizenship with consumption as the dominant, public and shared identity without making the effort explicit.[3] Two, it does so by embedding a fierce sense of aspiration among consumers. The drive to consume is kept alive by exposing people to the constant ease and benefits of consumption. The conversion of the citizen into a consumer is a political act which, curiously, tends to absolve the person from responsibilities of being political; it tends to make them 'apolitical'. Additionally, it tends to make this 'apoliticality' a normatively desirable condition. This insistence on the apoliticality can often be rooted in prudence. The market is an invasive force and it is unlikely that it spares the spheres of activity that belong to the state. The insistence on apoliticality of its activities apparently concedes the political domain to the state even as it really seeks to camouflage the political consequences of its own expansion.

With its relentless pursuit of consumers, the market encourages the idea of 'apoliticality' and seeks to create a view that being apolitical is somehow desirable because it places persons in the upper echelons of modernity. Being political, which, for the market, implies the domain of the state and its constituents, is relegated as the less desirable state of existence—parochial and messy, at any rate not in the zone of cutting edge modernity. The class that gets created in the course of market's expansion tends to generally support this view; indeed, the view is perpetuated primarily through its acceptance and subsequent derivation of values that flow from it. However, the middle class is also aspirational; and this ability to aspire for constantly improved conditions of existence for itself can sometimes spill over into arenas that are not properly its own. Since politics is contextual, the effects of the spill over depend upon the context in which the spill takes place.

The political domain in India belongs to the state in the generic sense. However, more meaningfully, it is an arena that has become constituted in the course of the workings of Indian democracy. In a superficial sense, it comprises the interaction between democratic institutions, such as legislatures, judiciary and electoral commissions and the people of India. With its curious assemblage of individualistic and group-oriented concerns about questions of rights, justice, entitlements and opportunities, it appears to be a hybrid of liberal and social principles of western democracy. This it may be on some readings. Yet, the political domain of Indian democracy also has another dimension, which, because it appears counter-intuitive to received wisdom on lives of democracies, has not been sufficiently explored. Barring a few attempts at unravelling its grammar, this dimension as yet remains little known even to specialists in the West.[4] Part of the reason for this limitation is its substantial openness: Indian democracy still continues to either create or confront new constituencies that lay claims to its vision; it refuses, to borrow from Ashis Nandy, to be fully defined.

In this deeper sense, Indian democracy appears to acknowledge as its primary constituencies those historical groups whose claims on its vision are necessary for holding together India as a nation and as a state. At the very core of India's democratic deepening has been an inexact but unmistakable empowerment of groups historically disadvantaged and overlooked during the forging of the nation. Groups debilitated by the caste system, indigenous people who have been hitherto overlooked, women and religious minorities remain primary constituencies of Indian democracy. The political domain in India implies the philosophical, discursive, institutional and the policy space created through the interaction between Indian democracy and its constituencies.[5] This obviously does not mean that other political claims have not been present or are not important. However, in the ordering of preferences that all meaningful politics necessarily entails, this version of the political domain has been the most basic, the most foundational, and the most non-negotiable for Indian democracy.

III

Political actors, whether individuals or groups, require a will to persist and an intention to bring about change in the prevailing ways of politics. Neither will nor is intention adequate for the emergence of political actors. In complex political contexts, political actors become important by harmonising their objectives with aspirations of a collective. Since harmony in politics is seldom achieved on its own, manipulation becomes a virtue.

The coordinators of the Anna movement have some claim to being virtuous manipulators of political variables. Their reasonable experience of working in, and thus expanding, the space between the state and the populations, seem to have guided a few crucial tactical elements. Since Gandhi, Indian politics has seen the prominence of centres of power that stay outside politics. This public separation between the executive and the ideologue is also hierarchical. The ideologue—either a Bal Thackeray or a Sonia Gandhi—always becomes someone 'above' or 'beyond' politics. This arrangement enables the ideologue to become an ethical (the term is contextual) bundle that does not yield to the corruptive influence of politics. The movement's coordinators identified the efficacy of this arrangement and installed as that ideologue someone who seems instinctively unintelligent for Indian politics. This helps. While Hazare's obscure antics at projecting himself in the mould of Gandhi somewhat compensate the need for an ethical centre in Indian public life, his innately limited political acuity ensures that he will not become a threat to more important manipulations. Close observers of Hazare's statements and demeanour cannot miss his reduction act: to Gandhi's quaint ideal of simple living and high thinking, Hazare responds by embodying his own, namely, simple living and simple thinking.

Hazare's projection as the leader of the movement also facilitates the less obvious process of the spill over of aspirations from one domain to another. It was earlier suggested that the organising belief of the market-inspired middle class is that apoliticality is both a morally superior and desirable condition of existence. If politics in these contexts is associated with a dirty, unclean, impure space and activity, then the apolitical becomes its opposite: tidy, clean, pure. These hygienic images form some kind of congruence with the person of Anna Hazare and the cause undertaken by the movement. Corruption in its generic sense is distortion, a move away from the ideal. It follows that getting rid of corruption requires individuals who are not corrupt, individuals who are closest things to the ideal. It is a comment on the average sensibility of Indian public life that Hazare matches that description. However, more crucially, Hazare's face allows the movement's real leaders to convert general aspirational energy of the middle class into a drive against corruption.

This drive against corruption indicates a strong spill over of the middle class into the political domain of Indian democracy. This is not a plain development. Appreciating its import requires explaining why this has come about—a task that would also help in normative evaluation of the movement.

The emulation of metropolitan political grammar by colonial and post-colonial political forces has been widely noted (Chatterjee 1986). The need for such emulation is felt when native resources are deemed either out dated or ineffective at providing solutions to problems a society confronts. Emulation is an implicit acknowledgement of the superiority of the emulated. Corruption as a social and economic fact may have existed in India on its own merit, but its conversion into *the* national political issue became possible because the middle class has been keenly emulating and internalising the values of governance. Why must it be so striking?

The political project of the newest form of capitalism, neoliberalism, has been to homogenise the political condition of the world, especially the Third World or the global South. This it has sought to do by seeking to replace *politics* with *governance* as the defining paradigm of the Third World state. Most of the ex-colonial world made their way to independence through political articulation of difference. Therefore, in post-colonial states, politics constitutes a domain of distinctive identity which also marks their sovereign independence. It is evident that articulations of difference, and thus insistence on politics, often obstruct the flow of capital. Politically strong states may also resist creation of conditions favourable for the market. Neoliberalism's response to this resistance has been to promote a worldview that governance and politics are antithetical conditions; that strong political commitments such as ideology, social justice, group welfare are obstacles to efficient governance. What it implies is that a politically strong state is also an involved and an invasive state, which, as the First World wisdom suggests, is inimical to individual well-being. Its criteria for judging governments are their smallness and limits of their political influence. To perform its functions efficiently, thus follow the policy recommendations, governments must concede their space, the political space, to private actors. Governments are inefficient, it further holds, because they are prone to corruption. Governments are corrupt because they privilege politics over governance.[6]

Market or neoliberalism conditions two forms of false polarities in order to self-perpetuate: a) of political and apolitical; and b) of politics and governance. It privileges apolitical governance over politics and promotes the idea as a desirable condition which can be universally achieved.[7] In some ways, this is an outward projection of the First World self-image. Many modernising societies are likely to fall for its charms, especially if the classes undergoing modernisation lose their traditional ideational resources and thus their self-confidence. Such classes are more likely to emulate and internalise the idea of apolitical governance. The Indian middle class has emulated the idea along with the underlying values. It holds apolitical governance to be empirically feasible and normatively desirable.

It is difficult to otherwise explain why it has identified corruption as the most important issue plaguing India. That there has been a felt resentment against corruption is undeniable. However, that popular sentiment has largely been due to a combination of conditions:

persisting inflation, exposés of multiple instances of massive corruption and the justified perception that the government did too little too late, thereby exposing itself to damaging implication of being complicit in corruption. Corruption *is* an important problem facing India. But it is not *the* most important one.[8]

Seen from the perspective of the traditional constituents of Indian democracy, justice, equitable distribution of resources, access to modes of life that strengthen human capabilities and recognition of structural vulnerabilities of certain groups are the most important concerns that Indian democracy must address. These concerns are rooted in the shameful aspects of India's past, its astonishing geographical and economic unevenness and the tragic denouement of formal colonialism in partition. Indian democracy must take the overcoming of these immense disabilities as its core task. These concerns form the content of politics in India.

Claiming that corruption is the most important issue in India enables the movement to spill over into the political domain of Indian democracy. By claiming that corruption threatens the country more than any other issue, the movement shows not only a disregard for the traditional constituencies and concerns of Indian democracy, it also threatens to dislodge them. The force and effectiveness with which this claim has been articulated make real the possibility that corruption could come to acquire centre stage in Indian politics.[9] It is here that the spillover becomes evident. The middle class, hitherto conspicuous by its absence from the core political concerns of Indian democracy, appears to be threatening to upset the traditional agenda altogether. This is possibly the first major political agenda that India's middle class has consciously adopted. In so doing, it is laying claims to the traditional vision of Indian democracy; not to be accommodated in that vision, but to alter it with its nouveau claims. Seen another way, it is establishing itself as a constituent of Indian democracy, in competition with the traditional constituents.

IV

Consolidation of the middle class into a political entity has been considered a sign of maturity for nearly all concrete expressions of liberal democracy. As agents of democratisation, they are the revolutionary classes in liberal democracies; for the political strengthening of the middle class greatly favours the constitution of a strong civil society. [10] There is a liberal component to Indian democracy, which, to a certain extent, would benefit from this strengthening.[11] However, the nature of politics espoused by the movement will have important consequences.

In the medium term, progressive consolidation of this movement or its variants is likely to create substantial conflict between the middle class and the traditional constituencies of Indian democracy. In a country marked by institutionalised dissensus, there will be strong resistance to any attempt at altering the somewhat established meaning of the political domain. This is because even though the spill over is thoroughly political, in the sense that all mass movements that seek transformations are, it is not being acknowledged as such at both ends. The leadership of this movement has claimed throughout that it is apolitical. This is in tune with the primary self-image of the middle class. The dominant intended meaning of the term is that Team Anna, so called, will not contest elections. But it does also mean it is apolitical in the sense that market-inspired middle class understands that term. Thus, the movement remains in self-denial, a position it is already finding difficult to sustain. Political goals are difficult to pursue while proclaiming apoliticality.

Even as the pressure to acknowledge its primarily political character grows, there would be resistance from the traditional constituencies of Indian democracy. As a political constituency, the middle class, if its acts as a somewhat coherent entity, will be an important force. However, the traditional constituents would be concerned at the articulation of a new set of national agenda: streamlining governance structures of the country to ensure efficient correlation between means and ends.[12] This *MBAisation*—I use the term to convey a technical orientation—of Indian politics is likely to unsettle traditional political configurations. Equitable rearrangement of hierarchical differences is often the best outcome of India's deep divisions. Any traction gained by the movement will put strains on the conventional ways in which that outcome has so far been scripted. For the traditional constituents, this movement primarily appears to be articulating an exclusionary vision.

Exclusionary tendencies are easier to contest when their contours are publicly identifiable. This is not the case with the movement in question since it excludes in insidious ways. Some of the prominent metaphors being relied upon by the movement are foundationally exclusionary in a pan-Indian context. The engendering of the nation in the image of 'mother India' must cause unease within women's movements in the country while embarrassing other constituents. The reliance on prominently Hindu symbolism, with its majoritarian overtones, likewise alienates religious minorities. Most damagingly, the movement relies on a strong binary between purity and pollution, identifying itself with an unpolluted zeal against the pollution of corruption. Expectedly, its Brahmanical overtones make Dalit voices resentful. It does not help that positions adopted by some of its top leadership, in response to positions of its other top leadership, in the context of Kashmir has close parallels with centre-right conceptions of nationalism. Indeed, there are strong suggestions of at least amorphous cooperation between the movement and Rashtriya Swayamsevak Sangh.

Most audaciously, the movement has shown open disregard for established political institutions. This has been evident in the sweeping provisions of the Jan Lokpal Bill, the undermining of parliamentary representative institutions during the August 2011 stage-in discourses and in the presumed moral superiority of the tone in which the movement's chief articulators engage public discussions. Emphasising this aspect in no way suggests that these institutions are flawless; to the contrary, the need for decentralisation and expansion of representative institutions in so deeply diverse a country is deep. The point rather is that undermining these institutions causes concerns among the traditional constituencies because these institutions have been the agents of their social and political, if not always economic, emancipation. A disregard for these institutions implies a disregard for the kind of politics they sustain. This disdain for politics is unwelcome for the traditional constituencies. Expectedly, there has been a concerted response from the political elite towards cornering the movement. That it has pursued this by proclaiming the primacy of the political domain in deciding the meaning of democracy and representative institutions in India is remarkable.[13]

V

The exploration of the movement's implications for Indian democracy would remain incomplete if it does not relate them to the international context. Examining the international dimensions involved in their dynamics would enable a sharper appreciation of the larger processes involved.

So influential and enduring have social and liberal forms of modern western democracy appeared that for long, and especially since the demise of the Soviet Union, it was considered to be the truly universal political philosophy for organising human societies. On occasions when democracy produced tragic deviations within the West, other democracies—the Allies—got together to reform such pathologies; post-War Germany being an example. This was the basis for western belief that their form of government, including its in-house variants, was the best for the world.[14] The claim is difficult to sustain now; so is the wish. Two overlapping sets of evidence strongly contest the desirability and the universality claim made with regards to western democracy. Firstly, major parts of the world are not necessarily democratising along the lines familiar to the West. Even accounting for internal differences, which may resemble western forms in patches, democratisation in South America, Russia, and South Asia appear more attuned to their specific contexts rather than inspired by supposedly universal ideals. Secondly, simplistic expressions of western style representative democracy such as crass majoritarian dominance have caused the West, uniquely perhaps, to doubt the inherent merit of their claim. The displeasure of the United States and some European countries with the democratic rise of Hamas in Palestine is instructive.[15] It is possible that a similar fear of democratically elected regimes that articulate strongly non-western values is behind the West's hesitant, unenthusiastic response to West Asian democratic movements.

Two features of these trends are salient for understanding the prospects of Indian democracy. The first is that despite being a process that bears fruit in the long term, democracy is given to transient tendencies of politics. Since in concrete expressions politics abides by contextual constraints rather than ahistorical ideals, it is important to consider the possibility that democracies may experience undesirable phases during their existence. The second is that the international distribution of political values is becoming increasingly unfavourable from the western perspective. Shifting power centre of the world from the Atlantic to the Pacific, from the West to Asia, is likely to further weaken the hold of western values. How will these two impact Indian democracy?

A general condition created by Indian democracy holds true even during its most confounding moments: perhaps never before in human history have over a billion people of such diversity had the right to simultaneously express their subjectivities. A billion subjectivities are a force by any reckoning. For a West that is swiftly declining, nothing would be more ideal than a billion voices sympathetic to its worldview. In their discourses during the last decade, the West, especially United States and western European countries, have singled out India's democracy as its greatest feature, its greatest asset, the glue that binds India to the West and, at the same time, entitles India to a great power status.[16] Economic considerations explain a great deal of this slant. India's emerging market is an engine that produces consumers at rapid pace. It suits saturated western capitalist economies to provide new, hungry markets for their businesses. However, there is a distinctness of the political explanation which cannot be ignored. Apart from its consumer base, the West likely finds in India a repository of its values in difficult times. It considers India a hedge for a set of political values that have their origins in West but can be more easily propagated in parts of the non-West from a non-Western location. This explains the western prescription to India that it should participate in global democracy promotion (see, Mohan 2007; Cartwright 2009).

This may still be the age of the nation-states, but there are large areas in world politics that seem least affected by boundaries that separate domestic and international politics. Thus, it is entirely possible that a global instance of democracy promotion may take place *within* the boundaries of a state. A reversal of our analytical gaze would show us that the kind of democracy promotion the West advocates is already being carried out within India. The steady growth in India of an understanding of democracy which privileges individual rights over group welfare, civic and political rights over social and economic rights, order over justice, greater trust in the judiciary than in the legislature and the executive, industry over agriculture, towns and cities over villages and governance over politics indicates that this democracy promotion has made substantial inroads. It is possible that the movement against corruption is the strongest public manifestation of this style of democracy promotion. We need not possess empirical evidence of the kind admissible in a court of law to advance this claim. Similarities between the western worldview of democracy, especially its emphasis on the market and civil society as catalysts of democracy promotion, and the views (either advanced or implicit) of the movement's leadership, along with its acceptance among the movement's enthusiasts provide sufficient contextual evidence.

When seen from this international perspective, the starkness of the spill over becomes evident. The movement is not merely laying claims to the vision of Indian democracy; it is not merely trying to redefine the content of Indian politics; it is doing so on the basis of a set of ideas that are not entirely internal to the vision of Indian democracy.

It is true that the formal vision of Indian democracy, elaborated in the constitution, was borrowed from the experience of western democracies. In the course of its deepening, however, Indian democracy has generated its own distinct vision. This vision may superficially appear to be a version of liberal or social democracy of the western mould. Yet, such caricaturing is to be avoided, especially because it ignores the efforts of some of the most disadvantaged groups of humanity to emancipate themselves in profoundly adverse conditions. Through their gritty participation, the traditional constituents of Indian democracy have given it a meaning that was perhaps both unintended and unanticipated at its initiation.[17] For a useful reading of this perspective, see Yadav (1999).

REFERENCES

Ablett, Jonathon et al (2007). 'The 'Bird of Gold': The Rise of India's Consumer Market', McKinsey Global Institute, San Francisco.

Bauman, Zygmunt (2001). 'Consuming Life', *Journal of Consumer Culture*, 1(1): 9–29.

Cartwright, Jan (2009). "India's Regional and International Support for Democracy: Rhetoric or Reality?", *Asian Survey*, 49(3): 403–428.

Chatterjee, Partha (2004). *The Politics of the Governed: Reflections on Popular Politics in Most of the World*, New York: Columbia University Press.

______ (1997). *A Possible India: Essays in Political Criticism*, New Delhi: Oxford University Press.

______ (1986). *Nationalist Thought and the Colonial World: A Derivative Discourse?* in *The Partha Chatterjee Omnibus*, sixth impression in 2007, New Delhi: Oxford University Press.

Ferguson, James (1994). *The Anti-Politics Machine: 'Development,' Depoliticization and Bureaucratic Power in Lesotho*, Minneapolis, MN: University of Minnesota Press.

Fukuyama, Francis (1992). *The End of History and the Last Man*, New York: Free Press.

Goldenberg, Suzzanne (2008). 'US plotted to overthrow Hamas after election victory', *The Guardian*, 4 March.

URL: http://www.guardian.co.uk/world/2008/mar/04/usa.israelandthepalestinians

Jayaraman, Nityanand and Ruchir Purohit (2011), 'The beauty of corruption is that, it converts any act of being into something which is rentable', interview with Shiv Visvanathan, *Tehelka*, 6 September.

URL: http://www.tehelka.com/story_main50.asp?filename=Ws060911Corruption.asp

Kaviraj, Sudipta (2011). *The Enchantment of Democracy and India*, New Delhi: Permanent Black.

Khoras, Homi (2010). 'The Emerging Middle Class in Developing Countries', OECD Development Centre, Working Paper No. 285.

URL: http://www.oecd.org/dataoecd/12/52/44457738.pdf

Klein, Naomi (2000). *No Logo*, London: HarperCollins/Flamingo.

Mehta, Pratap Bhanu (2003), *The Burden of Democracy*, New Delhi: Penguin.

Misra, B.B. (1961). *The Indian Middle Classes: Their Growth in Modern Times*, London: Oxford University Press.

Raja Mohan, C. (2007). 'Balancing Interests and Values: India's Struggle with Democracy Promotion', *The Washington Quarterly*, 30(3): 99–115.

Rice, Condoleezza (2002). 'A Balance of Power that Favors Freedom', *Wriston Lecture*, Manhattan Institute of Policy Research, 1 October, New York.

URL: http://www.manhattan-institute.org/html/wl2002.htm

Roy, Arundhati (2011). I'd rather not be Anna', *The Hindu*, Opinion-Lead, 21 August.

Varma, Pavan (1998). *The Great Indian Middle Class*, New Delhi: Penguin.

Yadav, Yogendra (1999). 'Politics' in Marshall M. Bouton and Philip Oldenburg (eds). *India Briefing: A Transformative Fifty Years*, Armonk, NY: M.E. Sharpe.

NOTES

1. Centre for Studies in Politics and Governance, Central University of Gujarat, Gandhinagar, Gujarat, India. Email: anticontic@gmail.com
2. Assuming market continues to expand, McKinsey Global Institute estimated in 2007 that by 2025 India's middle class will be around 583 million or nearly forty percent of population. Though a demographic minority even at that strength, it would be world's fifth largest collective of consumer humans (Ablett et al 2007).

   The global context of this possibility can be better appreciated when read along with the OECD Development Centre's hopeful projection. A 2010 Working Paper of the Centre suggests that by 2020, Asia would comprise half the world's middle class and Asian consumers could account for forty percent of global middle class consumption. India, apart from China, would be the core of that consumer base (Khoras 2010).
3. Sampling from the Indian consumer world: the preference for bottled or packaged drinking water in metropolises such as Delhi and Mumbai to the municipal corporation's water supply is instructive. Water is a basic resource and access to safe drinking water is the citizen's right. But the promotion of packaged water as an alternative relegates the citizen identity of the people and privileges their consumer identity. Had the alternative not been so easily available, would not the citizen assert her right to clean drinking water and struggle to ensure that supply rather than become a consumer of heavily-priced bottled water? Another trend: the proliferation of full front-page advertisements in newspapers. The space of the citizen—assuming that newspapers are meant to keep citizenry informed—is becoming a space of the consumer. Under the relentless pressure of advertisement, the first informed choices individuals make in a day are as consumers of LED television rather than citizens of a democracy. Unsurprisingly, the government too seeks to raise people's consciousness not as citizens but as consumers as the campaign jaago graahak jaago (literally, wake up consumer, wake up) suggests. For radical and rhythmic expositions, see 'No Choice' in Naomi Klein's *No Logo* (2000) and *Zygmunt Bauman* (2001), respectively.

4. For insightful counter-intuitive readings of the working of Indian democracy, see Chatterjee's A Possible India (1997) and some essays in *The Politics of the Governed* (2004), and those in Kaviraj's *The Enchantment of Democracy and India* (2011).
5. This does not imply that all constituencies have been equally attended to. Arguably, disadvantaged caste groups have fared relatively better than women, indigenous people and religious minorities, especially Muslims. Muslims, moreover, have been primarily approached through the prism of state security and patriotism rather than social welfare and capability enhancement, thus exposing the latent shortcoming of Indian democracy.
6. For a noted exposition of the concerted efforts to deny politics and history a space in framing of public policy and understanding of development, see, Ferguson's (1994) *The Anti-Politics Machine*.
7. Unlike economic dos and don'ts of the Washington Consensus, though, these prescriptions of apoliticality need not be listed. They can become cultural aspirations if a society finds the Consensus injunctions mostly acceptable, like the Indian middle class appears inclined to.
8. Long due arguments over what constitutes corruption have begun alongside the movement. Clarity about two aspects of the meaning of corruption may be foundational in this regard. The first relates to the understanding of the term by the middle class and its expression through the movement. Corruption here implies prevalence of petty briberies and colossal kickbacks in the governmental arena, forms of nepotism, duress caused to consumers of public service. The emphasis here largely remains on distortions in the functioning of the government. The resentment is premised on the image of the ideal governmental system—conceived in the West but seldom achieved anywhere. Except perhaps in Singapore, if we are to believe the Indian middle-class assessment. There are alternative perspectives critical of this governance-orientated, emulated understanding of corruption. It is a structural condition, argues Shiv Visvanathan, that controls access to rights and entitlements (Jayaraman and Purohit 2011). Arundhati Roy has likewise suggested that corruption may be 'the currency of a social transaction in an egregiously unequal society, in which power continues to be concentrated in the hands of a smaller and smaller minority' (Roy 2011). It could be added that what appears corruption from the middle class perspective, namely, unlawful siphoning off of public money by public functionaries for non-official ends, is also a form of redistribution—of resources and accompanying intangible

privileges. In a society marked by such historically entrenched unevenness, should it be surprising that public representatives of the disadvantaged groups, a Madhu Koda, a Mayawati or a D. Raja for instance, are suspected of diverting huge amounts of public money for other ends?

9. The movement received unparalleled media coverage whose significant feature was not the air hours but the concert or carnival-like production intent: wide-angle motion cameras catering to the fluttery waves of the Indian flag during its August protests in Delhi. It animated the Union government, caused a reluctant prime minister to intervene and a hurriedly-assembled parliament to convey a sense of the House. Perhaps no other movement in recent Indian history has achieved so much so swiftly; certainly not those involved in comparatively more life and death issues such as the repeal of abusive legislations from the north east and Kashmir, not the farmers protest movements, not the anti-nuclear protests.
10. Alexis de Tocqueville's *Democracy in America* remains the classic statement of this proposition.
11. Pratap Bhanu Mehta's *The Burden of Democracy* (2003) is an insightful liberal reflection on Indian democracy.
12. After, and if, the Jan Lokpal is clinched, IAC plans to pursue movements for judicial and electoral reforms too. Their outlines suggest the grammar of setting governance in opposition to politics will continue.
13. Among others, Congress General Secretary Digvijay Singh's frequent remarks are illustrative.
14. For a noted emphasis, see Fukuyama (1992).
15. There have been reported US plans and on-going encouragement from various sections of the West to topple the Hamas government in Gaza (see, Goldenberg 2008).
16. Thus, in 2005, when Condoleezza Rice declared that the US would help India become a great power, the idea behind it was to fashion a global balance of power in the favour of freedom. For an exposition, see Rice (2002).

12

Moment and Movement: De-hyphenating the Debate

Dhananjay Rai

Introduction

Over the years in Indian democracy, certain models have been developed wherefrom 'success and failures' have been envisioned. The year of 1947 has been set as a bench mark. The successes or failures have been measured intensively on the basis of continual institutional survival (Kohli, 1988 and 2001; Khilnani, 2004; Chandra, 2008). The span of success is delimited to 1947 onwards (Guha, 2007) while remaining silent over the continuity of pre and post-Independence India's legatees. Even the transfigurative revolutionaries like Jotirao Phule, B.R. Ambedkar and E.V. Ramaswamy have been construed as 'makers of modern India', as if modern India is a finished project and the role of these are limited heretofore, with the selective emphasis on a certain text (Guha, 2011) while negating their voluminous concern. The year of 1991 has been another watershed year. Now institutional success got new meaning. Institutions' successes and failures are contingent upon its their ability to negotiate with externality (global capital). In the pre-1991 era, the yardstick of success was 'internality'. Internality can be defined as a oppressive conglomeration of dominant social-economic and bureaucratic representatives. The *enabling* year of 1991 for internality to negotiate with externality has become a fulcrum of the measurement of 'India Unbound' (Das, 2000). The issue is 'sustaining India's growth miracle' (Bhagwati and Calomiris, 2008) by way of 'politics of change' (Singh, 2007) so that internality and externality become compatible for negotiation.

The post-1991 era wherein 'externality' is bemused is nothing but surrogated concern of 'internality' to ripen the fruits through shared negotiation and reconciliation with the former. Certain questions need to be answered. So, 'what needs to be asked'? Questions and answers are interlinked in many ways. Questions itself decide what would be the answers. There is a generic allusion that wrong questions will always have wrong answers. This is a premature understanding. Prefix 'wrong' does not suggest merely incorrectness but vantage points. There could be two types of questions. The first set of questions are needful questions. These are often being asked. Repetition of such questions circulates the belief and practices of their vitality. For example, liberal democracies over the years have become the acme of massive space for primitive accumulation of capital. Questions are being asked on the success of democracy/institutions while citing examples of periodic elections. Well-being/non-well-being are proven through circulation or circumvention of schemes/policies. Necessary questions are of a different nature. Foundational questions acquire primacy here. Questions like well-being and success of democracy in the context implementation of schemes and periodical electioneering will not be asked. These are not foundational questions. At best, they are 'outcome questions' and will always be the concern of needful inquiry. A foundational question will be, in this regard, whether beyond liberal democracy anything could be envisaged wherein accumulation and ascription-based subjugation could be made necessarily absent. It is time to ask foundational questions pugnaciously and not outcome questions meekly.

Biography and biographers of 'modern India' and postulators of success/failures have missed the fundamental question or ontological question of the Indian state. In fact, this is the question of prioritisation. In place of asking 'outcome questions' like how democracy/institutions are functioning, the questions should have been why they are functioning the way they are. 'Burden of democracy' (believing in social hierarchy and failure of the state) (Mehta, 2003) is not a scholastic concern; rather why this burden has touched new heights, is. Moreover, analysis of territory, the Constitution, the state apparatus, parties and regime change as 'political history of independent India' (Chatterjee, 1997: 1-40) and thereafter negotiation of marginal via formation of 'political society' with the institutions (Chatterjee, 2004) are important. But any such attempts would be abortive and partial because logic of institutions and manoeuvres to make a niche are being highlighted at the cost of the real ambitions of the marginal. Put differently, since Independence, various responses have grown and risen in respect of institutions. Do we find a changing nature of institutions, more specifically as desired by numerous struggles led by fettered social-material groups? Or are success/failures to be summed up on the basis of continuation/deviation of 'get-go' essentialities. Get-go essentiality is the pristine feature of institutions. Even this 'deviation', that is, corruption becomes justifiable on two grounds, as proposed by Micheal Walzer, if it serves the maximum benefits to the people while politicians express remorse concerning the act (Walzer, 1973: 160–80). This deviation is 'dirty hand' for Walzer and '[i]t is easy to get one's hands dirty in politics and it is often right to do so'. (ibid: 174)

Discerning continuation/deviation of 'get-go' essentiality is a flawed vantage point. There are two reasons. First, institutions' philosophy becomes sacrosanct which is, thereafter, followed by a long process of rigidification. Rigidification in toto, in turn, produces a benchmark wherefrom successes/failures are being adjudicated. In the ambit of institutional success, quadrupling numbers of billionaires, redrawing the calloused poverty level (₹ 34), ignominious aloofness for people who earn ₹ 20 per day, reincarnation of brahmanism in the form of nationalism are recurrent phenomenon. Some of these would be considered as successes while others might be considered as aberrations. However, it would be very rare to call a spade a spade from an institutional perspective which is: the institution is bound to produce such phenomenon since its edifices are intact and rooted in dominant material and social spheres to provide succour to them. Second, there is ipso facts relegation, rejection and endagerment of the collutive envisioning of numerous fettered groups whohave suffered or have been suffering from material and ascriptive subjugation and at the same time do not concieve institutions as infinite.

The entire rigmarole of 'India against Corruption', 'Team Anna' initiations and institutional responses to it just some inferences to delve into the deeper question of faith in institutions or otherwise. The most significant question is to understand the nature of response by the state to acts which either repose faith in institutions or become perilous to the institutions. Real democracy is not one which subscribes to the views of institutions; it is survival of those who wish to produce such conditions which could circumvent unfettered growth of billionaires and brahmanism/religio-techno fascism-led nationalism. This is a limited attempt by the author to understand the state's response to two different domains, 'moment' and 'movement', in order to evaluate the democracy/India which goes beyond cyclical success of institutional manoeuvres.

Moment and Movement: Need for Epistemological Diaphanousness

The problem with focus on 'get-go' essentiality and institutional success to carry forward the former in a robust manner, eclipses two contemporary dimensions. Firstly, ongoing struggles are omitted with the question mark (?) of their presence and being necessary. Secondly, desires of fetters are depicted anti-constitutional, thus suppressed. Ironically, voices are silenced through unconstitutional ways. Fetters' voices are not unconstitutional but beyond the constitution. The difference between 'unconstitutional' and 'beyond constitution' is an axiomatic one. Unconstitutional denotes the defiance of Constitution. Referent of beyond the constitution mobilisations suggests the limiting of it. Therefore, it becomes imperative to transcend the constitution. Between unconstitutional and beyond Constitution, here comes the third element which can be stated as a constitutional method which believes in the sanctimony of the constitution. The state's response is a peculiar one. The gap between promise of Constitution and its actual delivery got people into agitation. Even those who are unconvinced about the constitutionality wait for a seemingly eventual failure. It is true that after adoption of get-go essentiality, that is, basic principle of Constitution, a hegemony of dominant conglomerates gets established with the promise of a 'liberated' future. Hegemony comes with promises. Here, denial of a liberated future is not rejected, but the way of liberation is opaque. The tension between promise and opaque methods has to generate the situation of dismay. Dismay leads to mobilisation. The state's impromptu reaction is to dub it as unconstitutional but not beyond the constitution. Terming it unconstitutional helps to galvanise 'popular' opinion in favour of the constitution and emotional issue of ownership that is, the constitution is owned by everyone and helps the cause of the state. The state will never say that it is beyond the constitution. Doing so would entail the 'limit' of the constitution while generating a consciousness of its mortal character and thereby possible germination of a sense of unity amongst fetters. Institutional focus negates this chain of events where the state and people engage.

Institutional perspective also ignores the nature of mobilisation. Since they are too much occupied with go-get essentiality and the continuity, it is but an obvious outcome. In any 'constitutional society', anti-constitutional/unconstitutional and beyond constitutional always exist. They remain minor though more vocal. The fence line between these mobilisations and the the state is categorically drawn. We will focus here on two types of mobilisations: the first is for constitutional measures and the second desirously seeks going beyond the constitutional proviso.

Let's return to our discussion on the constitution. The constitution is nothing but complete hegemony of the subjects. It demands absolute surrender of the people. The absolute surrender in turn promises a 'liberated future'. This is of course a new development in contrast to the earlier period of feudal/monarchs wherein servitude was a fact of the day sans allusion to the future. The constitution will never function without allusion to the future. Maximum numbers of people by the name of 'citizen' are considered as fountain of the constitution. The issue is not whether they are or are not fountains of the constitution but whether they have been considered, adopted and treated constitutionally. Numerically, in any country, more than two thirds of the populace has to be actively/passively defenders of the constitution to cull the process of distanciation. The mobilisation often takes place 'passively' when the seemingly 'liberated future' remains a distant dream. One cannot remain passive for long. Churning inevitably takes place due to mismatch between liberated future and unfulfilling.

The first type of mobilisation takes place for pressing the demand for a 'promised' liberated future. The state response is atypical. Mobilisation is being termed as unconstitutional. Ruling echelons cite the philosophy of authorship. Since, they are authors of the constitution in terms of implementers, amenders and initiators, therefore more legitimacy lies with them. Here, authorship of the constitution gets contradicted with supposed ownership of people. Ruling echelons, however, cannot stretch the issue too much since legitimacy is required for hegemony. More so, various provisions of the constitution are being cited by mobilisers to augur the demand. Unconstitutional depictions of mobilisation cause two developments. The state commences some measures to appear as a genuine author. Mobilisers under the impression of 'ownership' tend to turn more constitutional after being dubbed as unconstitutional. These types of mobilisation are a fit case of moment. Mobilisation of such types must be depicted as moment because of its transient nature. The state also responds quickly to such moment due to two factors. Firstly, institutions remain intact. The more quick response, despite a slew of complexities, ensures quick reposing of faith in institutions. Secondly, quick response and quickened reposing of faith prevent moment's transformation into movement.

Movement represents 'beyond Constitution' mobilisation. Moment is rejuvenator of institutions whereas movement is transformer of institutions. The nature of moment is transient while on the contrary movement is intransient. Moment produces constitutionality and movement germinates utopia. Constitutionality is nothing but celebration of 'get-go' essentiality. Utopia is the first sign of rupture from the past and present. That is why movement and utopia are entwined. The utopia is worldly utopia. The desire and envisioning are rooted here in place of surrendering to the external world. The perennial question before movement is signification of 'transforming institutions'. This question has two purposive values. The first is to say, reveal and pronounce the referent of transforming institutions. This is important because adaptability and everyday 'progressive' changing of institutions are being highlighted even by institutionalists. Two major limitations and essential outcomes of liberal constitutionalism are germination of scaled accumulations and profundity of nationalism enmeshed with ascriptive assertion. The first sign of movement is to harp on these two non-negotiable entities in terms of rebuttal. The second purpose is to demarche the categorical difference between movement and moment. Scrupulous negation of scaled accumulations and nationalism enmeshed with ascriptive subjugations is a benchmark of movement.

Movements also construct 'political subject'. Moments bypass the process of construction. Before construction of the political subject, moments recede Political subject remains significant due to being conscious about duple demands. Duple demands are 'immediacy' and 'permanency'. Immediacy and permanency are dialectically linked. Immediacy represents everyday needs and strategies. It cannot be suspended till permanency that is, desired egalitarian order is achieved. Correspondingly, permanency cannot be jettisoned otherwise immediacy becomes only and absolute goal. The political subject reminds oneself and remains as a reminder for others of double demands. Transforming of institutions is not possible sans construction and presence of political subject. And political subject cannot be created without movements. Therefore, the distinction between moment and movement, apart from aforesaid two purposes, is vital to understand the nature of numerous mobilisations and the state's response.

The moment and movement dichotomy and categorical prioritisation can be located in Karl Marx and Frederic Engels and B.R. Ambedkar. *German Ideology* is the first attempt wherein revolution per se is envisaged. The two texts, *Manifesto of the Communist Party* and *The Class Struggle in France,* are vital to see choice before proletariats. 'Movement' is a categorical priority and celebration of it is writ large. The rupture between 'moment' and 'movement' is shown clearly. Rupture is stated in the following words:

> But it is just as empirically established that, by the overthrow of the existing state of society by the communist revolution ... and the abolition of private property which is identical with it, this power ... will be dissolved; and that then the liberation of each single individual will be accomplished in the measure in which history becomes transformed into world history'. (Marx and Engels, 1970: 55)

In *German Ideology*, 'political subject' is not omitted. 'The existence of revolutionary ideas in a particular period presupposes the existence of a revolutionary class...' (ibid: 65). The rupture is being again highlighted in *Manifesto*. They pin point that '[t]he communist revolution is the most radical rupture with traditional property relations; no wonder that its development involves the most radical rupture with traditional ideas' (Marx and Engels, 1999: 109–10). The celebration of *Paris Commune* is clearly visible in *the Civil War in France*.

> When the Paris Commune took the management of the revolution in its own hands; when plain working men for the first time dared to infringe upon the governmental privilege of their 'natural superiors', and, under circumstances of unexampled difficulty, performed it at salaries the highest of which barely amounted to one-fifth what ... is the minimum required for a secretary to a certain metropolitan school-board—the old world writhed in convulsions of rage at the sight of the Red Flag, the symbol of the Republic of Labor, floating over the Hotel de Ville. (Marx, 1993: 260)

In *On the Jewish Question*, Marx makes difference between 'political emancipation' and 'human emancipation'. According to Marx, 'political emancipation itself is not human emancipation' (Marx, 58). Explaining the irony, he states that '[t]he limitations of political emancipation are immediately evident in the fact that a state can liberate itself from a limitation without man himself being truly free of it and the state can be a free state without man himself being a free man' (ibid: 51). In fact,

> [p]olitical emancipation, Marx noted, is itself a great step forward, thus a necessary but not sufficient condition of human emancipation. Human emancipation does not require, as Rousseau thought, the adoption of 'alien powers' transform human nature but only the recognition that man is already a 'species being' so it is a question of organizing his existent social powers. The notion of human emancipation, them, is a particular specification of 'true democracy' as related to individual freedom in the rights citizenship. (Easton, 1999: 336)

In the case of B.R. Ambedkar, 'moment' and 'movement' division becomes clear. Emphasis on Ambedkar will also save us from reducing him to constitutionality and constitutionalism. Several of his schemas can be termed as 'movement' which while highlighting the need of the constitution, emphasise the role of the state in many sectors. The constitution and need of the state *differently* are two distinguish issues in Ambedkar. And both aspects need to be highlighted. In fact, nature of the state is impossible under the liberal constitution. Therefore, it can be construed that availability of the various mechanisms like protection and rights is needed. And a liberal constitution cannot overtly deny these rights for the sake of legitimacy therefore some effect can be envisaged amidst the incessant reminders. In *An Anti-Untouchability Agenda*, he emphasises he emphasises on ensurance and protraction of several measures like 'a campaign to secure civil rights' (water right, education, public convenience, et cetera), 'equality of opportunity' (opportunity in jobs and of market), and 'social intercourse' (live contact), and 'agency to be employed' (to look after implementation aspect) (Ambedkar, 2006: 359–68). *Political Safeguards for Depressed Classes* encompasses 'equal citizenship' (fundamental rights), 'free enjoyment of equal rights' (offence of infringement of citizenship), 'protection against discrimination', 'adequate representation in the legislatures', 'adequate representation in the services', 'redress against prejudicial action or neglect of interests', 'special departmental care', and 'participation of depressed classes in the cabinet' (Ambedkar, 2006: 369–81).One can construe that here also outcome is targeted. However, it would be a partial treatment. There were two targets of Ambedkar that is, accumulation and ascriptive discrimination/brahmanism. Regarding the latter, social intercourse is no way being promoted by the Indian Constitution that is, not *varna*/caste but discrimination is banned. This demand reminds one to move beyond it and also as a mechanism to augur the contradiction. Regarding accumulation, he categorically contrasts liberal constitutionalism from the *desired state*. The demand of the constitution is not finality in his schema but the nature of state. This particular aspect can be deciphered from *States and Minorities: What are Their Rights and How to Secure Them in the Constitution of Free India*. In this, Ambedkar is vociferous for the state ownership of industry, insurance, agriculture (Ambedkar, 1997). The movement in Ambedkar is movement to goad the process of contradiction in the Constitution while focusing on one desired goal.

Here, it is imperative to return to debate over 'populism', which is very important for moment and movement. The acrimonious debate started between Slavoj Žižek and Ernesto Laclau in *Contingency, Hegemony, Universality: Contemporary Dialogues On The Left* had reached its zenith over the French and Dutch refusal to accept a European constitution in 2005. Žižek argues that particularities (identity) can be assimilated well within capitalism while continuing their economic exploitation. He accuses Laclau of perceiving capitalism as the *only* bettering alternative (Butler et al, 2000). In response, Laclau negates the possibility of universalism (Butler et al, 2000). The mutual hostile response between Žižek (2006a, 2006b) and Laclau (2006), over French and Dutch, again highlights the significance of 'populism'. The publication of *On Populist Reason* by Laclau in 2005 was also at an apt time. According to Laclau, populism or a 'chain of equivalences' gets constituted when institutions are unable to absorb the existence of plurality of demands. Here, particularities are displaced by emergence of populist identity in form of imaginary unity of the people (Laclau, 2005, 2006). On this conception of populism, Žižek observes that he 'agree with Laclau's attempt to define populism in a formal-conceptual way, also taking note of how, in his last book, he clearly shifted his position away from radical democracy and towards populism (he now reduces democracy to the moment of democratic demand *within* the system)' (Žižek, 2006b: 197). He has also commented that 'Laclau and Mouffe … propose a new version of the old Edouard Bernstein's arch-revisionist motto "goal is nothing, movement is all" ' (Žižek, 2005).

If populism remains concerned about identification of enemy and formation of identity of people without much advancement beyond liberal institutions, it is bound to pass away eventually. And it becomes ipso facto case of moment. There are three reasons for it. Populism produces three conditions. The first condition is negotiation. It might be true that the state might not be able to absorb the demand of populism but it is also true that there cannot be sustenance of populism without the emphasis on negotiations. Negotiations take place within the ambit of liberal constitution. It creates the second condition that is bargains. Some demands are accepted which are not anti-institutions. The third condition is postponement whereby the demands which cannot be absorbedare simply delayed indefinitely.

As it happens, populism ends with negotiations, bargains and postponement.

Congruously, theorisation by Andre Gunder Frank and Marta Fuentes in form of 'Nine Theses on Social Movements' (Frank and Fuentes, 1987: 1503–10) and 'Ten Theses on Social Movements' (Fuentes and Frank, 1989: 179–92) reduce 'movement' to mere 'moment'. Frank and Fuentes explicate, while endorsing certitude, facets of social movements namely, ' "new" social movements are old but have some new features', 'social movements differ but share moral motivation and social power', 'social movements are cyclical', 'class composition of social movements', 'social movements and state power', 'social movements and social transformation', 'delinking and transition to socialism in social movements', 'the impropriety of 'good' outside advice to social movements' (Frank and Fuentes, 1989: 179–92). In 1989, by 'ten theses on social movements', one more thesis is included 'the new civil democracy' (Fuentes and Frank, 1989: 179–92) in previous 'nine theses on social movements'. According to them, far more than 'classical' class movements, 'the social movements motivate and mobilise hundreds of millions of people in all parts of the world–mostly outside established political and social institutions that people find inadequate to serve their needs-which is why they have recourse to 'new' largely non-institutionalised social movements' (Frank and Fuentes, 1989:1504). Moreover, soon upon realisation of a demand, social movement 'tends to lose force as its *raison d'etre* disappears' (ibid: 1505). The concern of social movement is 'not seek state power, but autonomy, also from the state itself' (ibid: 1506). 'The real transition to a 'socialist' alternative to the present world economy, society and polity, therefore, may be much more in the hands of the social movements' (ibid: 1509). The major criticism of social movement theses by them, as aptly explained by D.N. Dhanagare and J. John, is its division between social power and political power along with delinking both. In Frank and Fuentes' scheme,

> 'social power' is said to be self-generative ... [and] there exists two binary realms of power—social and political power –which are independent and opposed to each other ... Unless the social realm is depoliticized, an autonomous social realm and a corresponding social power cannot be conceived of. Here Frank and Fuentes are obviously committed to a

> process of depoliticization of the social realm. (Dhanagare and John, 1988: 1091)

There are, inter alia, three implications of these theses. Firstly, since 'social movements are "apolitical" Frank and Fuentes also reject the proposition that capture of state power is a necessary and an immutable law in the advanced stage of the struggle for social transformation' (ibid:1092). Secondly, they 'take away political consciousness from the exploited classes and bestow upon them a political force of morality and social power' (ibid). Thirdly, struggles are being reduced to 'moment', whereby transformation can be terminated any time; and if continued, it would be without much 'political'.

Here, the Michael Hardt and Antonio Negri notion of 'multitude' becomes significant. They put forth the category of 'immaterial labour'. According to them, '[i]n the final decades of the twentieth century, industrial labor lost its hegemony and in its stead emerged "immaterial labour," that is, labour that creates immaterial products such as knowledge, information, communication, a relation, or an emotional response' (Hardt and Negri, 2004: 108). Immaterial labour leads to creation of multitude that is, conglomeration of poor, peasants, wage-workers, the unwaged, migrants, and others. The multitude believes in democratic formation and transformative politics. Despite the problematique of 'immaterial labour', Negri and Hardt's multitude remains an important signifier against reconciliation and co-option. They suggest that '[o]ne initial approach is to conceive the multitude as all those who work under the rule of capital and thus potentially as the class of those who refuse the rule of capital' (ibid: 106). Hence, multitude remains the convenor of movements. There is no question of succumbing before capital/state.

On the basis of the aforesaid debate, it becomes imperative to dissect the nature of Indian intellectualism episteme on the Anna Hazare-led mobilisation. At the risk of generalisations, three strands can be fathomed modestly on mobilisation per se. Nonetheless, generalisation will have two caveats. Here, comments on the nature of the bill is excluded. I will focus on only those excurses where moment and movement are being hazed. In other words, those analysts are engaged with who have squarely bypassed the division of moment and movements. The first is 'institutional-constitutional' strand. Pratap

Bhanu Mehta (his was the earliest response) depicted it as a 'disturbing phenomenon' which is dissected against institutions. 'But the claim that the "people" are not represented by elected representatives, but are represented by their self-appointed guardians is disturbing' (Mehta, 2011). 'But the premise of so much accountability discourse is not just contempt of politicians, but contempt of representative democracy' (ibid). For Neera Chandhoke, the corruption issue 'needs to be fought, but according to procedures and norms, and in keeping with the mandate of the Constitution' (Chandhoke, 2011). Furthermore, she makes difference between revolution, social movement and event.

> Revolutions mount a challenge to the fundamentals of the system, and for that reason they constitute ruptural events in the political biography of a society. Social movements may not seek to overthrow the existing system, but they seek to transform it through sustained mobilisation, a clearly articulated ideology, a committed leadership, and the thinking through of alternatives... The four day gathering [April 2011] in support of Anna Hazare was nothing more than a political event.... (Chandhoke, 2011: 17)

Surprisingly and oddly, Arundhati Roy finds commonality between Maoist and the Hazare-led mobilisation in a sense that both want to overthrow the state and government is colluding with latter to overthrow itself (Roy, 2011). Even sympathetic commenters suggest that '[t]hey cannot claim to be representing all people. Representative institutions already exist' (Paul, 2011: 19).

The severe and amplified lacuna in the aforesaid strand is a hazed understanding between moment and movement. How is it anti-constitutional? Where is the demand which alludes to overthrowing the state? The suggestion to take recourse of constitutional measures become invalid since the Anna Hazare-led mobilisation has been ruled out from being a 'revolution' and 'social movement'. If this is moment, which is an obvious conclusion after ruling out other possibilities, then it remains a puzzled surmise concerning the invocation of the constitution. First, it is the constitution which provides the space for mobilisation. Secondly, mobilisations are often being turned into pro-Constitution under the guise of the 'ownership illusion' after the usage of 'anti-constitutional' remarks. The moments are not anti-constitutional movement but signs of a return of constitutionalism.

It is also surprising that the institutional-constitutional strand could not find fault in institutions while reposing faith unquestionably in them but finds problem in 'moment' which is nothing but necessarily an outcome of liberal constitutionalism. Two confusions are apparent here. Firstly, moment is perceived as movement. Secondly, if moment is not considered as movement then also it is termed as anti-state/ institution which is an oxymoronic theorem.

This second strand perceives it as movement so there is the arrival of possible rupture. The role of left is also envisaged. Nivedita Menon and Aditya Nigam are right when they reject epithets about the nature of movement like 'middle-class', 'upper-caste Hindutva', 'anti-politics' and 'fascists' (Menon and Nigam, 2011: 16-8). It is perfectly discernible that aforesaid criticism 'arises from a deep constitutive unease about mass politics per se' (ibid: 16). Criticism from democracy per se is also not tenable because 'democracy disciplined through representative institutions with "The People" entering the stage every five years' (ibid). The depiction of 'blackmail' is also not tenable since 'there is a tradition on the left of small lobbies and group trying to influence, or being actually involved in the drafting of law—on sexual violence and rape, against communal violence' (ibid: 17). They pose two questions. 'Does the movement express a goal that we agree with? We think it does, that is, the larger goal of making governments accountable to the people. And two: is there any expression by the movement of all those things that we oppose? No, there is not' (ibid: 18). Moreover, 'the stance taken by the left can be decisive here' (ibid).

There is no dispute that mobilisation by Anna Hazare's team expresses the angst against the promise and gap. The people's participation cannot simply be dismissed as fascist conglomeration. There are some more essential issues besides nature of participation. A mobilisation which seeks to make government more accountable and transparent by way of legalism is not movement wherein a possibility of rupture can be commenced. The problem is that the entire edifice which does not attempt to eradicate accumulation and nationalism, which are assertions of superiority of ascriptivity, cannot solve the riddle of corruption. Unfortunately, here also, moment is being perceived as movement which is not the case. Despite this overlapping, the role of the Left and its intervention carry important explication. There is always a possibility to transform moment to movement. However, it becomes difficult to transform moment which seeks legal remedies. A moment which starts with general distrust does have the possibility to be transformed into movement but the same cannot be stated regarding those moments which are issue-specific and seek solution by correction in deviational tendencies. There are two options left for the Left. First, there has to be massive participation in the moment which originates out of distrust. Secondly, movement is the best and only option for the Left to address immediacy and permanency. Unfortunately, absences of demarcation will only strengthen the return of constitutionalism via moments which are only issues-oriented.

The third strand suggests why inspite of corruption being thecore issue this mobilisation has been successful. '[T]he fact that the movement got even this far needs explaining' (Sitapati, 2011: 39). Middle class, according Vinay Sitapati, is the fulcrum of 'Anna Hazare's movement' precisely because 'Hazare was able to fire the idealism of the twenty-first century India's burgeoning middle class' (ibid). The uniqueness of this *movement* 'was that diverse middle-class activisms were able to craft a campaign that appealed to all their interests' (ibid: 40). There are four strands of the middle class, that is, Legal Activism, India Shinning (corporate middle class), Gandhigiri (Neo-Gandhians) and Independent Left. All strands except the Independent Left had supported the movement. The commonality amongst the other three is their opposition to politics and institutions. Legal Activists 'share contempt for elected institutions with India Shining...' (ibid: 41) who 'virulently dislikes the political class' (ibid: 42) while 'Gandhian techniques (though not ideology) are used to represent urban interests' (ibid: 43). Therefore, '[n]one of them have any problem with the unrepresentative nature of the movement or the draconian powers given to the Lokpal. No matter how earnest, India's middle class, has yet to view the political class as legitimate, the party system as the main way to achieve programmatic changes' (ibid: 44).

At the outset, it is difficult to disagree with the aforesaid postulations concerning expansion of the mobilisation. However the origin of mobilisation and its expansion cannot be delinked. If the origin of any mobilisation takes place against the deviational practices of the constitution, it thus becomes an exercise of the restoration or return of constitutionalism. If mobilisation is for the return of constitutionalism, then expansion must be for the strengthening of the constitution. Any mobilisation for the restoration of institutions or envisaging of new institutions under liberal constitutionalism cannot be termed movement but moment. More importantly, the middle class, or for all that matters upper class/brahmanism, is not uneasy with the representative nature of democracy but at those attempts which would possibly make liberal democracy more representative. And this is a mirage. Even a mirage is an attempt to destabilise by class and caste forces. Therefore, they are not against politics but politics of mirage which is equally worthless for the deprived sections. However, this is not being tolerated by the class-caste surplus usurper. The imminent sections attempt to fill the gap in explanations.

Moment, Movement and Constitutionality

Kisan Baburao Hazare's (popularly known as Anna Hazare and recipient of the *Padma Bhushan* in 1992), two hunger strikes (April and July–August, 2011) in the capital city of India, New Delhi and the Indian state's response have brought back the role of agitation/mobilisation and the nature of state act. Several questions are being incessantly asked. Does the state respond equally to all mobilisations? If variance exits, what could be the possible factor(s)? Do place and message producers and sender agencies like the print media and electronic media play an edgy role? These are needful questions but not fundamental questions. A repetition of such questions make them only dimensions which need to be fathomed. These are symptomatic questions not foundational one.

Constitutionality has been an effective weapon of the ruling echelons. Constitutionality lures have-nots and ascriptively subjugates social groups, and rightly so, due to promises of a better future. It is notable that with the envisioning and application of the Indian Constitution after India's Independence, recognition and rights were made available for the first time. People per se were recognised. A liberal constitution seeks legitimacy on the basis of certain modalities. It promises; it seems to act. Promise is a catch word and act is a future promise. The Preamble, Fundamental Rights and Directive State Policy of the Indian Constitution function differently with different purposes. The preamble is a microcosm of moral philosophy. Fundamental Rights (FRs) condition people with concrete minimum rights. *Directive Principles of State Policy* (DPSP) is a document of enactment of a 'liberated future' especially articles like 38, 39, 41, 43, 43A, 46 and 47. The preamble, before *Kesavananda Bharati v. State of Kerala* (1973), was not considered as a part of the constitution. The judgement delivered in this case made the Preamble an integral part of the constitution in terms of interpretation of several articles. In the Preamble, 'constitute' and 'secure' are important epithets. People resolve to constitute 'sovereign', 'socialist', 'secular' and 'democratic republic'. 'Secure' denotes an attempt towards 'justice' (social, economic and political), 'liberty' (of thought, expression, belief, faith and worship), 'equality' (of status and of opportunity) and promotion of 'fraternity'. The problem in moral philosophy is that moral actions are insulated from the socio-economic world. Here also, it has not been stated how people will resolve and secure such ideals. Fundamental rights are immediacy rights. Even they have been curtailed by way of non-implementations. DPSP promises the enactment of a better future. The problem here is that neither is the method revealed as to how these are achievable nor is the time framework specified in the constitution.

Put differently, close observation of the Preamble, Fundamental Rights and DPSP reveals the typical case of authorship and ownership. Moral philosophy generates hope without the method to galvanise the hope. Similarly, in the Preamble, 'constitute' and 'secure' generate hope without revealing a way of achieving it. It informs us about 'bettered' future without informing whether class-caste-gender influences are severed or not. The FRs are very important because here people become citizens and remain constitutionally empowered. The problem is that one has to remain a constitutional subject. However, this constitutional subject is not without rights. The constitutional subject enjoys rights constitutionally. DPSP seemingly suggests a liberated future. In fact, DPSP is the promised land. The real problem occurs due to the well established gap between implementation and promises. Authors (implementers) inform people that suzerainty of the constitution is in their interest because they are also owners of it. The widening gap between the real and the promise has to culminate into a mobilisation. This is an inherent and recurrent outcome of the Indian Constitution, like any other liberal constitution, where 'concrete' and 'abstract' remains at loggerheads. The ability of ruling echelons is to delay postponement and negotiate with mobilisations with the invocation of constitutional serenity. What is important is to keep mobilisation as moment and cull every attempt from making it movement. And moment responds back necessarily in the form of constitutionality due to the illusion of ownership.

The creation of a political subject remains a distant dream under the illusion of ownership. Yet, it generates a different phenomenon. The verbatim words, clause, articles and interpretation of the Constitution acquire supreme status. Immediacy (FRs) and permanency (the Preamble and DPSP) are being taken seriously. However, the state keeps postponing realisation of permanency (due to insufficient resources) with the phrase, the 'right time has yet to come'. The area of immediacy becomes a contested zone. However, it is difficult to postpone *Right to Equality* (Article 14, 15, 16, 17 and 18), *Right to Freedom* (Article 19, 20, 21, 21A, and 22), *Right against Exploitation* (Article 23 and 24), *Right to Freedom of Religion* (Article 25, 26, 27 and 28), *Cultural and Educational Rights* (Article 29 and 30) and *Right to Constitutional Remedies* (Article 32) without biases and so on. Authors do not even take 'immediacy' seriously because the method of removal of 'class' biases and 'ascriptive subjugation' are not envisaged except by stating, insertion and enactment of articles/ acts. In other words, sources of both the form of exploitation and subjugation remain intact and functional in the form of scaled accumulation, primitive accumulation of capital, landlordism and assertion of brahmanism by way of nationalism. The irony is that sources are not an issue but outcomes are talked about zealously. Therefore, mobilisation takes place to solve the riddle of immediacy. As soon as mobilisation takes place, the state, knowing very well its *inability* to address the grievances, terms the mobilisation as against-constitution. Its suggestive meaning is that people have turned against themselves, that is, the constitution, since they own it. The people, thereafter, respond constitutionally. The possibility of a construction of the 'political subject' and movement gets over here.

The ownership principle assumes that equality, freedom, right against exploitation, freedom of religion, cultural and educational rights and constitutional remedies are within the reach of people. Since the ownership principle is designed as such to ignore the source of problems, it tends to focus on outcomes. In the absence of focus on sources, the concrete minimum rights in form of FRs are not being taken seriously by ruling echelons. And it is bound to produce malfunctional implementation. Ignorance of the concrete minimum rights provokes 'citizen' to take the resource of mobilisation. The illusion of ownership paves the way for finding problems in 'deviational' practices not in the philosophical doctrine of institutions. Mobilisations for such kinds are moments whereby constitutionality becomes stronger with an initiation of some immediate measures. Hereafter, the deviational behaviour of the institutional gets primacy over sources of institutions.

One of the deviations of the institution is not implementing concrete minimum rights ipso facto. Sometimes one is being implemented while the other is not. Due to lack of obvious and calculated silence, realisation of equality, freedom and others go by mediating sources. Mediating sources are being termed as corrupted people who wield their authority to corrupt the people and practices while being corrupted. Their act to implement some of FRs in lieu of monetary resources is corruption. Mobilisation of the constitutional method is directed towards such people. That is why direct taxes and indirect taxes could not generate much debate. Governments under a liberal constitution and particularly in India evade the direct taxes against bourgeoisies but indirect taxes are being imposed through increasing sales taxes and cess on people. Even subsidies are being reduced and challenged. However, decreased direct taxes and sops to the bourgeoisie remain intact. The politics of direct tax and indirect tax is being done by legalism. Ownership illusion against decreased direct taxes stops people from revolt. However, corruption without legality agitates because it has no place in the constitution. And it cannot have a place tactically due to the legitimacy crises. So ownership and corruption cannot be reconciled in the absence of the constitutional mandate; therefore mobilisation often takes place in this regard.

In India, there are a plethora of signs of contestations and initiations on the issue of one of the deviations that is, corruption. In 1950, Life Insurance Corporation Scam took place. The alleged individuals were Haridas Mundhra (industrialist) and T. Krishnamachari (Finance Minister, Government of India) who caused Rs. 1.24 crore loss to the exchequer. The M.C. Chagla Committee was constituted. Krishnamachari resigned and Mundhra was imprisoned for 22 years. In the Bofors scam (1986), Martin Ardbo (former Bofors chief), Ottavio Quattrocchi (middle man), Rajiv Gandhi, S.K. Bhatnagar (former defence secretary), Hindujas and Win Chadha (arms agents) were alleged scam stars. The estimated loss was Rs. 64 crores. Win Chadha died in 2001. Rajiv Gandhi was cleared in 2004 posthumously. The case against the Hindujas was dismissed in 2005. 1992–6 witnessed the CRB Scams which cost an estimated Rs. 1200 crores. In this case, numerous charges like fraud, cheating and siphoning off of funds from SBI were slapped against C.R. Bhansali. In the infamous Harshad Mehta-led securities scam (1994), loss was estimated around Rs. 4000 crore. Continuation of fake stamp scam (1994–2000) led to a loss of an estimated Rs. 4300 crores. Abdul Karim Telgi was imprisoned for thirteen years. Inconclusive evidence in The Hawala Scandal (1996) paved the way for the dismissal of case. The fodder scam of 1996 accrued an estimated Rs. 900 crores and the case is still on. In this period, corporate scams (Home Trade of Sanjay Agarwal, estimated loss Rs. 600 crore; DSQO Software of Dinesh Dalmia, estimate loss Rs. 600 crores; estimated loss of Rs. 1500 crores in Ketan Parekh-led securities scam) scaled new heights due to proliferation and accumulation of capital in the post-liberalisation phase. The brazen and 'visible' loot in 2G Spectrum, Telecom Licenses Scam (2010; estimated amount Rs. 1.76 lakh crores) and Commonwealth Games (2010, estimated loss Rs. 8000 crores) have been 'stark' deviations.

In our everyday life, equality, freedom and right [EFR] make sense in three realms under the liberal constitution. The first realm can be identified as the 'survivalist realm'. The people associated with this realm are proletariats and ascriptively discriminated groups. They need the constitution more than others to realise EFR because even the illusion of ownership of the constitution was not offered to them previously. The second realm is the 'survived realm'. In this realm, people are from salaried groups/petite producer owners and for them EFR is needed for vertical elation. The third realm is of 'opulent survivors'. Here, survival is not an issue. They also need the constitution and particularly EFR for aggrandisement by way of scaled accumulation and in association with nationalism which is enmeshed in ascriptive assertion and domination since the 'sources' of both are not being questioned. Therefore, the survivalist realm and even the survived realm do *complain* about 'corruption' whereas opulent survivors ask for *reform*.

The interesting data can be obtained from *India Corruption Study* (2002–9). The study reveals affecting populace in respect of 'households reported paying bribe to avail any public service'. Karnataka occupies the first place where 40.1% households paid bribe to avail any services followed by Maharashtra (38.0%), Delhi (35.5%), Madhya Pradesh (29.7%), Orissa (29.0%), Tamil Nadu (28.6%), Uttarakhand (27.9%), Andhra Pradesh (23.7%), Chhattisgarh (23.4%), Gujarat (22.4%), Kerala (21.8%), Haryana (21.0%), Bihar (13.6%), Punjab (13.6%), Jharkhand (12.9%), West Bengal (12.1%), Uttar Pradesh (11.7%), Assam (10.7%) and Rajasthan (9.2%). There were several aspects for paying bribe to following PDS services. To take monthly ration, 22% people paid the bribe which was followed by other issues like 'permission for release of extra quantity during festivals' (7%), 'application for license to sell kerosene oil' (1%), 'deletion & addition of family members in ration card' (12%), 'change of ration shop' (1%) and 'preparation of new ration card' (58%) (Rao and Srivastava, 2010: 50–6).

The aforesaid data generates other complex questions. Why do people not revolt? Is moralism of constitutionality sufficient to subside the everyday hardship which is a recurrent phenomenon in the absence of concrete minimum rights? The answer has been given in the previous pages but here some more explanations are needed. 'Constitutional' mobilisation for non-implementation of FRs necessarily turns to find solace the ownership illusion. The state/institutions/bourgeoisie/ dominant caste-led parties necessarily remain active to keep mobilisation as moment not movement. The abovementioned survey also unearths how state actors and status quoist parties deal with citizens who are also 'voters'. Voting is decision, saying, assertion and confrontation. However, the constitutionality makes it as a mere constitutional exercise. Repetition of the constitutional exercise without substance is bound to become a moribund exercise. As soon as it becomes a moribund exercise, its philosophical value like 'decision, saying, assertion and confrontation' gets detached. Herein, ruling echelons attempt to corrupt people during 'voting' times.

The offering and accepting practices evince an attempt to 'corrupt' citizens who turn occasional voters. In Karnataka, the percentage of 'voters who took money to vote in favour of a candidate' is 48%. In other states such practices are 35% (Tamil Nadu), 34% (Madhya Pradesh), 33% (Andhra Pradesh), 32% (Bihar), 28% (Orissa), 26%(Delhi), 25% (Gujarat), 22% (Chhattisgarh), 20% (Uttarakhand), 18% (Uttar Pradesh), 15% (Rajasthan), 14% (Kerala), 14%(Maharashtra), 12% (Punjab), 8% (Haryana), 8% (Jharkhand), 8% (Assam) and 4% (West Bengal) [these are approximate values extrapolated from the table] (ibid:15). It also suggests that there was an attempt to corrupt maximum voters but the success rate remained to the respective figures.

Despite these overt attempts by ruling echelons, there have been response and concerted mobilisation at least for constitutional implementation. Lokpal has been one such attempt. It was introduced for the first time in the Lok Sabha in 1968 and was passed in 1969 but could not get through Rajya Sabha. Successive years like 1971, 1977, 1977, 1985, 1989, 1996, 1998, 2001, 2005, 2008 and 2011 also witnessed the introduction of Bill but to no avail on this issue. 'Jayaprakash Narayan in his movement had three planks. One of these was Lokpal Bill and others were electoral reform and an effective anti-defection law' (Noorani, 2011). These and more endeavours had to have some impact.

Institutional churning commenced with Independence. The state led response has been the formation of committees and institutions. 'Report on Reorganisation of the Machinery of Government' (1949, Goplaswami Ayyangar as Chair), 'Survey of Indian Administration' (1952, Chair: Paul H. Appleby), 'Re-examination of India's

Administrative System' (1956, Chair: Paul H. Appleby), 'The Committee on Prevention of Corruption' (1962, Chair: K. Santhanam), 'The First Administrative Reforms Commission (ARC)' (1966, Chair: Morarji Desai (1966–7) and K. Hanumanthaiya (1967-70)), 'Vohara Committee Report' (1993, Chair: N.N. Vohara), 'The Second Administrative Reforms Commission' (2005, Chair: Veerappa Moily) have been some of the significant committees. K. Santhanam and N.N. Vohara Committees are noticeable. Important suggestions of the Santhanam Committee were 'announcement of received funds and donations of political parties', 'declaration of private property' (Ministers, legislators and civil servants), and 'foundation of an ombudsman institution' and 'vigilance department in all organization' (Report of the Committee on Prevention of Corruption, 1964). The Vohara Committee enquired about nexus between crime syndicate and bureaucracy and politicians with indicting remarks (Vohara Committee Report, 1993).

Regarding institutions, the Comptroller and Auditor-General of India (CAG) is the oldest significant one. It derives its strength from Article 148 (1) and 149 of the Indian Constitution. According to Article 148 (1) '[t]here shall be a Comptroller and Auditor-General of India who shall be appointed by the President by warrant under his hand and seal and shall only be removed from office in like manner and on like grounds as a Judge of the Supreme Court.' Article 149 lays down the duties and powers of the CAG. The Central Bureau of Investigation (CBI) was established in 1963. It derives its legal power from the 'Delhi Special Police Establishment [DSPE] Act, 1946 to investigate crimes through 'Anti-Corruption Division', 'Economic Offences Division' and 'Special Crimes Division'. K. Santhanam headed the 'Committee on Prevention of Corruption' recommendation laid the foundation of the Central Vigilance Commission (CVC) in 1964 'to monitor all vigilance activity under the Central Government' and 'to advise authorities in Central Government Organizations in planning, executing, reviewing and reforming vigilance work'. The Administrative Reform Commission (ARC, 1966) was another landmark development for generating debate over Lokpal. The Lokpal and Lokayukta concretely get originated here. The last important institution in this regard can be termed as the Central Information Commission (CIC) which was founded on 12 October 2005 to provides right to information related to 'a) inspect works, documents, records; b) take notes, extracts or certified copies of documents or records; c) take certified samples of material; d) obtain information in form of printouts, diskettes, floppies, tapes, video cassettes or in any other electronic mode or through printouts'.

Formation of several committees, institutions and non- availability of FRs had to boiled down to mobilisation. The unprecedented coverage by print media and electronic media and significant mass mobilisation by Anna Hazare and his team provides an ample opportunity to analyse refreshingly moment, movement and constitutionality. Broadly, there are three methods employed by Anna Hazare and his team on corruption issue vis-à-vis government: hunger strike, mobilisation of public opinion and negotiation with the government. Longevity of hunger strike is known due to two reasons; firstly, issue is defined; secondly, a deadline is set for action. Put differently, issue and action are revealed. Corruption is an issue and passing the JanLokpal Bill is action. In the case of non-recognition of corruption and inaction regarding Jan Lokpal Bill, hunger strike is an eventual weapon. What is the nature of this demand? Here, recognition of corruption is a deviation from constitutional practices. The solution is passing a bill for making an act which will ensure the arrival of an institution. It is nothing but return of constitutionalism. Hunger strike for return of liberal constitutionalism presupposes its ephemeral longevity. It is because 'demands are likely to be accepted sooner or later'. Demands do not pose challenge and the 'source' of the problem is not an issue. Mobilisation of public opinion includes people's participation and usage of disseminative services like print media/ electronic media, social internet sites, blogs and 'individuated' bulk emails. Going to people is penchant and repeated acclimatisation. Surveying on Jan Lokpal in 'important leader's' constituencies and even campaigning against ruling party in election, as happened in Hisar by-election (2011) where ruling party at the centre finished third and lost deposit, are intrinsic part of mobilisation per se. The negotiation with the government to accept the desired end is the final recourse. Formation of committee and negation and negotiation in and outside are recurrent exercise.

The entire expedition of the Team Anna-led mobilisation which thrust upon 'hunger strike', 'public opinion by way of mobilisation' and 'negotiation' is a fit case of moment. Hunger strike and negotiations with the government have been built upon mobilisation. The target is set before people that are strike or negotiations or both. The ambition is well within the Constitution. Initial remarks by the incumbent government were depicting the mobilisation as anti-Constitution. The constitutionality was reposed by 'moment' by invocation of three slogans. These three slogans were/have been '*Bharat Mata Kee Jai*', '*Vande Mataram*' and '*Inquilab Zindabad.* The first slogan has been constructed, practiced and imposed on people by the right wingers. This ahistorical phrase has trans-imposed and metamorphosed in form of nationalism and regulation of everyday life of modern India. The second slogan invites lots of hermeneutic contestation even in progressive circles (see on communalism Noorani: 1999: 94–7; Pandey: 1999; on *why* secularist opposition see Chatterjee: 1997) In addition to these, the song has a biography of 'the communal war cry', 'national anthem', 'slogan' and 'the poem'. Each aspect is important to understand the sense of song. On this aspect and previous issue see the comprehensive debate in Bhattacharya, 2003. Sabyasachi Bhattacharya also explicates that

> [t]he nationalism that was imported from the West suffered from an adequacy. In the European mind there was a resonance created by a range of symbols which evolved historically in that civilization, symbols which were deployed latter in the nation-building process in Europe. In the Indian mind those symbols did not produce any resonance. India had to create them, or bring them back to remembrance and use them for a new purpose. It will be a mistake to believe that this was a strategy adopted with deliberation by Bankim and his peers in that enterprise. It was perhaps an intuitive leap towards an imagined future through remembrance of the past. (Bhattacharya, 2003: 94)

In contemporaneous context, appropriation of song and alienation of minorities cannot be washed off. The claimants seem to be only Right-wingers. The unwillingness of minorities, particularly Muslims is a fact. The imposition endeavour by Right-wingers is also a fact. Hereafter, the standpoint should become clear regarding what to do and what not to do. The standpoint from the Right-wingers is clear: 'The *Organiser,* an organ of the Rashtriya Swayamsevak Sangh (RSS), defined "Nationalist Muslims" as "those who refuse to adopt a separatist political policy raising issue of personal law, Vande Matram, *haj* and *madrasa...*"' (cited in Bhattacharya, 2003: 3). The third slogan is *inquilab zindabad* which can be translated as 'long live the revolution'. Repetition of such slogans without being linked to larger revolutionary practices turn into empty slogans which are not even capable of delivering original idea let alone abandoning original action.

It is time to return to our foundational question of 'why does moment function the way it is'. Put it directly, can we blame the Team Anna-led mobilisation for all its misgivings, erroneous methods and deliberate sloganeering? Should we not ask more questions rather than implicating moment for all sins? Moment, movement and constitutionality need to be discerned conjugately. The mechanism of constitutionality is such that only moment can be produced by constitutionally organised mobilisation. Time and again, the illusion of ownership is being invoked and the sardonic remark of 'anti-constitution'. These two weapons with the practice of 'corrupting' people are enough ground to inhibit the transcendence of moment to movement. The fate of constitutional mobilisation at the cost of beyond constitution mobilisation under liberal democracy is moment. Therefore, blaming moment for everything is not justifiable but celebrating it is also an erroneous move which is discussed in the following sections.

Epilogue

Mobilisation has two outcomes. It generates moments. It also generates movements. Moments end up with the germination of 'success' and success is defined under the ambit of liberal constitution. Here, the narrative of 'constitutional success' is generated, celebrated and expanded. On the other hand, movements go for transfiguration. It goes beyond liberal constitution. Here is the germination of transfigurative narratives. The emphasis *solely* on moment and considering it as success is goading the process of return of constitutionalism. Critics of moment when they do elide the nature of instutions/state also goad the process of liberal constitutionalism which remains silent over scaled accumulation and ascriptive superiority.

REFERENCES

Ambedkar, B.R. (1997). 'States and Minorities: What are Their Rights and How to Secure Them in the Constitution of Free India', in D.C. Ahir *Dr. Ambedkar and Indian Constitution*. Low Price Publications, Delhi.

Ambedkar, B.R. (2006). 'An Anti-untouchability Agenda', in Valerian Rodrigues (ed) *The Essential Writings of B.R. Ambedkar*. New Delhi : Oxford University Press.

Ambedkar, B.R. (2006). 'Political Safeguards for Depressed Classes', in Valerian Rodrigues(ed) *The Essential Writings of B.R. Ambedkar*. New Delhi: Oxford University Press.

Ananth, V. Krishna (2011). 'Lokpal Bill Campaign: Democratic and constitutional', *Economic and Political Weekly*, Vol. XLVI, No. 16, April 16.

Bhagwati, Jagdish N. and Calomiris, Charles W. (2008) *Sustaining India's Growth Miracle*. New York: Columbia University Press.

Bhattacharya, Sabyasachi (2003). *Vande Matram: The Biography of a Song*. New Delhi: Penguin Books.

Butler, J., Ernesto, L. and Žižek, S. (2000). *Contingency, Hegemony, Universality Contemporary Dialogues on the Left*. London: Verso.

Chandhoke, Neera (2011). 'Our Latest Democratic Predicament', *Economic and Political Weekly*, Vol. XLVI, No. 19, 19 May.

Chandhoke, Neera (2011). 'The Seeds of Authoritarianism', *Indian Express*, 4 April. Retrieved from http://www.indianexpress.com/news/the-seeds-of-authoritarianism/774794/

Chandra, Bipan et al (2008). *India Since Independence*. New Delhi: Penguin.

Chatterjee, Partha (1997). 'Introduction: A Political History of Independent India', in Partha Chatterjee (ed) *State and Politics in India*. New Delhi: Oxford University Press.

Chatterjee, Partha (1997). *The Present History of West Bengal*. New Delhi: Oxford University Press.

Chatterjee, Partha (2004). *The Politics of the Governed: Reflections on Popular Politics in Most of the World*. New York: Columbia University Press.

Das, Gurcharan (2000). *India Unbound*. New Delhi: Penguin.

Dhanagare, D. and John, J. (1988). 'Cyclical Movement Towards the 'Eternal' 'Nine Theses of Social Movements: A Critique', *Economic and Political Weekly*, Vol. 23, No. 21, 21 May.

Easton, L.D. (1999). 'Marx and Individual Freedom', Bob Jessop and Russel Wheatley (eds) *Karl Marx's Social and Political Thought: Critical Assessments of Leading Political Philosophers*. London: Routledge.

Frank, Andre Gunder and Fuentes, Marta (1987). 'Nine Theses on Social Movements', *Economic and Political Weekly*, Vol. 22, No. 35, 29 August.

Guha, Ramchandra (2007). *India After Gandhi: The History of the World's Largest Democracy*. New Delhi: Pan Macmillan, Picador India.

Guha, Ramchandra (2011). *Makers of Modern India*. New Delhi. Penguin/ Viking.

Hardt, Michael and Negri, Antonio (2004). *Multitude : War and Democracy in the Age of Empire*. New York: The Penguin Press.

Khilnani, Sunil (2004). *Idea of India*. New Delhi: Penguin.

Kohli, Atul (ed) (1988). *India's Democracy: An Analysis of Changing State-Society Relations*. Princeton: Princeton University Press.

Kohli, Atul (ed) (2001).*The Success of India's Democracy*. Cambridge: Cambridge University Press.

Laclau, Ernesto (2006). 'Populism: What's in a Name?', in Francisco Panizzav (ed) *Populism and the Mirror of Democracy*. London: Verso.

Laclau, Ernesto (2006). 'Why Constructing a People Is the Main Task of Radical Politics', 32 (Summer).

Marx, Karl (2000). 'On the Jewish Question', in David McLellan (ed) *Karl Marx: Selected Writings*. New York: Oxford.

Marx, Karl and Engels, Friedrich (1970). *German Ideology*. New York: International Publishers Co.

Marx, Karl and Engels, Friedrich (1993). *The Civil War in France: The Paris Commune*. New York: International Publishers Co.

Marx, Karl and Engels, Frederick (1999). 'Manifesto of the Communist Party', in Prakash Karat (ed) *A World to Win: Essays on the Communist Manifesto*. New Delhi: Leftworld.

Mehta, Bhanu Pratap (2003). *The Burden of Democracy*. New Delhi: Penguin.

Mehta, Pratap Bhanu (2011). 'Of the Few, By the Few', *Indian Express*, 7 April. Retrieved from http://www.indianexpress.com/news/of-the-few-by-the-few/772773/0

Noorani, A.G. (1999). 'How Secular is Vande Matram', *Frontline*, 15 January.

Noorani, A.G. (2011). 'History of Deception', *Frontline*, Volume 28, Issue 10, 07-20 May. Retrieved from http://www.frontlineonnet.com/fl2810/stories/20110520281003600.htm

Pandey, Gyan (1999). 'Can a Muslim Be an India ?', *Comparative Studies in Society and History*. London: Cambridge University Press.

Rao, N. Bhaskara and Srivastava, Alok (2010). *India Corruption Study: 2002– 09: A Comparative Scenario*: New Delhi : CMS Research House.

Report of the Committee on Prevention of Corruption (1964). New Delhi: Ministry of Home Affairs, Government of India.

Roy, Arundhati (2011). 'I'd Rather Not Be Anna', *The Hindu*, 22 August. Retrieved from http://www.thehindu.com/todays-paper/tp-opinion/article2380789.ece

Singh, Nand Kishore (2007). *The Politics of Change: A Ringside View.* New Delhi: Penguin.

Sitapati, Vinay (2011). 'What Anna Hazare's Movement and India's New Middle Classes Say about Each Other', *Economic and Political Weekly*, Vol. XLVI, No. 30

Vohara Committee Report (1993). New Delhi: Ministry of Home Affairs, Government of India.

Walzer, Michael (1973). 'Political Action: the Problem of Dirty Hands', *Philosophy and Public Affairs*, Vol. 2, Issue 2 (winter).

Žižek, Slavoj (2005). 'Object a as Inherent Limit to Capitalism: on Michael Hardt and Antonio Negri'. Retrieved from http://www.lacan.com/zizmultitude.htm#5x

Žižek, Slavoj (2006a). 'Against the Populist Temptation', *Critical Inquiry*, 32 (Spring).

Žižek, Slavoj (2006b). 'Schlagend, aber nicht Treffend!', *Critical Inquiry*, 33 (Autumn).

Part II

13

The Support of the People for Any Cause in a Democracy is Based on Popular Mobilisation through Political Education

Interview with Prof. K.N. Panikkar

Editors: ***Professor K.N. Panikkar*** *is one of the foremost historians of Modern India. His intervention in the sphere of the culture, communalism and secularism debate has shaped the contour of many disciplines. His work on the Malabar agrarian revolt has repudiated the communal interpretation of peasant mobilisations. Besides his academic contribution, Prof. Panikkar has shaped many generations of activists who have been fighting for an egalitarian world. Marxism has been greatly benefitted by him due to the localisation of it while becoming more relevant in the Indian context for an exploitation-free India. His interview with* ***Manu M.R.*** *evinces the political, the constitutional, democracy, Right wings, popular will and a historian's perspective on the Anna Hazare mobilisation.*

Manu M.R. [MMR]: *What is the politics of Anna Hazare's Movement?*

K.N. Panikkar [KNP]: Anna Hazare has described himself as apolitical. This description appears to be true only in the sense that he is not a member of any political formation. Whatever he has been trying to do during the last few years has undoubtedly been political.

He represents and practises politics of reform which aims to contain internal contradictions in society through compromises. That is the reason why the state accords him so much importance. Never in the past has the Indian state given the demands of an individual such consideration. That could only happen because Hazare's agitation suits the state. The success of whatever he has done in the village, Ralegan Siddhi, in Maharashtra is because of the social accommodation he has attempted. The agitation against corruption conducted in his name is an extension of those reformist politics. The state is not against his politics which do not question its power and hence the ruling classes are prepared to accomodate him. His main target is the bureaucracy, which is only the instrument of corruption. The really corrupt are the corporate barons who controls the wealth of the nation. They, in fact, are running the agitation. The politics of Anna Hazare or rather of those who run the movement in his name is politics aimed at preserving the interest of the rich and the affluent. In the globalised world, where the sky is the limit for the business class, they would like the bureaucracy and the politician to be tamed. That Anna has not taken up the cause of the eighty percent of the population who live on less than Rs.20 a day is not accidental. The claim that the movement is for the benefit of the poor is a joke.

MMR: *Do you think the movement is against the Constitution?*

KNP: The methods adopted by the movement are anti-democratic and anti-Constitution. The legislative function of the republic is vested in Parliament. There are well thought out and prescribed procedures for drafting and passing bills and incorporating them as Acts. Those procedures cannot be arrogated by a group of people to themselves, however eminent they are. In this case, Anna tried to bypass the authority of the parliament by taking on the responsibility of drafting the bill and giving an ultimatum to the parliament to sign on the dotted line. That people are supreme is indeed a good slogan, but in a democracy, people exercise their power through elected representatives. At any rate, how do he and his co-Magsashay award winners represent people? Incidentally, the Magsashay award is an American institution meant to nurture next-generation leaders in Asian countries. The corruption is not prevented, not because of the lack of rules and regulations or government agencies to deal with it, but because of the lack of political will to punish the guilty.

MMR: *Has Indian democracy been strengthened or compromised?*

KNP: Anna has tried to turn democracy into a mobocracy. The support of the people for any cause in a democracy is based on popular mobilisation through political education. It is not by resorting to emotional blackmail. Anna has undergone fast-unto-death twice. Now he has now announced the third! In a democracy, there is no place for coercion, which Anna and his team are resorting to. In all this, Gandhi's name is invoked. Gandhiji never undertook *satyagraha* as a political threat. Democracy would have been strengthened if Anna had led a national campaign against corruption. Without popular consciousness, corruption cannot be eliminated. It is most unlikely, therefore, that the Lokpal bill, however strong, would end corruption. It would only burden the system with another set of rules

MMR: *Can we consider the politics behind AHM as Right-wing? What will be the implication of such movement being supported by the rightwing forces?*

KNP: Two factors need to be considered. Firstly, the ideas of Anna himself. Secondly, who is running the show for him. Judging from what he has been doing at Ralegan Siddhi, his social and political ideas are very conservative and even reactionary. His method borders on the authoritarian. Such a demeanor is visible in the way he has conducted the anti-corruption movement also. Therefore, inherently the movement has the potential to assume Right-wing character.

Furthermore, he had sought the support of Right-wing religious forces. In the beginning of the movement Sri Sri Ravi Shankar and Ramdev were the main pillars of its popular appeal. It appears that the support was solicited by Anna. The RSS, VHP and a whole lot of communal forces joined the agitation. It was perhaps not accidental. The intention was to unsettle the democratic institutions and capture power. The political stance was a useful ploy. The movement is a potent mixture of religious Right-wing and the affluent middle class supported by the capitalist class.

MMR: *Is this movement representative of the popular will across India. Is it urban or rural?*

KNP: The movement does not have the sanction of popular will.

It is mainly an urban phenomenon, arising out of the emotional appeal of the middle class. The issues raised by the movement are not relevant for the rural poor, who are struggling for their livelihood.

MMR: *From a historian's point of view, does this movement represent any paradigm shift in the life of Indian polity? How, according to you, will history rate this movement?*

KNP: Not the least. It does not affect the corelation of forces in Indian polity. The movement does not raise fundamental problems of Indian polity, namely the marginalisation of the dalits, minorities and women. It does not address the issue of poverty and the concentration of wealth in the hands of a few. It does not question why bureaucracy is predominantly recruited from certain sections of society. Lokpal is not going to solve these problems. Therefore, social and political power would continue to be vested with the upper castes and classes. History will rate the movement as another attempt by the capitalist order to maintain social equilibrium.

14

Today You Have to Establish Your Democratic Credentials, Otherwise You are Making a Gift of the People to Dictatorship and Capitalism

Interview with Prof. Randhir Singh

Editors: *Professor Randhir Singh has been regarded as one of the greatest teachers of our time. His influence on political theory and Marxism can be felt enormously. His method of Marxism has been straight conversation with Karl Marx. He has been regarded as one of the leading Marxist commentators on Indian state, society and applicability of Marxism in Indian context. Generations of scholars and activists have been inspired and shaped by his arduous labouring as Teacher and omniscient availability for all. His interaction with* ***Rityusha Tiwary*** *dwells on issues like corruption, civil society, NGOs, methodology of protest, middle class and democracy.*

Rityusha Tiwary [RT]: *What are the political imperatives behind this anti-corruption movement?*

Randhir Singh [RS]: Anna has no broad perspective on corruption and lacks understanding of what is happening in India. Capitalism is the root cause of corruption. My serious objection to Anna is his not taking up the larger issue: the ideology of capitalism, which leads to structural alienation. Class issue is central to this problem. The Left in India should have intervened in a movement like this.

RT: *Has the movement showcased an effective way for the civil society to intervene?*

RS: I have expounded elaborately on civil society in *Crisis of Socialism*, volume 5/6. May be one can have a look. To understand the term it is necessary to go to its very origin as expounded by Hegel and Marx as non-political sphere of life; then dwell on Gramsci's explanation of civil society as an arena of strength which he viewed as an alternative to state powered revolution. But actually the real phase of civil society intervention is over. It is a question of 'power' and state remains the main repository of power. Civil society puts emphasis on taking up this power. So, on the one hand civil society is a good thing because it gives voice to people but on the other hand it creates illusion that all the problems can be solved at the local level, whereas for me state is important. It tries to intervene in variety of issues which creates a muddle. In this context, only bringing out the Lokpal bill will not mean that corruption will end. 'Humanism in Marxism' is one important pointer in this regard.

RT: *In the light of NGO led revolutions around the world in the last two decades, would you say that NGOs are highjacking the agenda of democracy?*

RS: I will not agree with James Petras who called NGOs as 'agents of imperialism'. All NGOs cannot be relegated to the position that Petras refers to. But such NGOs often do not have any guiding force behind them. NGOs perform variety of operations and they are effective as local level initiatives are decisive. But if you want to oppose World Bank and globalization you have to have a national perspective. And if you do not realize that these are the root cause of problems manifested at the local level, then you are missing the larger reality.

RT: *What are the implications that this movement holds for the methodology of protest in the context of Indian democracy?*

RS: I am a firm believer in old fashioned protest. The basis of all kind of protest needs to be a concerted effort to bring about the agrarian revolution. This alone is the key. Workers and farmers are the real forces of any revolution.

[RT intervenes] *What is the role of middle class then?*

RS: For me there is a place for middle class. As capitalism grows and expands, the middle class feels the squeeze in tremendous amount.

This is what happened in the US. For instances some of the new diseases that have come up, the psychological pressure emerging out of stress, various diseases like depression, heart attacks, tension; these are all the gifts of market to our society. The sense of competition, I don't know how you look at competition but, I take a very poor view of this. It is one of the many repercussions of expanding capitalism.

RT: *So, would you say that alienation is a concept more associated with middle class?*

RS: See, it is the kind of politics which holds a reason of its own: the very nature of capitalism, its growth trajectory and its natural offshoots. My writings in this regard can be referred to as this is something that I have written about.

RT: *Sir, in terms of urban and rural participation in current day protest, is it the urban sector that drives protest or is it still majorly, a rural prerogative?*

RS: For me the key question is still the agrarian revolution. There has been a lot of debate, for instance in *Economics and Political Weekly*, about how most of the research in social sciences is area-centric. For instance, the focus is only on looking inside the rural domain, not on people to people relation or people and their interaction with the ruling class. You go on planting the trees and miss the wood in these cases whereas it is better to see things in totality and not just in their specific particularities. There are so many inter-connections in this particular phenomenon that I would like to explore all the dimensions.

RT: *What are the implications of this type of movement in terms of democracy? The protest that arise in today's context, can they really be classified as constitutional or anti-constitution? And does constitutional protest serve any purpose?*

RS: I am very old fashioned. When people like me came into the Communist movement, say in 1939, it was taken for granted that socialism is superior to capitalism in terms of democracy and that it will give more freedom and better freedom than capitalism. Now, one negative consequence of Soviet experience has been that a gulf has opened between democracy and socialism. The Russian people did not say that we don't want socialism, they all insisted on democracy. In fact Soviet Union made a gift of democracy to capitalism. The restoration of capitalism in Soviet Union happened under the cover of democracy. So democracy is something that cannot be bypassed.

The question of constitutional and unconstitutional may not be directly answered by the following surmise but let us say we want a peaceful change. And then pose the issue to the ruling class whether they will accept this? There is a lot of evidence so far and I have given a lot in my book. The extra-parliamentary sanctions are needed to defend and justify even a democratic regime. A classic example is of Chile. The Socialists came to power and they were overthrown. Pinochet came in and so the Chilean government was faced with the problem of defending the democratic verdict of the people. Plenty of the examples are there. Starting with Mussadaf when he nationalized oil he was overthrown. So, are the capitalists willing to accept the peaceful means? Today you have to establish your democratic credentials otherwise you are making a gift of the people to dictatorship and capitalism. At the moment democracy is in crisis so you persuade the people to move through their own experience towards the kind of political solutions that suit best. When Naxals say 'boycott election' they forget they are getting isolated from the people. It is like that report in the British media that 'there is storm in the English Channel and Europe is isolated from Great Britain', while it is the other way round. So it is not that simple and let people through their own experience move out of these democratic solutions. Therefore, all the extra-parliamentary/unconstitutional methods have to be defended because they represent peoples' aspirations. Even Cromwell was compelled to make revolution which he did not want. He said 'trust in god and do the needful'. This means that he was not willing to give up his army, so trust in the constitutional process; but do not entirely rely on it; tell the people that ruling classes are willing to betray the democracy whenever it suits you.

The main criticism of the Anna Hazare Movement is that they are allowing the government to ridicule and reject any kind of extra constitutional practice. If you translate in Marxian terms, it is the question that India faces today: of that of building socialism.

15

To Be Progressive, One Has to Have Critical Consciousness

Interview with Prof. G. Haragopal

Editors: *Professor G. Haragopal is widely known for being one of the few academicians who has transcended the boundaries of the university and involved himself in the issues directly impacting the people on the margins. He is widely known for his commitment to issues of human right. His active intellectual and political interventions have contributed to the shaping of its discourse in India. His critique of neoliberal policies of the Indian state from the vantage point of people-centered democracy has influenced the academics and activists alike. His long association with the struggle for democracy, equitable institutions and transformative movements has inspired successive generations of students, teachers and radical political activists. His interview with* ***Dhananjay Rai*** *unearths numerous critical aspects of the ruling echelons and Anna Hazare Movement [AHM].*

Dhananjay [DJ]: *What do you think of the politics of the Anna Hazare Movement?*

G. Haragopal [GH]: I have a feeling that the timing of the Anna Hazare movement coincides with a series of scams and scandals which came out as a part of the Comptroller and Auditor General report and also the public debate from the 2G Spectrum resulting in the arrest of a minister from the cabinet of the present government. There is a widespread feeling among the people that whole political classes have become thoroughly corrupt. One can also see the frustration of the middle class about the very nature of the state and political elite reflected in various forms of expression. I think the Anna Hazare movement springs in a very refreshing way and demands for institutional correction to the political distortion. One should also note that this movement enjoyed wholehearted support particularly from the electronic media. In a way, the system permitted it and patronised it and legitimised the movement and to that extent, the faith in the institutions and politics that was being lost was restored. I think Anna Hazare has helped the ruling classes in restoring their credibility at a time when they were on the verge of collapse. I am not saying it was a deliberate design, rather, it might have happened without the knowledge of so called civil society. This is how I would understand the politics of the Anna Hazare movement.

DJ: *Do you think that it was basically a middle class movement and therefore, not of any important consequence?*

GH: I think there was a positive side to the movement. There was mobilisation of the people and the passive middle classes became activated. And the movement also unexpectedly got support from even the relatively poorer sections of society who were suffering in the hands of petty bureaucrats; this was not really a settled issue in the Anna Hazare's movement to start with. In fact, it was much later that they brought the lower level bureaucracy into the picture because as they could see rickshaw pullers, food vendors, vegetable vendors, slum dwellers, pavement dwellers being attracted by the issues the movement was raising. Perhaps these people also imagined that their issues were lined with whatever the movement was representing. All these sections were looking to Anna and many of them physically reached to the venue, from far off distances that too. I think that's what in a way the movement gave some kind of hope to the people that they can struggle; they can collectively struggle for some public issues. The politics of movement and politics of mobilisation, which were getting eroded in the public life of India, in a way got revived because of the Anna Movement. In fact, the middle classes found a new meaning and perhaps a way to redefine its own role in public life. I think to that extent it has positively contributed to the process of democratisation. To some extent, it has contributed to the strengthening of the civil society, or if we may call it, public life, as I am not comfortable with the term 'civil society'; I think it is a very problematic term. Another interesting point is that the movement was unexpectedly planned and organised. On the whole, I think Indian society and Indian democracy have slightly benefitted from this movement.

DJ: *Do you think that the movement is against the Constitution?*

GH: It all depends on how one understands the Constitution of India. If the Constitution of India or sprit of the Constitution is reduced to formal institutional arrangements and structures then one can perhaps even interpret that Anna's movement is the negation of the way that power is organised, structured and institutionalised because Parliament is supreme, it is a law-making body and it is a representative intuition of the popular will of India. And therefore asking for an institution which can oversee all constitutionally structured institutions can be interpreted as extra-Constitution or beyond the constitution.

Instead, my understanding of the Indian Constitution is that it is not an arrangement of institutions. Institutions are only one part of the constitution. I think there is a larger vision that is represented by the Indian Constitution. We must remember that unlike many constitutions of the world, it has deep philosophical foundations. For example, one should look at Part III of the Indian Constitution. It makes it possible for people of India enjoy lots of freedoms, that is, freedoms to resist unhealthy and undemocratic threats in society. It is remarkable to note that people retain their ultimate sovereign power to question the governments in office. The Constitution of India also gives a vision informed by an egalitarian value. One can read for this in Part IV of the Indian Constitution: Articles 38 talks about reducing inequality in incomes, status, opportunity and facilities; Article 39 talks against the concentration of wealth in few hands. It suggests that wealth should be used as such that it will not detrimental to interest people of India. One way of looking at Anna's movement is that it is using freedom guaranteed in Part III of Indian Constitution to ensure the realisation of Part IV of the Indian Constitution because corruption leads to concentration of wealth. Corruption destroys an institution from carrying on the constitutional goals; corruption, in a way, hijacks power through the members of Parliament and members of Parliament become more representatives of concentrated wealth than of the common good and general will of the people. All this is detrimental to the interest of the people of India. I think whoever is raising the voice against corruption is, in fact, carrying the constitutional mandate and constitutional vision forward.

DJ: *Is there any limitation of the movement?*

GH: Yes. The only limitation or negative side of this movement is that when institutions of India are crumbling under the heavy weight of corruption, reposing one's confidence in one more institution with a naïve believe that this supra institution will be free from corruption and it will be totally committed to public ethics seems to a misplaced understanding. I think this faith in the institution of Janalokpal comes more from Anna's moral sensibility than his political understanding of the realities of India.

On the other hand, I would expect that Anna will not restrict his movement too much to Delhi and to the corrupt electronic media but will go to the honest masses of India who labour very hard in villages, living an honest life of high dignity. In fact, he should look for the social base of the anti-corruption movement in the rural India. Mobilisation of those masses would have served the constitutional purpose than merely asking for an act and finally ending up with an institution whose working will be conditioned by the same political and economic culture of India that has produced corruption. No institution can be above its historical and socio-economic context. Expecting today that an extraordinary individual or *avatar* like a Lokpal will clean the administration and cure the cancer of corruption is not possible. We have seen the Central Vigilance Commission and the controversy related to the appointment of Commissioner. We have also seen some of the judges becoming vulnerable to corruption which we never thought in our dreams. We should not forget the way the National Human Rights Commission has been mode totally devoid of its power and it has turned to be an institution of no value for the people of India. So what are these institutions? Even if it is given a constitutional status I do not think that the Lokpal can have a better composition than the NHRC, which has a former Chief Justice of the Supreme Court as chairperson and former judges and outstanding public figures as members. What else can Lokpal have other than what the NHRC has? Why has the NHRC failed to perform its expected role? Therefore, I do not say it is against the constitution but to superimpose an institution on all institutional structure is to repose too much of confidence in one institution.

DJ: *Has Indian democracy been strengthened or compromised by the movement?*

GH: This question was raised by Justice Santosh Hegde during the debate on this issue at Bangalore National Law School. A simple answer to this is that it all depends how one defines democracy. If democracy is defined as a formal-institutional framework and reduced to mere representative democracy, that in my view is an inadequate, incomplete and incorrect way of looking at democracy.

The evidence of the last six decades demonstrates beyond doubt that there are moments when representative democracy ceases to be represented. If Parliament has 300 millionaires or billionaires and we believe that they represent the poor, starved and suffering Indian masses are deluding ourself. At best, it can be considered as merely a formal democracy but certainly not a substantive one. Democracy is not merely a form of government, but also a way of life. There is a possibility of having so called democratic institutions in a highly undemocratic society.

So, any movement or demand made on the parliament or on a greater accountability from the members of Parliament should not be viewed as decline of democracy or compromise of with democracy. I would rather say that it has in one sense compromised with the formal democracy. However, it has perhaps contributed in its own way to the strengthening of certain democratic forces, if not the masses of India at least certain urban, middle and professional classes by slightly activating them.

DJ: *One of the charges against the movement has been that it has been orchestrated by the Hindutva family. What would be your response?*

GH: My reaction to this question is that Anna Hazare like many other personally honest people has no formidable world view, a sense of history or vision for the future. I do not credit him with any of these articles. Such persons by default end up with Right-wing politics. In order to be progressive, one has to have critical consciousness, which I think is absent in his case. The other limitations are not personal limitations but contextual. There is a big constraint that the political arena parliamentary politics is constituted of only two major players, therefore, whatever he does necessarily has to be either in favour of or against one of these parties—BJP or Congress.

The Congress Party is in power and the responsibility lies with them to enact this bill so any hesitation on its part tends to help the Right-wing forces. BJP, as a party, has abandoned its nationalist agenda and is indulging in communalisation of society in turn contributing to the strengthening of global economic forces. Given their opportunistic politics devoid of any solid agenda, ethics make them to fish in these troubled waters. So, Hindutva forces are using Anna for their political gain and Anna knowingly or unknowingly ended up consolidating those political forces.

DJ: *What is the nature [caste/class/gender/minority perspective] of AHM?*

GH: I do not know whether there can be a complete answer to this question because one really does not know. My own view is that it is urban middle class, professional, elite and media driven. I do not think that this movement ever touched the lower castes, deprived classes and disempowered women.

DJ: *Is this populism a product of neo-liberalism and global capital to drive away the structural attention?*

GH: My response to this would be similar to that of the earlier one. The support of the English national media makes one suspect that global capital is somewhere behind this movement. Media as a corporate world would not like the state functionaries to share their profits legally through taxation or illegally through corruption. In fact, Kaushik Basu's argument about legalising corruption or viewing corruption as speed money suggests that global capital might be benefitted by Anna's movement.

DJ: *Are corruption and germination of protest quintessential capitalist phenomena?*

GH: I think in India, if you look at the range of social movements in post-Independent India, many of these identity movements are supported, financed and patronised by either local capital or global capital. The same capital which promotes social movements is extremely upset with struggles which question the existing structures.

The Anna Hazare Movement in no way challenged the existing structures, capitalist framework and development model. Movements of this kind which are organised within the given structural framework are always supported by process of globalisation. Global capital also believes in delegitimising the state in favour of the market.

Anna's movement fairly fits into this thinking as it questions the corruption of the state and is totally silent on corporate exploitation. And I would think that corporate capitalism is the cause and state corruption is the consequence. Any anti-corruption movement confined only to an anti-state stand also ends up legitimising the corporate capitalist.

16

Civil Society, Movements and the Democratic Theory

A Conversation with Prof. D.L. Sheth

Editors: *Prof. D.L. Sheth, a leading socio-political theorist, belongs to a rare genre of intellectuals wherein dissent occupies the central role. His originality lies in the deep and sceptical unravelling of the relationship between social sciences and social realities. His scepticism and dissent are imbued with the urge for a positive future. In a conversation with* ***Dr Manindra Nath Thakur****, Professor Sheth unties the complexity of the relationship among civil society, the state, political parties, globalisation and democracy. We are grateful to* ***Ruchi Shree*** *and* ***Shashank Chaturvedi*** *for transcribing the conversation for the book. This interview is a part of a series of conversations with Prof. Sheth.*

I. THE IDEA AND POLITICS OF CIVIL SOCIETY

Manindra Nath Thakur [MNT]: *How do you view popularisation of the idea of civil society in the context of the ongoing movement against corruption under the leadership of Anna Hazare?*

D.L. Sheth [DLS]: Although an established concept in political philosophy, the term civil society entered public discourse in India almost abruptly with the rise of the Anna Hazare-led anti-corruption movement. Until recently, people who belonged to what is today called civil society did not see themselves as civil society; the terms used were NGOs, voluntary associations, micro movements, grassroots organisations, social movements, and so on. The term civil society was rarely used. But the phenomenon was there, which is today identified as civil society; the media and the internet have particularised this term to refer to Anna Hazare's anti-corruption movement.

More precisely, in the 1990s, when India began to enter the globalising world and adopted new economic policies for its 'integration' with the world economy, the term came into circulation. The foreign funding agencies used this word frequently. The term they used was CSO (Civil Society Organisations) for their partners, the Indian NGOs who received the grants. Besides, identification of the NGOs with civil society enabled foreign funders to justify, even if semantically, their direct dealings with the Indian NGOs. The partners, too, accepted the civil society tag with great alacrity. It is interesting to note in this context that a change in the political climate, and emergence of a new political discourse may infuse an old established concept with new meanings. It may even reverse the meaning retrospectively by making its prominent meaning recessive. Something like this seems to have happened to the term 'civil society'.

The term 'civil society' became popular also through international politics of the Cold War. Especially towards the end of the Cold War, the idea of civil society was embraced by the Soviet intellectual and political dissenters. The central argument of the protesters against the Soviet regime, and the one that was then widely carried out to the rest of the world, including India, by the American academia (the journal, *Problems of Communism* comes to mind), went like this: the Communist state has not only lost touch, but has in fact become the enemy of the people, thanks to its intrinsic tendency to totalise power in a small coterie by whatever populist name it may goby. The state has moved away from the people. It now rules sitting imperiously above and over their heads. Only the revival of civil society can bring the state back to the people. Thus civil society which was considered in Marxist lore to be a passive, anti-revolutionary and retrogressive phenomenon, integral to bourgeoisie democracy was now being given new, democratic-revolutionary content. The dissidents believed that bringing the state under the command of civil society was necessary for the emergence of a multi-party democratic system, and the attainment of political freedoms, both of which the Soviet state denied them firmly and ruthlessly. The term, now loaded with a specific meaning acquired in the Soviet political discourse of dissidence – political action against the state—soon became a favourite concept for the Indian social activists and academics. Some of them, without giving much further thought, began to use routinely the term 'civil society' in the place of 'society', even when that usage was not at all appropriate. When Anna Hazare's movement mobilised people in significant numbers against governmental corruption, the term got quickly fixed to it, along with its meaning—political action against the State.

Q. MNT: *You seem to be saying that there was a civil society, before civil society. So how that arena of politics was seen by the activists and the academics?*

When the term civil society descended on the Indian political scene, a fairly clear conceptual thinking and a vigorous debate was on about the sector of democratic politics that operated outside the representational institutions of state (elections and political parties). The debate was initiated by the activists and public intellectuals, associated with the Lokayan movement. They conceptualised and popularised the idea of non-party politics and characterised this sector of democratic politics as non-party *political* (formations) groups and movements. Compared to civil society, the non-party political formations was a more focussed and appropriate conceptualisation of the phenomenon. This idea of non-party politics, however, was not the same as that of the party-less democracy developed by Jayaprakash Narayan, in the early 1960's. Here, the idea is not the replacement of parliamentary democracy by direct, participatory democracy. The thrust of the debate raised by Lokayan to carve out and to highlight the aspect/arena of politics, in the parliamentary democracy, that represented the phenomenal world of democratic politics. But the practitioners of institutional politics (the party politicians) were sceptical of this idea and a section of political theorists saw it as if it represented some archaic idea of democracy and perhaps also a threat to liberal democracy itself. The non-party political formations referred to individual actors (social activists) and groups whose intentions and programmes, were essentially political, but eschewed the politics of parties and elections. The debate reminded the citizens that democratic politics was not all about parties and elections.

The role non-party politics performed was largely in terms of raising and communicating specific issues of people to the political establishment and compel it to address them, by mobilising popular support. These were also called grassroots movements. Then, there were state-level *support organisations* of the grassroots movements; their main terrain of activity was to engage the state in a dialectic of opposition, protest and cooperation. They worked with and on behalf of the people—a vast number of marginalised groups of people in the economy and society all over the country, whose needs and rights were not even perceived by political parties, and when seen, the parties did not find them important enough to articulate these as issues of electoral politics. The kind of problems the people faced simply were not amenable to creating votebanks. For the local, rural communities governmental corruption had become so rampant that it virtual became a life and death issue for them. A non-party political group (MKSS) worked hand in hand with the affected people in Rajasthan and succeeded in compelling the officials to administer development works, in a corruption free manner. Eventually, it developed into a national level campaign for right to information as a means to fight governmental corruption—and the MKSS succeeded again, this time at the national level. This is the kind of non-party political process and movements that typified the Lokayan's concept of *non-party political formation*. I have in mind MKSS: the Mazdur Kisan Sangharsh Samity founded by Aruna Rai and her colleagues. Other examples are: a network of non-party groups and movements NAPM (National Alliance of Peoples' Movements) led by Medha Patkar and the Manushi movement for economic rights of the poor, especially the cycle-rickshaw pullers and the *rehdy patriwallas*, founded and led by Madhu Purnjima Kiswar. There have been many more such micro-movements in the south, east and other parts of India. I have mentioned the above only as illustrations.

The debate on non-party political formations was sidelined as the idea of civil society became fashionable. Significantly, however, the idea of people's grassroots movements survives in an important section of the activist world in its Hindi name: *Jan-andolan* (Samuh).

The tendency of Indian academics to readily give up what they are doing if a new fashionable word comes up from the West is a known fact. There is ofcourse no harm in adopting a new term from wherever it comes, but it must be linked to our experience so that we could correctly and more appropriately use it in our own context; the kind of thing we perhaps have done with the concept 'secularism'. The problem arises when a clearer concept, describing appropriately the reality at hand, is abruptly dumped in favour of a catch-all term.

MNT: *Did the political parties take note of the debate on non-party political formations?*

DLS: Political parties were not happy with the academics and activists privileging the 'non-party' organisations. Even in those days, (in the early 1980's) they thought that such movements and organisations undermined their political salience. Left parties, in particular the Communist Parties, did not like it at all. In fact, in the mid-eighties, the leader of the Communist Party, Prakash Karat, wrote an article in his party organ arguing that the rise of non-party political organisations represented yet another strategy of the bourgeoisie to counter the revolutionary politics of the Left.

Some of us, however, saw this development as one containing seeds of a new politics of democratising the Indian democracy. It not only raised political participation and awareness of people at large but energised political action of groups, leading to a high-intensity politics of rights in the country as a whole. A phenomenon that was latter described by V.S. Naipaul as: a million mutinies. It, was a phenomenon radically different from the established public institutions and organisations conventionally identified as 'civil society' such as the universities, colleges, philanthropic organisations, social services and welfare groups. The Left-Communist parties were not unhappy with the academician confining the idea of civil society to such apolitical spaces as it did not threaten the Left monopoly of radical/revolutionary politics. Their eye-soar was the public intellectuals and academics who recognised and supported (and some even led) non-hegemonic, democratic radicalisation of politics.

The political parties' discomfort with non-party politics was however not confined only to the Left parties. This was easy to understand. The non-party political groups were seen by almost all political parties as usurpers of party-political spaces. They raised new issues in politics. They made demands on the state, which were pressed politically and processed and converted into rights. A kind of politics the parties had left behind when they ceased to be movements. A significant amount of theoretical and empirical work was done describing and analyzing this phenomenon that acquired the shape of a movement led by Jayaprakash Narayan. But it developed and expanded in the 1980's and 1990's, into a myriad micro-movements at the grassroots engaged in the politics of rights for marginalised and socially and economically deprived rural as well as urban populations. This spurt in grassroots politics captured the political imagination of the Indian youth and significant innovations were made in the politics of protest, and in devising programmes for alternative developments. Today, all kinds of political initiatives and campaigns in the arena of non-party politics are lumped into a singular idea and given the name—especially by the media—the civil society. This is what has happened with Anna Hazare's campaign against corruption. It has been virtually personified by the media, and that too with an address: civil society @Jantar Mantar! It is high time we pay serious theoretical attention to democratic politics and conceptually clearly differentiate between politics of civil society, of movements, and of the parties.

MNT: *You talked about the media. Would you like to comment on the academic writings and discussions on the issue of civil society in recent years?*

Indian academicians, especially the sociologists and political scientists, began to make serious use of the term 'civil society' sometime towards the end of the Cold War, more specifically in the post-Emergency era: the former in their attempt to make sense of changes democratic politics had brought in the Indian society and the latter, perhaps to make up for the deficit in the democratic theory caused by its excessive concern with formal, institutional democracy and neglect of substantive politics of movements. This neglect, in fact, continues to constrict the theory's view of political power to mainly the power of the *modern* democratic state especially to its institutions. The focus on institutional power (and, ofcourse, the concern for its legitimacy) daunts the theorist from boldly inserting the non-institutional forms and processes of political power, emerging from non-party democratic *politics* as a phenomenon relevant for theorising (Indian) democracy. Consequently, the theory's focus remains *primarily* on the modernity of India's democratic state and, only secondarily, on its democratic character. As a result, the democratic theory has been badly entangled with the theory of modernity. This has led to a tremendous loss of perspective—involving non-recognition of those forms of political participation which do not revolve around elections and political parties. This has created a peculiar dialectic in India, between democracy and modernity which the democratic theory cannot afford to bypass. Further, the theory does not easily bring in its ambit the non (pre)-modern sources of political power—which also are presumed to be non (pre) democratic. The fact, however, is that the non/pre modern forms, get transmuted into new, contemporary forms of power which the institutions of democracy have to constantly cope with. This antecedent structure of power, even though modified and tempered by democratic politics, is represented in the power of the contemporary elites. It is the play of this *elite power that* constitutes a big challenge to India's democratisation, even as it works as an engine for its modernisation. It is a formidable challenge verging on a threat to democracy because the historically persisting elite structure of power is constitutive of the institutional power of India's liberal democracy, and, ironically, the harbinger of its modernisation.

MNT: *How would you like to trace the genealogy of the concept and the phenomenon of civil society in the academic discourse in India.*

DLS: One important strand of intellectual genealogy of the concept civil society in India could be traced to political philosophy—the writings of Marx, Hegel, Gramsci and their derivations and renderings by the Indian academicians. Another strand could be found in writings of some British and the North American thinkers who highlighted civic functions of public organisations and institutions in fields of philanthropy, welfare, education, health and lately development. And, of course Toquevel' studies of the American democracy constitute an important influence in thinking of non-state, civic associations as integral to a functioning democracy. The phenomenon attracted attention of Indian academicians, mainly the sociologists and political scientists, as late as in the early 1980's. They, by and large, locate civil society in the modern-secular sector of public life in India. As such, its emergence could be traced to colonial modernity

When the colonial regime needed to link the government, especially its administrative apparatus, to people, it promoted creation of sets of intermediary organisations and institutions at the interface between the rulers and the ruled. The agenda was to moot the idea, and support initiatives for social, economic and welfare activities in the provinces and, in the process, build a degree of political support in the Indian population for the (modern) colonial regime. This included formation of cooperative societies, public trusts and voluntary social organisations in the area of education, health and welfare. In the area of local administration a series of district level organisations, such as district development boards were also created; they were all manned by the 'notable' and 'respected' persons in the area selected by the colonial administrators. I have in mind the nineteenth and early twentieth-century India, when the awareness of *colonial publics* grew, thanks to the regime's policies implemented in collaboration with the English educated, as well as the traditional social elite. The creation of and participation in the intermediate bodies came also on the agenda of social reformers. In Gujarat, for example, Narmadashankar Dave (Narmad), an influential social reformer and the founding father of modern Gujarati literature, wrote an interesting small essay titled, *Mandali Banawana Phayda* (Benefits of Forming Associations). Thus, associations in various fields were promoted by social reformers, even as they were adopted as a policy measure by the colonial state. The society registration act of 1860 gave a legal basis and recognition to such organisations,

The point is, colonial modernity was crucial to understanding the relationship between the civil society and the state. One could no longer talk of civil society and not refer to the state. Although it worked relatively autonomously for the welfare, and in general interest of the people civil society appeared as penumbra of the state. By locating it in the sphere of the modern state, the social scientists began to view civil society almost exclusively in secular terms, and caste and religious organisations as existing outside its pale. It was thus seen as a para-political structure of public organisations *aligned* to the state. In short, civil society for them represented primarily the modern sector of India's social and political life, and derivatively, an aspect of democracy.

Once again, we find here theories of modernity and democracy being intertwined, to the point of inter-changeability where the sphere of democracy coterminates with modernity. In today's world with the phenomenal growth of diverse *political publics*, especially in the post-War democracies, civil society has, in fact, come face-to-face vis-a-vis the state, in a dynamic relationship of conflict and collaboration. The churnings in the civil society interrogate the long term modernist project of crating a democratic polity consisting of deracinated citizens. Civil society politics also makes it difficult to take a simplistic, black and white view of state-society relationships according to which the civil society can exist only in a purely secular space, created by the state; and as if there is no society beyond civil society.

The fact is that the caste and religious organisations have conventionally performed secular functions for their (social) constituencies, especially in areas of education, health and general welfare. Nor did they stay aloof from some kind of political influences in the course of performing these functions. They never confined their activities to only managing ritual statuses and sacral roles of their members. It should be noted that similar kind of functions—social as well as political (vis-a-vis the state/king) were performed by the social and religious centres (temples) even in pre-modern times. All this suggests that the task of conceptualising civil spaces and drawing boundaries around civil society is yet to be accomplished.

In the meanwhile, in my view, a more urgent theoretical question that awaits attention is: what has been the primary source of the tremendous political energy we witness in India, today: democracy or modernity? It is crucial to address this question if we wish to begin disentangling democracy from modernity—theoretically and phenomenologically. This might also help us situate civil society in the midst of ongoing, para-institutional democratic politics, rather than in the supposedly exclusive and passive middle-class (elite) politics of influence and networking. Civil society politics is not a politics of cabals, nor an informal (even though non-institutional) politics of favour banks where accounts are held of the favours done and received in the course of using one's official power for unofficial, pecuniary purposes. I forget the name of the author who devised this term 'favour banks'. I find the term quite useful for characterising the *informal* elite politics where favours are internally exchanged among bureaucrats, politicians and businessmen benefiting each other. Such a Mutual Favours Society does not carry a civic, *public* identity in a real sense. It cannot be called in any sense a civil society. I would like to think of civil society as the third kind of politics, expanding and making spaces between the politics of vote-banks and favour-banks. We will have to find some other name for internal intrigues and deals made in the corridors of power. Of course, this network of exchanging huge 'gifts' (for work done or expected to be done), when becomes thicker and grows wider it comes in 'public' view and is seen for what it is: crony capitalism. In another context, we have seen such cliquing together of bureaucrats, big-businessmen and the politicians for pecuniary and party-political benefits under an ideological veneer of socialism, but did not give it the name it disserved: (bureaucratic) crony-socialism.

This is one way of understanding civil society which has mainly unfolded in the academic and ideological discourse. It's actual politics is another story—developing, open ended and multifarious. In part, the story is of marginalised peoples' struggles and movements for right to life with dignity and in the process democratising the institutional structure of the state. The constitution recognises this aspect of democratic politics, but in general terms—as a part of political rights of individuals and groups. The political legitimacy of movements which continually innovate programmes and mechanisms for protecting rights of citizens when encroached upon by the state or undermined by its highly power-endowed institutions of the Executive and the Parliament, (as was revealed during the Emergency), and by the non-state power centres in the society routinely trampling the economic and social rights of ordinary citizens is yet to be established—legally and politically. Many more constitutional mechanisms and provisions need to be made to *realise* the rights that are technically given/provided in the constitution, but remain substantively unachieved. Possibilities of achieving these lie not in the mainstream politics of civil society; it lies in the non-party politics of movements.

The protest politics is officially regulated even today, in the age of democracy, by old colonial laws—comprised by and large in the Indian penal code—for example, the rules pertaining to unlawful assembly.

The short point is: It is the politics of non-party groups and movements that has lent intensity and vibrancy to Indian democracy. This politics need to be brought into the focus of political and theoretical debates so that the current, amorphous, amoeba-like concept of civil society is unpacked, hopefully opening up the theory to the phenomenal world of non-party politics which it has so far dimly perceived and only partially taken into account.

MNT: *How can we relate the concept of civil society to our own social and political experiences, particularly those of non-party political movements you talked about earlier.*

The basic issue is, how can the people (the ruled) achieve maximum degree of representation and a say in governance. The concept of representation needs deeper, theoretical—philosophical probe. Since electoral politics has been taken as the defining feature of democracy and the elections constitute the main source of its legitimacy, the elected political leaders often fail to recognise democratic role the other, 'non-party' public leaders play and in a different but democratically crucial sense also *represent* the people in the nation's politics. It is the fear of such representation by non-elected leaders that perhaps explains why the party politicians and some media leaders tried to project Anna Hazare's movement as constituting a danger to India's democratic polity.

We have thus one kind of scholars and political commentators who still use the term civil society with its conventional Western trappings and feel unhappy when the concept is being extended to incorporate protest movements. It is essentially the fear of politics itself. The fear turns into a terrifying thought, a nightmare, when protests assume the form of direct action politics. We have no inbuilt mechanisms, nor sufficient clarity of (theoretical) thought as to what kind of politics could people resort to when the democratically (electorally) acquired political power of legislators and constitutionally sanctioned power of the government administrators are used 'illegally' albeit in the name of Executive, that has been systemically allowed to monopolise governmental power. The situation becomes worse when such power is used for, and on behalf of a clan or a family which rules the party that numerically dominates the government or has a power to hold it in balance: (read ransom). Preventing the decline of institutions should therefore acquire utmost priority for the theorists as well as the its practitioners of democratic politics. The issue is what kind of political means are available to people in such a situation. It is in this context that the idea of direct political action become relevant, demanding serious theoretical attention. The overall practical challenge is: how to invest the reality of non-electoral power, which sometimes may take undemocratic populist forms, with democratic content. Innovating new forms and mechanisms in the practice of democratic politics and developing a comparative theoretical understanding of its principles and functioning (in different social-cultural, and historical contexts) is therefore crucial: at the minimum, to prevent further decline of its institutions and, in the long run, to evolve broad-based, alternative forms of representation and participation.

MNT: *How would you then describe the growth of Civil Society in the Indian context?*

DLS: In post-colonial India, 'civil society' evolved in three phases: during the Freedom movement; during the JP Movement; and in the post-globalisation era. In its present form, the development of 'civil society' took place only in the post-Emergency phase. After the JP Movement, various kinds of NGOs came on the scene in different parts of the country. With this development, it became increasingly difficult to confine the idea of civil society only to the charitable organisations or to organisations like universities. As the term civil society is being popularly used in the present context, the meaning has gone beyond this initial stage, which was closer to the Western notion of the term. In its new meaning, the term civil society incorporates what we used to call non-party politics. If we want to understand the meaning of civil society today, we should not neglect this conceptual evolution that took place in the post-Emergency India. I would like to again emphasise the idea of 'non-party political formation' particularly because it does not hide the political content of the movements. This concept is necessary for unpacking the complexities of various forms of democratic practices in India. I find it strange that people in anti-corruption movements call themselves non-political. In fact, it is political in every sense of the term, except that it is not electoral and party-political.

MNT: *Do you think that all the trends of civil society which history has thrown are available to us?*

DLS: In a sense, yes. The crucial point is that a democratic state can't remain confined to its own organisations and institutions. It needs civil society so that political action which can often turn lawless and violent is brought in the frame of democratic protests and dialogues. This is why, since colonial times, the state has looked for, even promoted organised form of protests and co-operation it can deal with. It therefore should not have surprised us that Planning Commission recognised non-governmental and voluntary organisations for implementing developmental schemes as well for seeking their advice in the planning process. The National Advisory Council (NAC) today is in fact an outcome of this process. And now there is a new buzzword, thanks to the overriding presence of the market in politics: the public-private partnership!

MNT: *Are the people and their organisations in the villages also part of the civil society or does it limit itself only to the urban middle class?*

DLS: In the civil society arena the rural space is in continuity with the urban. There does not seem to be a distinct space for villages as such. These are, in a manner of speaking, the people behind the bush involved in the 'Naipaul's million mutinies. Civil society has spread all over India in the form of micro-political movements identified as NGOs, and various other names.

MNT: *Does civil society act against the state?*

DLS: Civil society , as we saw, is in a dialectical relationship with the state—democratic or otherwise. It does not have to be, necessarily, always against it. Here, we are talking about a democratic state. In the tradition of Marx, Hegel, and Gramsci civil society is a part of the bourgeois state. Even Partha Chatterjee in his critique of civil society is not talking something drastically different from this. His contribution lies in devising the concept of 'political society' and thus recognising an aspect of democratic politics which need not be discarded in the name of civil society. He, in a manner of thinking, conceptually saves an aspect of liberal democracy from the ongoing Marxist theoretical onslaught on it.

MNT: *People are even saying that the state itself has organised civil society and it is visible only at places where the state is not able to reach.*

DLS: We have earlier talked about this in another context. Yes, it is true that where the state is not able to reach, civil society is playing its role. And where both are absent, the Naxals rule. We can see today that there is a big change in the role of civil society after the anti-Emergency movement led by Jayaprakash Narayan. Most of the contemporary progressive legislations have been initiated in the civil society and then taken up by the government. This is reflected in legislations such as the right to information, right to education, et cetera.

MNT: *What is the impact of globalisation on civil society, keeping in mind that we have now bigger global players interested in our economy?*

DLS: Two important impacts one can see of globalisation on civil society. The first is the emergence of the politicised and growing middle class and its entry into the global civil society. With this development the liberal democracy, which was always linked to the idea of liberal or liberalised economy, has now acquired, in a manner of speaking, the character of a market democracy. It is in this sense I understand the word neo-liberal when prefixed to the term economy, and democracy.

The second is implicit in the first, namely the reduced legitimacy of representative governments. Thus, the global democracy is conceived as democratic but not in the sense of being *representative*. It is so more in the sense of being consultative. The idea has certainly shifted from a representational to consultative, expert based governance which is non-representative but democratic in the sense of making governance transparent and *procedurally* accountable. We can give the example of increasing credibility of such institutions as the Election Commission, the CAG and the higher judiciary in India or the global watch type of organisations in areas of environment, civil rights and other trans-national institutions. In this context, trust rather than representation has become more important. At the same time this would increase the power of 'international' experts and technocrats. It is an open question as to what form the global democracy as well as the nation-state democracies will assume with progressing globalisation. The emerging concern is: how democratic will be the global democracy, and what that would do to democracies in the nation-state.

17

The Most Important Aspect is to Understand the Nature and Agenda of Capitalism Today

Interview with Prof. Imtiaz Ahmad

Editors: *Prof. Imtiaz Ahmad's contribution highlights three significant roles. Firstly, he is one of the early academicians in India who blurred the distinction between politics and sociology as separate disciplines thereby ventur into the realm of political-sociology throughout his academic life. His continuous defence of minority rights has highlighted the initiation of immediate and robust intervention by the state for the former's betterment. Moreover, he has long back rejected the Muslim as a homogeneous category which is devoid of internalconflict. According to Prof. Ahmad, Muslims are being divided and exploited in the name of caste internally and religion externally. His interview with* **Manjur Ali** *highlights the 'critical vantage point' vis-à-vis Anna Hazare and his team.*

Manjur Ali [MA]: *How do you look at the politics of the Anna Hazare Movement [AHM]?*

Imtiaz Ahmad [IA]: People have grievances against the Indian political class for not fulfilling their expectation. They feel that leaders and representatives are in the nexus with the business class who exploit the resources of this country which are common property. Indeed, people feel that politicians are the source of corrupt practices. The Anna Hazare movement gathers momentum in this circumstance by way of exploiting the anger. However, this particular movement forgets to focus on the role of big business houses and corporate loot. Thus, it is against the politics itself, which is a dangerous trend. We should be aware of this dimension.

MA: *What is your view on whether agitation against corruption is against the constitution or not?*

IA: One cannot be against people's mobilisation against the government and the state. In democracy, everyone has a right to demand and protest. Nonetheless, it is important to understand the nature of these mobilisations and demands. So, technically it wasn't against the constitution but this fact should not stop one from critically analysing the whole farce in the name of a so called 'people's movement'. The Anna Hazare Movement was not a people's movement by any definition. For instance, movements related to livelihood, environment and land acquisition can be categorised as people's movements. The POSCO struggle against the land grabbing by the state for a Korean company is a people's movement. I prioritise, among the whole gambit of struggles, the struggle against land acquisition. The most important aspect is to understand the nature and agenda of capitalism today.

MA: *How do you judge Indian democracy after this Anna Movement?*

IA: As I had said earlier that it is not a people's movement and certainly not a democratic one. It is a most undemocratic movement with a demand which, if implemented, may weaken the structure of Indian democracy. For instance, Right to Reject is a very problematic one. It may end up in a vacancy of a large number of seats in parliament and the Legislative Assembly. It means many constituencies without representatives. Just imagine what will follow. A similar result follows up with Right to Recall. If a certain law or democratic policy has worked for European or smaller countries like Sweden and Norway, it doesn't mean that it will work for India. Look at the bigger democratic countries like US, UK, Australia and Canada. There is no such provision of Right to Reject or Right to Recall. Hence, I think democracy will be compromised if Anna Hazare Movement succeeds.

MA: *Is Right-wing politics behind the Anna Hazare Movement?*

IA: My answer is yes. Anna Hazare is a RSS man. He is backed by these communal organisations. RSS, BJP and ABVP cadres have participated in large numbers in this so called 'apolitical' movement.

Moreover, one should understand the take of RSS on democracy. Their central command politics is imbued with casteist and communal aspirations. Therefore, in place of strengthening democracy, they will hamper its prospect.

MA: *What is the nature (caste/class/gender/minority status) of Anna Hazare Movement ?*

IA: Before anything else, we must not call it movement. The word has a bigger connotation. As far as the nature of this mobilisation is concerned, it has missed the larger and most important chunk of population. The minority, dalit and Scheduled Tribes were continuously missing from the scene against the media hype created around the lakhs of mobilisations. According to Bal Thackrey himself, the number was between 30,000–35,000 only.

The deprived sections (whom you are categorising as caste/class/ gender/minority) of India are more important politically than elite mobilisation. These sections make or break any government through their votes and not the middle class. They have given this country so much. In and around the country they are part of people's movements against capitalism whose real beneficiaries are the Indian middle class.

MA: *Is it an urban or rural phenomenon?*

IA: It is certainly an urban phenomenon with the middle class at the axis of mobilisation. This class has a grudge against the politics especially after the so called second wave of democratisation in India which has seen a political rise of rural India. That was possible with the positive discrimination policy implemented in the process of national building. The rise of an alternate middle class threatens the very control of the upper caste middle class which fill the hatred within them against the politics. Then the propaganda started that politics is the business of criminals and politicians are *gundas* and uncultured. That is why any mobilisation against the politics is not supported by deprived sections.

MA: *Can we perceive this populism as a product of neoliberalism and global capital crisis to drive away the structural attention?*

IA: I feel that capitalism is the root cause of all problems in and around the world. If capitalism is not a part of our discussion while delving upon the current crisis, then we are not landing anywhere near the solution. We have to make an autopsy of capitalism. Otherwise it will keep the people's movements divided and will not let a unity to build against them.

MA: *What is the way out of it?*

IA: I must say that a strong Jan Lokpal Bill will not solve the problem of corruption. Corruption is a moral question and a sign of degrading social value, which no bill or law is going to address. We have to build up a democratic movement having the participation of deprived sections, if not that, at least such a movement which brings a majority of people together on one platform. The movement on must engender social value into the society. M.K. Gandhi, B.R. Ambedkar and Jotirao Phule have once led such movements.

Today, we are lacking even a glimpse of such movements. As of today, despite the enemy being common, we do not see the presence of people's movements whose character is national.

MA: *Dalits and Muslims have two different reasons for being away. Regarding dalits, they felt the threat to constitutional rights which might undo various safeguards. Muslims are apprehensive due to RSS support. What is your comment?*

IA: I agree that dalits and Muslims, who constitutes larger section of deprived masses, have different reasons not to join AHM. Unlike Muslims, dalits have a social and political agenda or goal drawn from the thoughts and writings of Dr Ambedkar. They are continuous and persistent in their fight against social discrimination and to achieve social equity. Once AHM sprouted on the political scene, dalit intellectuals and organisations felt that it was diverting from the struggle. It was a 'clash of interest' between an agitation which has a metropolitan 'middle-class' character and the deprived sections. That's why you saw a parallel protest rally against AHM under the banner of save the constitution. That was to save the 'politics'.

On the other hand, today Muslims have no such agenda to achieve from the politics. Muslims don't relate, since Independence, with the state much. They feel the state has never addressed their interests. The social psyche is of 'statelessness'. So they build up a parallel system which is managed by the community itself without any help from the state. That's why you see self-funded health, education and welfare institutions. So the movement against corruption led by Anna is not attractive enough for them. In short, this agitation lacks Gandhi politics of 'symbolism' like the Khilafat movement.

MA: *Is it true that Muslims masses were part of the mobilisation but Muslims leadership was reluctant?*

IA: No ! Not at all. There was no participation of common Muslim masses. Look there is a genuine concern over corruption in the country. It is affecting every citizen whether he/she belong to any region or religion in even manner. But individual participation could not be termed as community acceptance of AHM.

MA: *Can we expect from any movement that it should plan the inclusion of all from the very beginning or that it should happens along the way?*

IA: Both could happen. One can plan to include all prior to any movement. Also, people do join in the process. In this case, it was not planned at all. In fact, after the attack on the movement, the core team decided to make it inclusive. If you remember, initially the AHM used symbol of *'Bharat Mata'* and slogans like *'Bharat Mata ki jai'* and *vande matram* dominated the scene. This wasn't going down well with the downtrodden masses that are averse or feel indifferent to such markers. It is typical RSS brand of politics.

Earlier, the RSS was an urban Hindu middle-class phenomenon. The lower caste (dalits) had the inheritably bottom place reserved in the RSS political schema. So they never thought of bought them into the main framework of society. However, this strategy of RSS failed miserably, which forced it to contemplate the social equation. Hence, they started welfare projects among the SCs/STs population, which eventually paid them off. Shiv Sena, BJP, Hindu Yuva Vahini and other RSS family members have a large support base in these sections. This is also a consequence of the failure of progressive politics in India. You can see some of these similarities in the AHM.

MA: *What is the possibility that opposition to Anna and his team was orchestrated by the Congress by using the fear factor of RSS/BJP?*

IA: No, it's not correct that opposition was led by Congress, initially. First you have to understand that the Indian state has different strategies for different problems. The state has ready-made solution to the problem like communal violence. There are laws against the ethnic cleansing and riots. The government can deal with it at any moment. It is another matter that the decision to deal with communal violence is mired by politics.

However, the state doesn't know how to deal with class violence like corruption. As I have said earlier that corruption is a middle-class agitation. So the state was ready to compromise at all levels. That is why it first sent a minister to receive Ramdev and later on to deal with Anna's team. It is only when Anna and his team insisted on passing the Jan Lokpal Bill and started blackmailing them, that government began to use the 'exposed' game to deal it. This agitation was about 'eroding morality' in public life. Now look at the corrupt practices Anna's team members are involved in. Shanti Bhusan in the land scam, Kiran Bedi in airfare issue and Arvind Kejriwal in non-payment of taxes and others. So, today even the AHM movement has lost the necessary moral high ground. Today, people have begun to question the politics of the AHM.

MA: *Do you see the emergence of alternative movement on behalf of dalits and Muslims vis-à-vis Anna and his team-led mobilisation against corruption?*

IA: No, the AHM has been fading day by day. It is becoming weaker. The team members are under trust deficit. Off late, they have started blaming each other. The government will further strangulate the AHM. Therefore, I do not see the emergence of any alternative movement on behalf of dalits and Muslims.

In the end, I would like to say, there are two types of movement in human history. First, believe in the complete overthrow of the old political system and establish a new one. For instance, the French Revolution, Russian and Chinese revolutions. Second, never aim at the destruction of the state. Its only aim is to push the interest of the 'broader good' but certainly not to challenge the establishment. Today, we have a few movements of the first kind in India such as naxalism, Kashmir and the North-East. However, the Indian state is too strong for any such movement. It can crush it militarily any moment. That is why the government does not bother them.

Yes, we have the second type of movement, which wants the state to be more responsive. I called such movements 'middle range' or transformative movements (TM) for which state show its soft character. The basis of TM is negotiation. During the negotiation, transformative thrust increases as well as decreases. This particular element is missing in the AHM, hence, it is making it dictatorial.

18

In Fact If the Left Was a Part of the Movement They Could Have Done à la 'Wall Street': 99 per cent against the 1 per cent

Interview with Prof. Manager Pandey

Editors: ***Professor Manager Pandey*** *has contributed significantly in Hindi literature. His contribution especially lies for the development of social science criticism of literature. Including Hindi, in all languages, there has been no development of social science criticism of poetry. He has recognised the development of social science criticism in this regard. He has also seriously pondered over the historical vision of literature. Sensitivity and knowledge obtained from aesthetics and the senses are streamlined by ideology. He is a well-known Marxist critic. He is president of Jan Sanskriti Manch. His interview with* ***Rityusha Tiwary*** *unravels politics, constitutionality, democracy and media in the context of the Anna Hazare-led mobilisations.*

Rityusha Tiwary [RT]: *Can some decisive inference be made as to what kind of politics drive the Anna Movement?*

Manager Pandey [MP]: Only speculation is possible and based on facts and incidents, some inferences can be drawn. Broadly speaking, the disenchantment and despair the of middle class has been used as the force behind the movement. The Anna Hazare team has not announced any political future or political strategy and the only topic of their discourse has been corruption. Over the past two-three years, the scenario created by finance capitalism has been one serious issue of concern. The issue of corruption herein affects the labour as well as the middle class and the root cause of such a problem is big capitalist houses/firms. Corruption seeps in from top to bottom in the finance capitalist system and big-level corruption gives nutrition to the lower levels. World over, the upper class has no nation or national interest. Certainly this movement has not been the politics of the upper class. The first phase had students, teachers, employees and shopkeepers of the middles class participating in it and their collective discontent was expressed. All the political parties have proven to be corrupt and hence not one came out in support of the movement initially. In the later phase, some parties like the BJP tried to use it because of which the movement got mistreated and misnamed by the Congress, for reasons of political rivalry. The Indian National Congress has proven itself to be as corrupt as the BJP and the entire political class is seeped with this culture. So it is a political class versus civil society struggle. Therefore, the other political parties did not come to the aid of the movement initially. Some with the cleverer strategies decided that mass discontent would harm them as well. As the momentum gathered, these fence-sitters like the RJD, SP had to support it, owing to the political demand.

In essence, it is middle-class politics. Its boundary is usually till a demand for more effective administrative and judicial system and does not want any big political change. Since corruption affects these organs of polity and all the welfare mechanisms become skewed, the middle class is opposed to the phenomenon.

RT: *There are allegations that the movement has become extra-constitutional. Can such categorisation be ventured? Is it even possible?*

MP: Any mass movement is not anti-Constitution. It cannot be. It is the government that becomes anti-constitutional if it fails to cater to the peoples' hopes and aspirations manifested in the constitution. In fact, is not the government already anti-Constitution as in the preamble to the constitution the word 'socialist' is explicitly mentioned? It should be struck down as the present-day political class and has no commitment or relation to socialism either in principle or in practice. The same masses are trying to move forward their hopes, aspirations and interests through this movement so how can it be categorised as anti-Constitutional? Nothing is sacrosanct, not the constitution either. If so many amendments can take place then what is the problem in amending it further to make it more democratic and accommodate the will of the masses? In fact only those misusing, abusing and duping the masses are calling the movement unconstitutional. I mean, look at the 'vote for cash' scam. Now that is unconstitutional and why cannot the populace demand for amendments to curb such practices?

RT: *With regards to this movement and its politics, what are the imperatives for democracy in India?*

MP: The present-day administrative, political, economic, social system has been abusing and exploiting people. After Jayaprakash Narayan it is for the first time that large scale discontent has come to surface. If Arab revolutions can be termed as 'springs' then why cannot this popular movement be labelled as favourable to the democracy?

RT: *How far is it correct to say that the movement has leaned towards Right-wing political tendencies? Having said that, what should have been the role of the Left parties?*

MP: This is an allegation by the Congress party to discredit the mobilisation and the demands forwarded by the movement. Ideally the whole thing should have been the prerogative of the Left parties in India. Since they are not doing anything, the demands emanated from other quarters. Anyone doing so would influence the politics and would face support or opposition since it became an intensely political question. Just because the Left did not participate in the movement, it does not mean that it has become Rightist. In fact, the Left lost an opportunity. It is an irony that at least in India; the Left has never stood by any movement that they did not start. Since this movement is against Congress by default (because it is in power at the centre), the BJP tried to gain political mileage by being associated with the movement through popular propaganda, lending its cadres to the crowd and using slogans associated with the Party.

The Left have lost an opportune movement to participate and steer it towards the right kind of political direction. They could have exposed the centrality of capitalism as the root cause of corruption and they could have challenged undisputed, unbound capitalism. In fact, if the Left was a part of the movement they could have done a la 'wall street': 99 per cent against the 1 per cent. Then the movement could have made a structural and systemic change which would have been more far reaching then its current limited mandate. There would have been only two courses possible: either the intellectuals would have supported it or rejected it. Even if the latter would have materialised (which in any case was more likely), the Left would have gained sympathisers. I agree that a revolution would have not happened but that does not mean that change for the better cannot be an agenda in itself.

RT: *It has been said that very few people participated in the movement and hence it cannot be termed as the 'country's aspiration'. Is it plausible argument against the movement?*

MP: Who barred the other people from participating in the movement? And more specifically who has stopped the others from mobilising even a bigger crowd and a more voluminous movement? Today, the sociology of the Communist movement in India is majorly driven by the middle class and it is steadily losing its traditional base in worker/labour/ agricultural classes. People like Arundhati Roy have their politics embedded in the economic/social strata even above that. So she cannot decide whether the workers/labourers/agricultural classes are represented by the movement. Today, intellectually, anything original means 'disagreeing with others'. Such arguments are in sync with this popular practice.

RT (intervenes): *Is it a hype created by the media?*

MP: All the political parties carry forward their political agenda through the media, so this allegation is unfounded. The middle-class centrality in this movement has attracted the attention of the media which is good for the movement at least. Anyway, all the problems that have the sympathy of the intellectuals are the only problems or what? Why is there no support for Irom Sharmila who has been fasting for more than a decade? If this movement has garnered attention at least it will do some good to the culture of protest and popular demands.

19

[A]s Opposed to the Western Belief That Socialism Will Die with the Collapse of Soviet Union, Voices against Capitalism-Induced Crisis are Reviving Demands for the Socialist Pattern of Development

Interview with Prof. Tulsi Ram

Editors: *Professor Tulsi Ram is one of the important signposts of the synthesis of Marxism, dalit discourse and Buddhism. Trained as a social scientist, which includes specialisation in international politics with reference to the former USSR and Russia, his intervention has all along been remarkable in the field of literature. His recently published autobiography* Murdahiya Volume One, *has laid the foundation for looking at lived experience from the social science perspective in which context, system and surrounding institutional set-up are more explicated than the 'mere self'. His interview with* ***Rityusha Tiwary*** *vividly reveals numerous facets of movements and implications.*

Rityusha Tiwary [RT]: *Do you think Anna Hazare's anti-corruption movement is influenced by the current pro-democracy movements in the Arab countries and the surrounding region?*

Tulsi Ram [TR]: Frankly speaking, I don't like this kind of a movement. Anna is raising the issue of corruption but he does not raise the issue of poverty, unemployment or education. Of course, his movement is influenced by movements particularly in North Africa and recently in Yemen and Tunisia, where NGOs are playing a very dangerous role, aided by American [the US] foreign policymakers. The US is using a lot of NGOs to dislodge so many governments across the world which do not subscribe to American policies, particularly the foreign policy. It all began in Georgia a few years ago when the twice, elected President Eduard Shevardnadze was forced to resign in the aftermath of boycott of Parliamentary elections, orchestrated by the George Soros Foundation—a US-led NGO. The people, empowered by funds from the foundation, claimed that the elections were not fair. Mikheil Saakashvili, who subsequently won the Presidential elections, was a US citizen. In international politics, this was interpreted as the Georgian trend by the Western scholars—a spate of coloured revolutions following Georgia's Rose Revolution. It is not difficult to trace the connection between the Soros Foundation and the US, George Soros being one of the largest shareholders in the US. He funds hundreds of NGOs across the world and dislodges governments through them; it is quite a known fact out in the open. He is the biggest shareholder in America and he is what is popularly known in India as *suttebaj*. A decade ago when he announced that he was going to provide 10 billion dollars to different NGOs in America out of his personal earning for a year, his name became known to people as the man who was funding NGOs for very nefarious reasons. Owing to this strategy, Ukraine, Kyrgyzstan the former Soviet Bloc and East European countries have all become NATO members. In fact, none of these countries can see any irregularity or instability as even the Baltic States have become NATO members.

One needs to see this as a larger game plan of the US which initially concentrated on the former Soviet /Trans-Caucasian Region. Long ago in 1889, Lord Curzon, when he was a correspondent for *The Times* in London, mentioned in his Trans-Caucasia Report that this region was a chess board and a game was being played here for domination in international politics and the region was a centre of East–West rivalry.

Today, Egypt, Tunisia, Libya and other countries are also being influenced by the US-led NGOs because of this rivalry. The way the Libyan government was overthrown by the people, funded and armed by such NGOs, is providing incentives to other NGOs in the world to intervene and dislodge governments. And I think Anna Hazare's Movement is badly influenced by this trend in North Africa and Egypt recently.

RT: *Can you throw some light on the political premise of Anna Hazare's movement? Do you think it can be categorised as extra constitutional or anti-Constitution?*

TR: In the name of opposing corruption, when Anna decided to launch propaganda against a political party (Congress) in Hisar, it became clear that it is not a social movement, rather a political movement and they have their own long-tern ambition to acquire power for themselves, by dislodging the government. Initially it does not look so but any movement raised on populism ends up being a way to dislodge the existing government and capture power for oneself.

They are developing themselves as an extra-constitutional authority. There is existing constitution under which any government has to work. They are anti-constitutional which is evident from some of the statements made by members of team Anna like Kejriwal — 'Anna is above the parliament'. These kinds of statements smack of dictatorial overtones. No individual can be above parliament or constitution. For centuries there was no constitution in India and hundreds of princely states existed. Post-1947, India is integrated due to the constitutional government otherwise it would have been divided into many parts. So the constitution is the basis of any democratic system in the world; if constitutional provisions are violated, then even if the whole attention is purely on democracy, it cannot be a success.

If an extra-constitutional authority like Anna emerges in our country, it is a dangerous trend even if it does not seem that they are going to pose any danger initially. They are influencing the people by raising popular demand of removing corruption. In fact, the media propagated such speeches round-the-clock and in turn played a very poisonous role. The media hailed Anna's statements against Parliament, political figures or constitutional provision. It is the parliament which is authorised to make any law. Any individual cannot impose his personal opinion on the parliament. The members of Anna's team were forever in a threatening mood, claiming to go on agitating, which is very undemocratic. Any changes in the legislation need to be authorised by people through legitimate channels of the parliament and judiciary. Any such movement initially looks popular but by and large, it is a dictatorial movement, and in this case, Anna's demands are nothing short of *fatwas*. It is a very one sided movement. The real mandate of this movement is barely in thousands and this is precisely the way Maoists function. They take sanction from a few thousands to kill anybody.

A basic social movement should raise real issues—unemployment, poverty, lack of education, health facilities— and raising these will benefit people and they can be served better. The Issue of corruption, as raised by this movement, only catches the mind of people and is far from practical. Black money and corruption cannot be checked by making stiff laws. Look at the case of laws punishing murder. There are a number of stringent laws against it but that has not stopped this particular crime in our country. Therefore, to think that issues of corruption and black money can be dealt with by making laws is wrong. It is a question of large scale moral education for changing the mindset and this is a reform required in the education system right from primary level.

RT: *Over the years, has democracy strengthened in India?*

TR: The Indian democracy has been strengthened in due course of time and today, politically many strengthening measures like 33% reservation for women in the Panchayati Raj Institutions, Right to Information [RTI] and many other democratically enlarged rights have been provided to people, expanding the scope of democracy. In fact, through RTI, we have been provided with tools to weed out corruption. Though corruption has seeped into every institution in our country, still democracy is expanding ... which is good. If women are given reservation in the parliament, it will change the entire historical development in India because women have lagged behind in every area. The main concentration of NGOs or any social organisation should be on strengthening the democratic system first without which any further development is impossible.

RT [intervenes]: *So, Anna's movement has strengthened the Indian democracy? What is the role of the NGOs in this?*

TR: Practically, this particular movement is not going to help the common people by raising the issue of corruption. It just catches the mind of middle-class people living in the metropolitan cities. Common people have nothing to do with it. They are concerned with unemployment, price rise, poverty, lack of health facilities, illiteracy. So this anti-corruption movement is normally concentrated in metropolitan cities and by using the mass media they are forwarding their propaganda. The media changes the psychological thinking of the masses. Otherwise, members of Team Anna like Arvind Kejriwal, who is always threatening and demanding, would not become popular. In fact, it is a practice for ex-bureaucrats to resign from their jobs and open NGOs, the biggest money-making enterprise today. Even Hazare's NGO gets millions of funds which would have been scarce when Anna was serving in the Indian army. The same applies to all the members of his team. The NGOs are indeed becoming the biggest source of corruption in India. Just to invest in this field, people open NGOs on any and every issue since the funding from various sources like Sorros Foundation, Switzerland, Denmark and others is abundant. The nexus between funded money and corruption is obvious everywhere: one example is the Soviet Union under Gorbachev and Russia since 1991. They just have to cater to populist demands and these demands need not necessarily have any logic. This is evident in so many populist movements like the one raised by Medha Patekar. On the one hand, the lack of electricity deprives common people from getting proper basic civic amenities; on the other hand, the construction of any and every dam is opposed by NGOs. This reveals their dual character. The need for large scale electricity production is imminent in India, yet NGOs in the name of ecological preservation oppose such developments tooth and nail. They hamper any developmental issue and many times such nefarious activities are funded by the developed world. The social mandate of NGOs gets severely limited due to such dubious activities and now they are infringing on the political space as well with equally dubious claims.

RT: *Is Right-wing politics behind the Anna Movement?*

TR: Yes of course. The Right-wing party like BJP is out of politics and that is why it is trying to make use of any such movement to reap political benefit. The party cadre that becomes the crowd in rallies organised by the party is seen everywhere in the Anna movement.

The slogans used in the movement like '*Bharat Mata ki jai*' or '*Vande Matram*' are diverting the attention of the masses to Right-wing political propaganda. In fact, such trappings have converted Anna's movement as a typical political movement which is against the spirit of NGOs. In any country, the clear mandate of NGOs has been limited to social movement and social development.

RT: *What conclusions can be drawn in terms of the class/caste/gender/ minority component of the movement? Can any inference be drawn regarding its urban/rural landscape?*

TR: It has nothing to do with any of these. Some elites and former bureaucrats have joined with a sense of making money out the whole practice. It has no bearing on these problems. The movement does not show any cognizance to communal divide or gender bias or class disparities. They are openly giving statements that they have no problems if communal forces are joining them. India has suffered under communalism over the years and if organisations like Sangh Parivar are allowed to come in the forefront through movements and forums like these, it is very detrimental to the democratic fibre of our political system. These communal forces use religion to instigate people along populist notions and this is against the spirit of democratic or secular systems.

The rural is totally absent in this movement and it is essentially an urban phenomenon, very restricted in its mass appeal.

RT: *Is capitalist crisis a tangible force behind reinvigoration of protest? Is corruption a capitalist phenomenon?*

TR: It all began with the collapse of the Soviet Union in 1991. It was a kind of a shield for the defence of third world countries against all kinds of nefarious ideologies emanating from the USA like liberalisation, privatisation and globalisation. Poverty, unemployment, illiteracy all have risen very fast under globalisation. Under the so-called economic crisis, the entire concentration of the Western developed world is on developing economies like India and China. Though the developed world is making profits, it is just not enough and hence the 'crisis' of not making more money. So, this corporate capitalism has developed very fast after globalisation. Rich people are becoming richer overnight and others are getting poorer by the day. This is exposing the inherent weakness of capitalism and as opposed to the Western belief that socialism will die with the collapse of the Soviet Union, voices against capitalism-induced crisis are reviving demands for the socialist pattern of development. This is happening in the developed Western world itself on the streets of the US, the NATO countries and others.

Yes, corruption is inherently a product of a rigid capitalist system and the people within this very system are raising their voice against it. It is intrinsically linked to moral degradation as well. The globalisation artificially creates economic crisis and thus a chain of morally debunked practices like corruption follows.

20

The Anna Movement could not Produce a Counter Hegemony

Interview with Dr. Hilal Ahmed

Editors: ***Dr Hilal Ahmed*** *is one of the sine qua non signposts of modern India with reference to political Islam, politics of symbols and masques as monuments. He is intensely engaged with Muslim political representation. Currently, he is working on the political reflection of Muslim identity formation through Hindi Quran and reading Waqf politics. Regarding Muslim Identity formation, he has two postulations: there is a limitation of uni-identity or fragmented identity approach; secondly, Muslim identity formation takes place by way of global embeddedness along with localisation. Both global and local constitute intrinsic aspects of Muslim identity formation. This interview has its own trajectory. The questions sent to him for this interview on the Anna Hazare agitation by* ***Dhananjay Rai*** *were dubbed as 'Typical Marxist' questions by him. He emphasises on 'more' creativity on the 'Marxist standpoint'. These questions were verbally put to him and recorded by* ***Shashank Chaturvedi. Rityusha Tiwary*** *hastened the process of transcription.* ***Pavel Tomar*** *has transcribed this interview.*

Shashank Chaturvedi [SC]: *What is the politics of the Anna Hazare Movement?*

Hilal Ahmed [HA]: In my opinion, before making any comment on the politics of Anna Hazare, it would be important to look at the manner in which the idea of politics itself has been used by the movement in its two phases. In the first phase, it stays as completely apolitical, and that's why they felt that they would not allow any political party to speak from their platform. The symbolism of the movement is equally important, because if you look at that first phase, the figure of *Bharat Mata* is there, as if politics is corrupt, politics is a dirty game. And you need some kind of a pious representation of something, by evoking that [which] you can answer to those who are actually running the business. So that was the spirit of the movement, or the understanding of the idea of the political in the first phase. But surprisingly, in the second part, this has gone out. Here you will find a picture of Mahatma Gandhi, as if the so-called movement is actually trying to interpret or create a new meaning of politics around the issue of corruption. And that is precisely what happened when several people, including Kejriwal and others, made speeches repeatedly trying to avoid the apolitical tag which they were using in the first phase. So, in order to understand the politics of this, it is, in my opinion, important to look at these two important interpretations of the idea of the political in the movement itself. So, that is one point.

The second point is how to understand the politics of the movement. Now the conceptual question in this is what a movement then is. I am not going to take you to the debate on the idea of movement and various things. But what is a movement? Today we have to be conceptually very clear when we use this term, because we have got a 'campaign'—another important term—you have got a 'movement' and a 'political party'. So all the organised forms of social action are there, and unfortunately in India, we do not have any conceptual take on these terms. As a result, we are actually dealing with these things in a no man's land. We take it as granted as to what is a movement along with politics. So, if we understand, two things I would like to emphasis: first is the understanding of these people in relation to the idea of the political. That is important. And second is their own organisation structure. And is it appropriate to call it a movement, or not? I have a problem with this whole concept of 'Team Anna'—what does it mean? Because it is a media creation. What is the meaning of 'Team India' for the Indian cricket team? We have been hearing this word 'Indian Cricket Team' for a long time. But suddenly in 2008 or 2009, this term—'Team India', 'Team Australia'— became very popular. What does it mean? Is there any conscious move to make sense of something which is different from the 'Indian Cricket Team'? Or is it something to recognise or underline a group identity in a different way? We do not know. So, when media says that these are two things which are interchangeably used—'Team Anna' and 'Anna Movement'—my question is if we are conscious of various kinds of social actions at the moment. It would be important for us to make a distinction between popular terms like 'Team Anna', 'Anna Movement', 'campaign' and other forms. Only then, will it be possible for us to make sense of what we call as politics of this 'movement'. So this is unpacking of something given to us: 'Anna Movement' and whatever. Now this question has got a moral dimension as well. What is my understanding of that? Before taking a position, it is important to look at the way in which they define themselves. For example, who is Anna Hazare—an individual or a phenomenon? So, you know, before conceptualising these terms, as students of politics, this is our responsibility to look at the way in which they prefer to. For example, I was reading that thing, 'Students' Report to the Nation'. The manner in which they call themselves secular is problematic. Because 'secular' is a term which comes in relation to communal in our context, and it has got a politics of its own. Now you are saying you are secular, and at the same time you are underlining your apolitical character, as if whatever you are saying is apolitical and it has got a legitimacy to be accepted as a final truth. Now, this is something happening with the Anna Movement as well. They are actually projecting themselves as the final truth of some kind. The moral dimension of these things is that we really do not know about these things. So I would stick to the manner in which they define themselves, rather my own sense of that, quite similar to Osama Bin Laden: I do not know him. I do not know his organisation. I know only his. Now acts are crucial. And my criticism or support or whatever, is in relation to the act, which we actually receive through the media. When I visited Ramlila Maidan, there were two or three kinds of people. There were people who were actually hoping for some kind of breaking news. Now this whole idea of 'breaking news' is very interesting. You need something sensational, which is extraordinary. There is a difference between 'every day' and 'critical event'. Every day is something which is 'normal', which is given, which does not have the so-called 'excitement'. But this was something 'exciting' for the media, because they were creating something very different. So, how to do that? How to do things differently? Somehow they managed to do things differently. I can answer this question with reference to Antonio Gramsci. There is a very interesting distinction between spontaneity and consciousness. What is spontaneity? He says that when people are not happy with their own lives, they have got a genuine anxiety, genuine resentment against the system, something like that. But this resentment cannot be considered as something like a consciousness to overthrow a system. Here, he talks about an organic intellectual whose responsibility is to create a counter hegemony. Only then something like consciousness emerges.

So, from that point of view, the resentment is there. What the Anna Movement did, and virtually failed at, in my opinion, was that they could not produce a counter hegemony. And that is why, I would say, to answer this question morally, they are intellectually very weak because they do not know how to translate such resentment into a genuine politics of genuine change. So this is what I would say is my opinion of Team Anna or the Anna Movement, whatever.

And precisely because they were very weak intellectually, they kept on repeating 'Lokpal Bill', trying to reduce everything to that. They could have looked at, for example, at the manner in which Gandhi used the Khilafat. Khilafat was just a minor scandal. No Indian Muslim could ever visit Turkey; they were completely unaware of that. Gandhi used it very strategically—in such a way that other kinds of issues could be answered through this, which this movement did not, for example, rising prices, farmers' suicides. The Anna team make some kind of an assertion, but that assertion is some kind of a tokenism. And that's a problem with the Anna Team. They did not say anything about the land acquisition debate. Farmers' suicide is something which is very crucial and also the issue of Structural Adjustment Programmes and Occupy Wall Street movement. They could link to these. But they failed. Why? Because intellectually, they do not have courage. They are intellectually very weak. There are three or four kinds of people: retired bureaucrats, who have got their own mentality and way of functioning; They have a very non-structural meaning of corruption, like if I take a bribe, this is corruption. Time and again Kiran Bedi says that now onwards you keep a *topi* in your pocket whenever someone asks you for a bribe. It is something like *jaago re* type of an advertisement of Tata Tea, as if that very act is enacted in that way. The point is that, they were intellectually very weak, and that's why they virtually failed to link or establish a link between different issues and the so called Jan Lokpal Bill. I am not saying that they are weak precisely because they are not interested. This is something clearly reflected in the coalition of non-party political actors. One kind of coalition is done by Priya. They are everything which is non-political. They put everything in one category. The second example could be the National Alliance of People's Movements. They are not interested in those issues which are overlapping each other. You can talk of dalit, but what about dalit women. You can talk of women, but what about Muslim women. You can talk about minorities, but what about the Parsi minority. These are crucial issues and they present them as if they are not interested in critical issues. The conclusion we get is that we are a very goody-goody kind of a coalition, where we come, meet and say that the state is bad, system is so and we go home, that's it. So there is no urge to develop an intellectual critique of the system, and precisely because of that there is a no alternative discourse in which the question of alternative is already reduced from its potential. Nobody is interested in talking about the alternative. Nobody is interested in making a coalition, making bridges. So, that's clearly reflected in the movement.

SC: *Do you think that the movement is anti-Constitution?*

HA: This is a very interesting question. What is constitutional? Unfortunately, when we refer to the constitution or when we refer to religion, we assume that the constitution and religion are fixed entities: they never change. But the fact is that the meaning of constitution, and religiosity are discursively constituted, and because these are discursively constituted, it is very important to recognise the manner in which we talk about the constitution and in what context. When we talk about constitutional validity of this kind of movement or whatever, I have a great difficulty in understanding this kind of happenings or collective action as movement, because then, as I have said, then you have to make a distinction between what is campaign, online campaign and the movement and where the boundaries lie—how these things are getting into it. I am not entirely sure. So that's why the question of Constitution is very important. The question of representation is coming in a different way, through this movement. Now they are saying that they are the 'people'. But if we look at the constitution, it is also of the people. So who are the 'people' and who is the best representative of the people: MPs, MLAs, whatever? And when I was watching the parliamentary debate, this kept coming that 'we are the true representatives of the people'. But when I went to the movement, they also said that they were the true representatives of the people. So when we say the constitution, at that very moment when these two parties are criticising each other, one referring to the idea of democracy, and the other was referring to the idea of constitutional democracy. Now what is Constitution in this? The constitution comes up as a kind of text, which is free for various kinds of interpretations. So what was Anna's understanding of that? That is important because thereafter Kapil Sibal came into picture, saying that if they have courage they should fight elections. Kejriwal made an equally interesting point, that they were not interested in electoral politics and that is why they were actually doing this movement. And when they went to Hisar, they made another important argument that Anna is above the constitution because he is representing the people. Now these are polemical arguments and these statements are not at all serious, and we need not take them seriously. But the point they raise is very important. Now, from this point I would like to link it to the idea of representation which is given in the Constitution: what is the meaning of representation there? As I said, the Constitution is not fixed and has multiple forms of interpretation. In the 1950s and 60s the idea of representation was primarily in relation to electoral bodies: you are represented through these bodies. At that point of time, the Indian people were not mature in playing politics of electoral games. But in the 1970s, when the electoral system got lost in some kind of, JP movement is the best example to demonstrate the fact that there is a possibility of an alternative politics of representation which can be constituted outside the electoral politics. And this is precisely what happened in the 1970s. From the late 1960s, you have some kind of a model. Rajni Kothari's entire argument is that the Congress system is accommodating different identities into it, precisely because there is a constitution and the interpretation of the constitution is coming as a form of the the Congress system by which you accommodate different identities into it. But the same Rajni Kothari made a different argument in the post-Emergency period, so the second form of representational politics emerged in post 1970s when the civil liberty movement started. Before that, if we look at the Communist Party movement, before the emergence of naxalites, it decided to participate in the electoral politics. I took a long interview of late Harkishan Singh Surjeet in 1996, and I asked him the reasons behind that decision, and the kind of Marxism they were following when they declared participating in electoral politics, and he said that they realised that the Constitution was an outcome of a struggle, and we had to recognise the potential of national movements in the 1950s, so they decided to participate into it, but it does not mean and it did not happen that they discontinue to struggle outside the parliament. So that outside Parliament constituted a different form or representation which was given in the parliament. In the 1970s, that got dispersed, and then you have got a parallel kind of a civil liberty movement, which you might call fashion-group kind of a representation where you need not get into parliamentary form of representation to say that I am a representative of someone. And new social movements, particularly women's movements, adivasi movements and minority movements actually intensified this kind of phase which was opened up by the civil liberties movement.

But in post-globalisation India what really happened was that because political parties realised the fact that their form of representation is not the only one or electoral forms of representation is not the only form of representation in India, they were keen to create a structure which could be accommodated in the formal institutional set up. And that is why in my opinion, the NAC (National Advisory Council) came into being. What is this? You have got people into it, and these people are coming from many different backgrounds, they have got resentment against government policy, but these people are not fighting election. So, the discourse of creating an alternative platform, for politics and for representation, was made available to people like Anna Hazare in 2005–6 by UPA. Now what Anna Hazare and his team are doing is that they are trying to manipulate the structural changes introduced by the UPA through the NAC. So, my argument is that the Constitution is interpreted in order to create structures which could accommodate voices which are accommodated in a conventional manner. That is, precisely, what I would say on this question.

SC: *Has Indian democracy been strengthened or compromised?*

HA: What is democracy, then? If democracy means what Lalu Yadav has to say on the Jan Lokpal Bill in the parliament, if that is the meaning of democracy, then obviously that form of democracy is reduced to electoral form of democracy. I do not believe in that. But the real sense of the idea of democracy in India is more than this. And this is precisely where, apart from all other things, what the achievement of this movement is. This movement actually brings the question of democracy into the realm of the media-dominated public sphere, which was earlier dominated by cricket, Bollywood and sex. Now these things are replaced by the serious question of democracy and politics. In that sense, this is an achievement of the movement, and that is precisely what happened when England came to India for a return tour of the one-day series, and the movement had just finished. The media was not interested in that series. And the media is completely driven by market. So something serious happened, which is quite evident in that. So, now the question of democracy and politics has become the question of everyday. That's why I'd say it provided a great push to the idea of democracy.

SC: *What is the nature [caste/class/gender/minority status] of the AHM?*

HA: This is a problematic area.

SC: *Can you link it there to the Right-wing politics in India?*

HA: Yes. There is a formal or informal idea of mainstream in India. And somehow we adhere to it. And interestingly, we are so keen to have that mainstream reflected in almost everything of our public activity. You have got institutes that would ask you how many dalits you have got into the movement, how many women you have. You have an Indian cricket team; you ask how many regions are represented in that. The point I am making is that is it possible to have a completely non-identity oriented question, on which you can do any kind of politics, without giving up your identity. You cannot. It is completely absurd to assume that people will somehow give up their identities and participate in completely secular politics. But there is a possibility, and this has happened during the time of Emergency, but fortunately or unfortunately, this is the beauty of Rightist politics, and a weakness of Leftist politics, that we never realise the fact that whenever the question of a grand coalition comes up, and there is no clear representation of identities in these coalitions, we suddenly allege that, look, this is your game plan, you are into it. We do not know what really happens behind the scene, but my question is: is it very important to actually ask this question, because the question of corruption, and the question of privatisation, these affect all of us?

Because we are conditioned to the idea of mainstream, and precisely because of that, we are conditioned to look at how many faces we have in such a coalition. And that has been the problem with the movement. The movement could have said that we are not interested in showing totems. There is identity in all movements but because these allegations come in, somehow they respond in the same language which was given already to them. I find it hard to understand this question. Do we really need this question?

Now come to the effect part. Suppose I am leading a movement against globalisation. The effect of globalisation on different identities could be one way of understanding it. But it does not mean that when you oppose something larger and comprehensive, do you need to organise people in their own shell? I find it a bit problematic. You recognise one's identity. But you do not need to confine him to that identity.

And, precisely look at your question. The question is, again: the Hindu is completely absent from this, as if the idea of Hindu is acceptable.

SC: *Is Right-wing politics behind it?*

HA: Yes. I do not think we actually force one to give their identity. But at the same time, we ask people to actually assume a new identity, and participate in the issue, and oppose a larger question. So if we could do that, then there is a possibility to do that.

Now the question of class is different. The question of class is opposed to identities. From a Marxist point of view, it can be said that this is a class-based movement because there is upper class representation. But again, is it possible in the kind of society in which we live, do a purely class-based movement? Look at what Communist Parties are doing, look at what trade unions are doing. And what was Marx's understanding of the relation between trade unions and political parties. Do we find that reflected today in the acts of Communist parties and trade unions now? I do not think so. And that is the difference between our kind of Marxism, and the Marxism we saw in China. The Chinese interpretation of Marxism was completely internalised in that milieu. We were so brahminical in our attitude towards Marxism that we stuck to the classical formulation which was completely abstract, and we stick to that, and this is precisely the problem. Obviously the AHM has a class background if its own. But look at the class background of all revolutionaries who participated in revolutionary politics throughout last 150 years. They all came from the middle class. So, can we say that the Communist parties have got a class background?

De-classisation was essential, but somehow, if we look at the practices of all the Communist parties, including ML (Marxist Leninist), I think this idea has disappeared. How can we put that question, then? So, what should be the take of those who are inclined towards Marxism, people like me? I would say that is true that AHM has a class bias. But this is a very popular kind of a movement. Again, Gramsci is relevant for me: resentment is there, people are actually cultivating the resentment, and as an organic intellectual, this is my duty to put the class question into it. But Communist parties, and people with Communist background have virtually ignored that. Nobody went there. How many Communist party people did go there? They were completely apathetic. They did not make any statement on this. Something which is happening at a grand level, media is hijacking it; people from every part of India are participating in it. This is democratic, some kind of a democratic upsurge, and this upsurge we, who claim to represent 'people and class', did not go there and hijack it. But they went, RSS people went and participated into it, without showing their banners. Look at their way of functioning, and our way of functioning. Because we are still 'very' Marxist, we are very brahminical. For us, the question of revolution is like the Day of Judgement, and we are waiting for that, as if the God of Marxism will come, and the Day of Judgement will happen. But this is not the case. What Marx told in his writings, he provided some kind of an outline of a theory of critique, but he never suggested that this is the route and you must take it. This is very important from a methodological point in Marxist politics, that most of Marx's writings talk about an idea of dialectic. What is dialectic? He was very critical of those who were instrumental economists; he was not an economist of that kind. What was his take on this: there is something called matter and consciousness, and their mutual relationship is very complex. He knew matter well— the entire *Capital* is about knowing that matter—but he was equally interested in the question of consciousness. That's why Lenin and Mao took it very seriously, because they were practical politicians. They understood that realm where consciousness is played out as politics. So, critique of matter is one part; we need not stick to that. This question is coming from that point of view. It is sticking to some kind of an economic explanation of the system, globalisation et cetera. What Marxist politics is not understandable to me? Because what we have is a critique of capitalism, politics is to die for a common cause. Cause is not a critique of capitalism. Cause is to make an egalitarian society, for which you do not have any blueprint. So, for the construction of the blueprint of that utopia, political parties somehow fail to recognise that utopia. Precisely because of that, we explain it beautifully. Those who are well-versed with Marxism, explain the critique very well. We are caught up in a methodologically binary framework; we see things in binaries— there is a capitalism, there is a globalisation, there are certain imaginary people on that side, and others on this side, but politics is played out in between, in various way in which people and system get mixed up. This is the problem identified by Partha Chateerjee. But he failed again, because of his rigid Marxist framework, in his recent 2008 *EPW* article, to understand the complexity that this is not a fair. You cannot say that if the state cannot participate in the realm of the people, and the people won't take advantage of the state, so the making of an egalitarian society is never talked about. Markandey Katju, in his article in *The Hindu*, asked a very stupid question, 'What is India', and answered it in schoolboyish manner. But I liked his stake that we have forgotten to talk about a good society. The beauty of Enlightenment rationality is its control over people, but there is something more to it. That is in Kant: reason. Through this control we can create a world which is free from all bad things. Part of our criticism of Enlightenment is because of that, but that madness of a consciousness imagining a huge emancipatory society we do not bother to talk about.

What is important in the AHM? That, it is forcing us to think of something positive. You need not to look at *Hind Swaraj*—a beautiful text, in which there is a promise that is possible. We all remember Gandhi for his critique of modernity, but he said that it is not necessary that something which has not happened in the past should not happen in the future. This is his commitment in the ability of man to change the society. That commitment is completely missing in our political discourse. Precisely because such kind, of questions are coming up. This much is on class.

Now over to the gender question. I am not very sure about it. I am not sure how to deal with this question. I am not the right person to respond to it. But consider the impact of the AHM, It happened in the month of Ramazan. I decided to stroll around the Ramlila Maidan and talk to the people. No one was interested in that. Some interesting arguments came out, like corruption is good for Muslims. Why? Many thought that if communalism prevails, corruption is the only way they could survive. Young, very young old, shopkeepers all made such kinds of arguments. Generally, people from Islamic backgrounds oppose taking bribes. But this is an accepted norm. For them, this movement is some kind of a *dikhava.* They are projecting something else while they are interested in seeking a place in the structure. What was the reason behind that?

If we talk about Dalits, or about what dalits say about Mayawati, the impact of this discourse on corruption is very deep, particularly on urban Muslims, because most of them are in the paddy kind of business where corruption alone ensures survival, because you cannot ignore the nature and caste character of the administration.

SC: *Is it an urban or rural phenomenon?*

HA: Again, this binary is problematic. These are creations of the media. If I reformulate the question like this: is it a media-created movement, or is there something more to it. Many people from rural areas participate in it. Recently I was in Maharashtra, and Anna Hazare is very popular in the countryside there. We cannot say that it is entirely an urban phenomenon. But they came out on the question of farmers' suicides. But because of the media, it transcends the boundaries of that. The movement actually travelled a lot.

SC: *Is this populism a product of neoliberalism and global capital crisis to drive away the structural attention?*

HA: This is a very typical, instrumentalist type of a question. The vocabulary is coming out from a certain understanding of Marxism. I'd say that not all capitalists would sit down one day and prepare a strategy on how to survive. There are things which we do strategically. There is an unsaid consensus on this, and that is the beauty of politics, that I did not say anything, you did not say anything but we did the thing in the same way. I am not talking of individuals, but structures. When we say structures of capitalism, there is a consensus in that. If we believe in a certain Marxism, and that there is contestation at every level, how could we say that there is an instrumental relation between a movement and the enterprises. These are some peculiarly contested manners. There is a question commonly raised against NGOs, that they are products of neoliberalism et cetera. But if you look closely at the relation between NGOs, the states, and the corporate world, you will find a different kind of contestation happening. Not all NGOs are funded by corporate houses, not all of them are protected by the state. The NGOs which receive such funding find it rather difficult to survive.

If I were to do an alternative Marxist politics, I would do away with such categories. These categories are completely misleading, and these are actually polemical categories. We say such things when we mobilise people, but in an intellectual discussion we have to be very truthful about the way in which the question is asked. I would say that the best way to understand these things is to unpack structural linkages. I would say that this question is right in one respect: in seeking the relation between ex-bureaucrats and some kind of politics. I came to know recently that Harsh Mander did not resign immediately after the Gujarat riots. He waited till the time his twenty years in service could be completed, so that he could get the benefits in his next life. Then he was offered a very lucrative job in Action-Aid. Then he mobilised people through his colleagues in other states to his rallies. Is it not something we need to understand closely? These may be completely wrong, but we have to understand these linkages, and then their politics. Without that, simple deductionism that this is happening because of this structure, I do not think that this is an appropriate way to understand things.

SC: *Are corruption and germination of protest quintessential capitalist phenomena?*

HA: This is a good question but good in one respect. Again it is coming out of a certain understanding of Marxism, I would not criticise that because I have already made so many comments upon that. It is a good question if we take the instrumental logic out of it, and then contextualise it—contextualise it in the Indian context, especially in post-global India. Look at the ways in which this idea of corruption is understood. Then we can establish a link between the crisis of capitalism, and the corruption which we get to hear.

But again, saying that there is a crisis of capitalism and that is why corruption is happening, I would not support it, because I do not see any evidence to support this kind of a claim. Some kind of hard work is needed. Some kinds of questions are very legitimate questions. I would have to dedicate two to three years of my life to understand such issues. Without doing any empirical research, any investment into the conceptual realm in which these kinds of questions are constituted, this exercise would not be able to produce the desired result. We all have some kind of views on these questions, but what is essentially important is that we have to have evidence. Evidence is of two kinds. One is empirical. We require some kind of data, some happening, and conceptually we have to make ourselves acute. For example, we talk of India-specific capitalism, is it not appropriate to investigate into what is India-specific corruption? For example, the book *Foul Play,* is actually a compilation of previous cases from 1952–2000, all the corruption issues which came into public discussion.

SC: *Final Comments!*

HA: Nothing is final. Whatever I have said is very preliminary, very general and common-sense things. I wanted to write on a theoretical part of it, and contextualising it in the Indian debate and so on. But I am not fully satisfied with these questions. Because these questions are quite typical, interpreted either as per common sense, or in one sense of Marxism. I consider myself a Marxist, but as Manindra Nath Thakur says, it is important to understand Marx's method. It is important to look at class, capitalism and correction in his way, but we have to contextualise them in our times.

21

Reflections on the Anti-Corruption Movement of Anna Hazare

Reflections with Manindra Nath Thakur

'The movement has to realize that the real enemy is capitalism. Therefore, struggle against corruption will have to be a struggle against capitalism and struggle for socialism'.

Self-reflection is one of the oldest ways to engage with surrounding and distant questions. The advantage in this way is to reflect dually in the form question and answer. Seeming contradictions get reconciled or reconciled in answers. It exhibits that there are certain queries which can be reconciled but others cannot be. Either way, the author has an opportunity to bring a slew of concerns while solving or not solving many puzzles. Autonomy in this method is self-imposed which is a difficult terrain. ***Manindra Nath Thakur*** *has chosen this particular way of engagement which covers the entire gamut and concern from people to movement and movement to people. He has been engaged on diversified issues ranging from Indian polity to Indian political theory and Indian philosophy. Marxism and religion are constant concern in his academic pursuance.*

Ed: *How do you look at the Anti corruption movement of Anna Hazare (now onwards ACM)? Do you think it is a specific moment of Indian democracy that has triggered off this movement?*

MNT: I think the movement is an important intervention in the theory and practice of Indian democracy. Let us have an overview of the situation. We know that the economic policies pursued almost for last four decades have produced a difficult situation for Indian democracy. We started with the idea, 'India that is Bharat', but we have reached a situation where India and Bharat are two different worlds. It is no more about the difference in rural and urban India; rather it is difference between the classes in Indian society. This issue has been raised by many people. Look at the difference between the two. According to Credit Suisse's assessment, the top 1 per cent of the population own 15.9 per cent of India's wealth, the top 5 per cent own 38.3 per cent wealth and the top 10 per cent have 52.9 per cent, more than half the wealth of the county. In contrast, the bottom 20 per cent own 1 per cent and the bottom 10 per cent own only 0.2 per cent of the wealth.[1] Remember that this data is only for the year 2002–03. In fact, one would not deny the fact that it must have become worse in last few years.

I want to bring home the point that such a situation is against our democracy and against the preamble or directive principles of the constitution. Therefore, I see such a movement as an important intervention in the malfunctioning of both.

Ed: *But how do you link this growing inequality with ACM?*

MNT: I think the average Indian is not able to explain the hardship that he is facing in her everyday life. On the one hand they now have access to the information about goods and services available for quality of life but have no money to access them. Whatever used to be available in the sectors of health and education even that has been either withdrawn or reduced to skeleton services. One of the most visible explanations for this growing inequality and hardship is corruption. In last few years so many scams have been exposed that people take that as symbol of system to protest against. That explains multiplicity of reasons for participation in the movement given by participating people when they are asked by the electronic media.

Ed: *But why do you think the system is being symbolized by corruption? We have probably a clean Prime Minister and the UPA government has taken action against the ministers engaged in corrupt practices.*

MNT: I can only talk about the people's perception as I have no access to the information regarding the involvement of political leaders in the recent scams. I think people have got this perception that such huge scams cannot take place without the knowledge of the top leaders of the party. They do not have evidence for this but people's perception does not wait for the evidence. The burden of proof in this case remains with the leaders. There is a general perception that many of the top leaders work in close interaction with the multinational corporations and the interest of the other global capital. They work on their behalf and they work for money. The growing wealth of the members of the parliament works as evidence. The attitude of the government towards the issue of black money deposited in the foreign countries also raises doubts in the minds of the people. There is a common perception that UPA-II has used the present PM merely as a night watchman and he is working only as a rubber stamp. I am not saying this is true but this is what people talk on the streets.

Ed: Can I ask a specific question about the PM? Don't you think he is quite committed to the economic growth of the country?

MNT: I am tempted to think so because he is an eminent economist. However, in the last couple of decades people have started doubting him. He has not been able to convince people of his policies. He shows that his heart bleeds for the poor of the country but he never puts his foot down when it come to take position in their favor. He has only acted firmly on the issues like Nuclear Treaty or any other issue that forces us to open our economy for the exploitation of the global capital. When it came to the nuclear safety bill he could only give promises to the people. His government's policies of opening up education and retail seem to put people in doubt. He has to work hard to convince that he would like to put the national interest as defined by the marginalised people above than that of the same defined by the big capital.

Ed: *So you think that this the general discontent of the people has worked as major reason for massive mobilisation of the peopl?*

MNT: I do not think this is the only reason but this is one of the most important reasons. This discontent against the system has got accumulated. And now the discourse of development has taken the front stage; therefore the earlier strategies of the ruling classes may not be effective. I am hinting towards the strategy of raising the feeling of nationalism by provoking Pakistan or China. Interestingly, the ACM has even appropriated that slogan of nationalism. I think for the first time it has happened that the slogan on '*Bharat Mata ki jay*' or '*Vande* *matram'* is linked with anti-corruption slogan. I think nationalism has taken a back seat and it has become a junior partner. This is quite symbolic.

Ed: *But don't you think adopting this slogan has become quite counterproductive too as it is said that this has alienated the Muslim population?*

MNT: I do think that Muslim participation in the movement was not much. It is also possible that the slogans adopted might have alienated them. This is very natural in the background of the Gujarat genocide. However, I do not think it was deliberate on the part of any one of them. The fact is that Muslims suffer more due to corruption; as a community they are not only in minority but also poor. So, they were facing a dilemma as they wanted to join but were not sure. The ACM took several steps to make its intension clear and gradually space was being created for them. It is possible that a movement of this kind has many streams. Since it was not based on any explicit political ideology, it was difficult to know how many people were adhering to it and which party was there. When we say Muslims were not there, we basically mean either Muslim leaders were not there or the stereo type Muslim who could be distinguished by their dress were not there. It would be difficult to say if Muslims in general were not there. However, it would be interesting to see in which ways such a movement breaks this division of the citizens which has been used by the ruling classes for several decades in India.

Ed: *But not only Muslims, it said that even dalits were not part of the movement. How do you explain that?*

MNT: Well, dalit politics has gained new grounds in the contemporary times. It made significant advance in the desired direction of sharing institutional power. The initial reaction of Mayavati was to support the movement, but in the second thought she withdrew the support. Many intellectuals advocating dalit cause came out with their articulated opposition to the movement quite late. This only shows that they were taking time in evaluating the movement. Two issues were highlighted in their opposition. One, that such a movement is challenging the Constitution of India, which was supposedly written by Baba Saheb Ambedkar. Two, that such a movement is men by many people known for their anti reservationist positions. It also recalled the memory of anti-reservation movement of 1990.

Engaging with dalit politics is a big challenge for this movement. The issue of challenging the constitution is not a big one. Amendment in the constitution is a normal thing and that does not challenge the vision of Ambedkar in any case. Perhaps, even the dalit intellectuals know that this is a trivial issue. Also the AMC has to make the dalits sure that this movement will not touch the reservation policy. But more important issue is creating a space for dalit leadership in this. As dalit politics is on its rise, it will not become a subordinate partner to any movement. It would require lot of innovative talent on the part of the leadership of AMC to engage with the dalit leadership.

Ed: *And what about tribal population?*

MNT: That does seem to be difficult as ACM has already incorporated the issue of *Jal, Jameen* and *Jangal* in their slogan.

Ed: *Some people are suggesting that it is just a middle class movement and poor people never participated in this. Do you agree with this?*

MNT: I think it is partially correct. The new economic policies gave big hopes to the middle class of India. One section of this class also became global in a true sense. Some of them could manage to earn huge salaries. But for many them, not only did nothing great happen but also the earlier job security became a dream. For this section, the fruits of new developments in the services remained a virtual reality. It is this section of the society which got attracted towards the movement. The level of their dissatisfaction with the system is directly proportional to their commitment to it. It is difficult to imagine how huge numbers of people without much organisation decided to stay on despite heavy rain to support Anna Hazare when he was arrested in Delhi. Even the Anna team did not imagine this.

However, to think that it was only a middle-class movement would be undermining the strength of the people of India. Gradually, with the passing of time, the awareness about the movement spread all over the country and the media played an important role in this. People in different parts of the country started showing interest. The movement was attracting people for many different reasons and like any other mass movement, it allowed people to imagine their own connectivity with it.

Ed: *There is a view point that the middle class cannot do a sustained political movement. Such a movement will also not raise any issue of fundamental change.*

MNT: I am tempted to agree with this viewpoint. But I think we should not forget the importance of the contemporary middle class which has a very wide spectrum. This class is not only well informed about the system, but is also located in the urban centers and influence the opinion of the people. Moreover, their active participation is a symptom of the fact that classes below them must be in anger because dissatisfaction in them must be very high. Any effective political movement in India will have to develop strategies to bring these classes together. One has to understand the sociology of the middle class in India which is quite different than the same in the European and American societies. India needs a political leader who can understand this and develop a political philosophy to this effect.

Ed : *Do you see such a model of leadership in Anna Hazare?*

MNT: There is no point in comparing Anna Hazare with great leaders of India like Gandhi or Jayaprakash Narayan. Gandhi had a wide exposure. He had a project of liberation not only of the people in the colonial India but in other parts of the world too. He was capable of thinking of universal human liberation. Hazare has no experience of politics like Gandhi and he has not been able to project himself as a great philosopher. Having said this, one has to accept that at a time when political class has lost its legitimacy, he has proved that Indian people appreciate a Gandhian model of leadership. Despite having many weaknesses, what made Anna Hazare attractive is the trust factor and the honesty of intension. His simplicity and transparency has impressed people. One would like to recall the argument put forward by sociologist J.P.S. Uberoi in this context. He has argued that Indian society has figures like Sanyasi and Faqires who have great legitimacy among people and at times in the past they dared to challenge the king. I think Anna Hazare, like Gandhi people of there faquires. The problem is that the modern discourse of politics does not have this category and therefore fails to understand the popular support. Hazare's work has been appreciated by national and international agencies and the massive support that he commands from people of Ralegan Siddhi is an example of his inner strength.

However, I think a leader under whose leadership we can imagine any major change in Indian society has to be much more capable compared to him. Though the overall model might be the same, he or she must possess the intellectual and moral strength of Gandhi, Ambedkar and Marx together. Probably, the Hazare phenomenon only indicates towards this model.

Ed: *There is no doubt that the Hazare model seems to be attractive but do you think he will be able do anything without the support of a political party? Don't you think that he has to either take support from one of the political parties or form a party to carry forward the movement?*

MNT: It seems we are entering into a new era in the history of democracy in which three major modern institutions are passing through deep crisis. I would like to call them the three Ps: party, parliament and property. As we know, the party system has emerged with the modern bourgeois democracy. Probably people are losing faith in this institution. Parties in India are mostly family affairs. Instead of people making parties now parties are looking for people. The Anna movement shows that there is distrust against political parties. For some time, the ideology of caste or community may hold the political parties but they are not parties in the true sense. Rajni Kothari has been talking since long about non-party political actors. It seems this is going to be one of the main actors of democracy in the future.

Ed: *But what do you mean by parliament being in crisis?*

MNT: This is the crisis of legitimacy that Parliament is facing. If one has watched the debate on the Lokpal Bill in the parliament can one easily understand this problem. Though most of the parliamentarians were trying to defend the right of the parliament to make laws that was the symptom of more of a decline of the parliament. This movement was not saying that Parliament does not have the right to make laws; it was only suggesting that a law should be made soon and should be made in a particular form. Any citizen or a group of citizens do have this right. The real tension was the way the movement was making a mockery of the parliamentarians publicly. The demeaning comment on the political elite was the real concern and the fact that people were enjoying or approving this was much more demeaning. Their claim that they were elected representatives made no difference to their bad image. Anna Hazare's trust factor is much stronger compared to that of the democratically elected representatives. Despite all efforts, the Congress Party could not malign his image. So the movement has raised a question regarding the model of representation itself.

Ed: *And what do you mean by the crisis of the institution of private property?*

MNT: It seems the liberal euphoria that emerged after the collapse of the Soviet Uinion is gradually getting over. Throughout the world, the discontent against capitalism is growing. Initially, it seems to be a revolt against a particular set of policies of the government but the logic of this discontent leads to the idea of private property as a model for relationship between human and the nature. No wonder this kind of movement hides within itself may have seeds of destruction of capitalism. The contradiction between democracy and capitalism is so obvious nowthat the governments are unable to contain the discontent. Probably the world is pregnant with epochal transformation of this relationship.

Ed: *Let me ask you a rather difficult question. What do you think of the idea that the movement was, if not raised, at least supported by the Bhartiya Janta Party?*

MNT: I know lot of people think that this movement is a kind of proxy war against Congress. It is managed by BJP or the Hindutva family. I would like to make two points on this. One, that whenever any movement targets the party in power the other party-in-waiting becomes natural friend of the movement. One can recall the anti-Mandal agitation. Many of us who were supporting the reservation policy found to our surprise that the movement was funded by many important leaders of the Congress Party. This does not mean that the movement was raised by this party. In fact, in today's world, parties are unable to raise movements. We know many of them claiming to be the people's representatives take help of film personalities or bar girls to attract crowds. It is surprising that the ACM has been quite firm on its non-party character. That is its USP.

Second, initially many people though that Anna Hazare was being used by the Congress Party to divert the attention of the people as the front pages of the newspapers were full of the party's involvement in corruption. It was taken as a tension releasing act of the party. Similarly, now the other argument that is being put forward is that he is an agent of the BJP. I think, it is possible that the BJP will corner the advantage of people's discontent but it does not mean that it can use it as it wants. In fact, people who think from the window of a party will fail to capture the dynamics of this emerging trend in politics.

Ed: *Many people think that the media has played a very important role in converting a protest into a mass movement. Do you think the media can play such a big role?*

MNT: This is the most difficult puzzle to solve. Anyone who has a little bit of understanding of Indian politics knows fairly well that the Indian media does not have enough of autonomy vis-à-vis the corporate world. Now, if the AMC has an anti-government agenda, how can the corporate world allow this to be supported by the media as it is more than obvious that this government is working on behalf of the capitalist class. Many of the important ministers are well-known supporters of the Indian and global bourgeoisie and are following the dictates of World Bank and IMF at the cost of the welfare of the people. Is it a strategy to divert the attention of the public? There is another possibility and I want to talk about it merely as a possibility. It seems in the last few years there is wide spread acceptance of the naxal viewpoint in the middle classes too. It is not unlikely that the government has open up another window to ventilate the anger and discontent of the people.

There is no doubt that the media supported the movement in a big way. But, as one of the NDTV correspondents rightly commented, we do not know if the media made the movement or was it forced to cover it to raise their TRP. One thing is sure that the media cannot raise a movement; it can only raise the scale of it.

Ed: *Some of the intellectuals have criticised the movement and particularly the hunger strike as a strategy. They have gone to the extent of calling it a kind of 'blackmail'. What do you think of it?*

MNT: I think this is too strong a comment. Hunger strike has always been one of the important political weapons, particularly when the political actor is sure of attracting huge crowds in its support. One of the problems has been that some of the Indian intellectuals are totally disconnected from people's idioms. The English-speaking elite of India has no meeting points with the people. It is difficult for them to make sense of a Gandhian model of politics. They can only see such people either as *sanyasi* or as *sansari*. Bhikhu Parekh has rightly commented about the problem of understanding Gandhi who was neither sansari nor sanyasi. That is why many intellectuals were in a fix. I think, they have to develop new categories to understand these actors in Indian politics.

Ed: *Do you think ACM is part of the global trend of protests against the state?*

MNT: I think so. The protest against the new economic policy started with the spontaneous action in Argentina in 2001. There was not political party, no organisation when people came on the streets and protested almost for three days. Now we know that Egypt, Israel, United States of America, London and almost everywhere in the world people are protesting. ACM seems to be one of the forms of such protests. It is possible to think that this is indicative of a turning point in the history of the world. I would agree with Perry Anderson's argument in his editorial of New Left Review (March–April 2011) that the Arab revolt of 2011 belongs to a rare class of historical events. I think it is important see ACM along with the Arab revolt.

Ed: *What do you think are the major challenges before the movement?*

MNT: There are many challenges before the movement. The first and the most important is the problem of the understanding. It seems the movement has no idea about the nature of capitalism. So it treats the issue of corruption in isolation. It fails to understand that capitalism cannot survive without corruption. You see, even in USA there is an anti-corruption movement going on. The movement has to realise that the real enemy is capitalism. Therefore, struggle against corruption will have to be a struggle against capitalism and struggle for socialism. the ACM has to expand itself and involve people from all community, caste and religion. Second, it has to incorporate more fundamental issues concerning people. Though it has responded to the issue of *'jal, jangal jameen'* the real challenge is to take it seriously. All will depend on how quickly and to what extent it transforms itself from city based, middle-class, anti-corruption movement to an anti-capitalism movement. I am not sure if this transformation will take place. There is possibility that the movement will collapse and nothing great will happen. It is too early to make these observations.

NOTES

1. http://www.livemint.com/2010/10/13203814/Distribution-of-wealth-of-nati.htm

Contributors

Editors

Manindra Nath Thakur (manindrat@gmail.com) is Associate Professor, Centre for Political Studies, School of Social Science, Jawaharlal Nehru University, and New Delhi.

Dhananjay Rai (jnudhananjayrai@gmail.com) is Assistant Professor, Centre for Gandhian Thought and Peace Studies, School of Social Sciences, Central University of Gujarat, Gandhinagar, Gujarat.

Contributors (Articles)

Manoranjan Mohanty (drmohantys@gmail.com) is Professor (retd), Department of Political Science, University of Delhi, Delhi; Presently, Professor at the Council for Social Development, New Delhi and Chairperson of the Institute of Chinese Studies, Delhi.

Mahendra Prasad Singh (profmpsingh@yahoo.com) is Professor (retd), Department of Political Science, University of Delhi, Delhi; Presently Honorary Senior Fellow, Centre for Multilevel Federalism, Institute of Social Sciences, New Delhi.

Manoj K Jha (manojmeeta@gmail.com) is Associate Professor, Department of Social work, University of Delhi.

Vivek Kumar (vivekambedkar@yahoo.com) is Associate Professor, Centre for the Study of Social Systems, School of Social Sciences Jawaharlal Nehru University, New Delhi.

Satish K. Jha (satish_k_jha2005@yahoo.com) is Associate Professor in Political Science, RLA(E) College, University of Delhi, Delhi.

Ajay Gudavarthy (gajay99@rediffmail.com) is Assistant Professor, Centre for Political Studies, Jawaharlal Nehru University, New Delhi.

Anand Teltumbde (tanandraj@gmail.com) is a renowned commentator, academic and political analyst.

Shailaja Menon (shailaja@aud.ac.in) is Assistant Professor, School of Liberal Studies, Ambedkar University, Delhi.

N. Sukumar (suku69@yahoo.com) is Associate Professor, Department of Political Science, University of Delhi, Delhi.

Sukumar Muralidharan (sukumar.md@gmail.com) is a freelance journalist based in New Delhi.

Harish Wankhede (enarish@gmail.com) is Assistant Professor Political Science, RLA(E) College, University of Delhi, Delhi

Atul Mishra (anticontic@gmail.com) is Assistant Professor, Centre for Studies in Politics and Governance, Central University of Gujarat, Gandhinagar, Gujarat, India.

Contributors (Interviewee)

K.N. Pannikar (knpanikkar@gmail.com) is Professor (retd.), Centre for Historical Studies, Jawaharlal Nehru University, New Delhi.

Randhir Singh is Professor (retd.), Centre for Political Studies, School of Social Science, Jawaharlal Nehru University, New Delhi

G. Haragopal (profharagopal@gmail.com) is Professor (retd), Centre for Human Rights, School of Social Sciences, Central University of Hyderabad, Hyderabad.

D.L. Seth (dlsheth@csdsdelhi.org) is Professor, Centre for the Study of Developing Societies, 29, Rajpur Road, Delhi.

Imtiaz Ahmad (profimtiazahmad@yahoo.com) is Professor (retd), Centre for Political Studies, Jawaharlal Nehru University, New Delhi.

Manager Pandey is Professor (retd), Centre of Indian Languages, School of Language, Literature and Culture Studies, Jawaharlal Nehru University, New Delhi

Tulsi Ram (tulsiram@mail.jnu.ac.in) is Professor, Centre for Russian and Central Asian Studies, School of International Studies, Jawaharlal Nehru University, New Delhi.

Hilal Ahmed (ahmed.hilal@gmail.com) is Associate Fellow, Centre for the Study of Developing Societies (CSDS), 29, Rajpur Road, Delhi.

Contributors (Interviewer and Transcriber)

Manu Puthur (manuputhur@gmail.com) is Doctoral Candidate, Centre for Political Studies, Jawaharlal Nehru University, and New Delhi.

Manzoor Ali (manzoorali.ali@gmail.com) is Research Consultant, Centre for Budget and Governance Accountability (CBGA), New Delhi.

Rityusha Tiwary (rityushatiwary@gmail.com) is Doctoral Candidate in Chinese Studies, Centre for East Asian Studies, School of International Studies Jawaharlal Nehru University

Contributor (Transcriber)

Ruchi Shree, (jnuruchi@gmail.com) is Doctoral Candidate, Centre for Political Studies, Jawaharlal Nehru University, New Delhi.

Shashank Chaturvedi (jnushashank@gmail.com) is Doctoral Candidate, Centre for Political Studies, Jawaharlal Nehru University, New Delhi.

Pavel Tomar (paveltomar@gmail.com) holds Master Degree in History and pursuing research from Centre for Historical Research, Jawaharlal Nehru University, New Delhi.